Sociology of "Developing Societies"
Southeast Asia

Sociology of "Developing Societies"
General Editor: Teodor Shanin

THEMATIC VOLUMES

INTRODUCTION TO THE SOCIOLOGY OF "DEVELOPING SOCIETIES"
Hamza Alavi and Teodor Shanin

SOCIALIST "DEVELOPING SOCIETIES"
(in preparation)

THEORIES OF SOCIAL TRANSFORMATION
(in preparation)

REGIONAL VOLUMES

SOUTH ASIA
Hamza Alavi and John Harriss

SUB-SAHARAN AFRICA
Chris Allen and Gavin Williams

LATIN AMERICA
Eduardo P. Archetti, Paul Cammack and Bryan R. Roberts

THE MIDDLE EAST
Talal Asad and Roger Owen

CENTRAL AMERICA
Jan L. Flora and Edelberto Torres-Rivas

SOUTHEAST ASIA
John G. Taylor and Andrew Turton

Series Standing Order

If you would like to receive future titles in this series as they are published, you can make use of our standing order facility. To place a standing order please contact your bookseller or, in case of difficulty, write to us at the address below with your name and address and the name of the series. Please state with which title you wish to begin your standing order. (If you live outside the United Kingdom we may not have the rights for your area, in which case we will forward your order to the publisher concerned.)

Customer Services Department, Macmillan Distribution Ltd
Houndmills, Basingstoke, Hampshire, RG21 2XS, England.

Sociology of "Developing Societies" Southeast Asia

edited by John G. Taylor and Andrew Turton

MACMILLAN
EDUCATION

First published 1988

Published by
MACMILLAN EDUCATION LTD
Houndmills, Basingstoke, Hampshire RG21 2XS
and London
Companies and representatives throughout the world

Typeset by Wessex Typesetters
(Division of The Eastern Press Ltd)
Frome, Somerset

Printed in China

British Library Cataloguing in Publication Data
Taylor, John L.
Southeast Asia.—(Sociology of
developing societies).
1. Southeast Asia. Social conditions
I. Title II. Turton, Andrew III. Series
959′.053
ISBN 0–333–29277–4 (hardcover)
ISBN 0–333–29278–2 (paperback)

Contents

Series Preface

The question of the so-called "developing societies" lies at the very heart of the political, the economic and the moral crises of the contemporary global society. It is central to the relations of power, diplomacy and war of the world we live in. It is decisive when the material well-being of humanity is concerned; that is, the ways some people make a living and the ways some people hunger. It presents a fundamental dimension of social inequality and of struggles for social justice. During the last generation it has also become a main challenge to scholarship, a field where the perplexity is deeper, the argument sharper and the potential for new illuminations more profound. That challenge reflects the outstanding social relevance of this problem. It reflect, too, an essential ethnocentrism that weighs heavily on the contemporary social sciences. The very terminology which designates "developing" or "underdeveloping" or "emerging" societies is impregnated with teleology which identifies parts of Europe and the USA as "developed". Images of the world at large as a unilinear rise from barbarity to modernity (or vice versa as a descent to hell) have often substituted for the analysis of actuality, as simplistic metaphors often do. To come to grips with a social reality, which is systematically different from that of one's own, and to explain its specific logic and momentum, is a most difficult conceptual and pedagogic task. It is the more so, for the fundamental questions of the "developing societies" are not of difference only but of relationships past and present with the countries of advanced capitalism and industrialization. It is in that light that we encounter as analysts and teachers not only a challenge to "sociology of development", but also a major challenge to radical scholarship itself.

The Sociology of "Developing Societies" series aims to offer a systematically linked set of texts for use as a major teaching aid at university level. It is being produced by a group of teachers and scholars related by common interest, general outlook and commitment sufficient to provide an overall coherence but by no means a single monolithic view. The object is, on the one hand, to bring relevant questions into focus and, on the other hand, to teach through debate. We think that at the current stage "a textbook" would necessarily gloss over the very diversity, contradictions and inadequacies of our thought. On the other hand, collections of articles are often rather accidental in content. The format of a conceptually structured set of readers was chosen, sufficiently open to accommodate variability of views within a coherent system of presentation. They bring together works by sociologists, social anthropologists, historians, political scientists, economists, literary critics and novelists in an intended disregard of the formal disciplinary divisions of the academic enterprise.

Three major alternatives of presentation stand out: first, a comparative discussion of the social structures within the "developing societies", focusing on the generic within them; second, the exploration of the distinct character of the main regions of the "developing societies"; third, consideration of context and content of the theories of social transformation and change. Accordingly, our *Introduction* to the series deals with the general issues of comparative study, other books cover different regions, while a final volume is devoted to an examination of basic paradigms of the theories of social transformation. They therefore represent the three main dimensions of the problem area, leaving it to each teacher and student to choose from them and to compose their own course.

The topic is ideologically charged, relating directly to the outlook and the ideals of everyone. The editors and many of the contributors share a broad sense of common commitment, though there is among them a considerable diversity of political viewpoint and theoretical approach. The common ground may be best indicated as three fundamental negations. First, there is an implacable opposition to every social system of oppression of humans by other humans. That entails also the rejection of scholastic apologia of every such system, be it imperialism, class oppression, elitism, sexism or the like. Second, there is the rejection of "preaching down" easy solutions from the comfort of air-conditioned offices and campuses, whether in the "West" or in "developing societies" themselves, and of the tacit assumption of our privileged wisdom that has little to learn from the common people in the "developing societies". Third, there is the rejection of the notion of scholastic detachment from social commitments as a pedagogy and as a way of life. True scholarship is not a propaganda exercise even of the most sacred values. Nor is it without social consequences, however conceived. There are students and teachers alike who think that indifference improves vision. We believe the opposite to be true.

TEODOR SHANIN

Acknowledgements

The authors and publishers wish to thank the following who have kindly given permission for the use of copyright material.

American Anthropological Association, for "Rice Harvesting in Kari Loro: A Study of Class and Labor Relations in Rural Java", by Ann L. Stoler, *American Ethnologist*, 4:4 (1977).

The Anti-Slavery Society for the Protection of Human Rights, for material from *The Hmong of Thailand*, by Nicholas Tapp (1985).

Associated Book Publishers (UK) Ltd., for "The State and Capitalist Development in Thailand", by Kevin Hewinson, from *South East Asia: Essays in the Political Economy of Structural Change*. R. Higgott and R. Robinson (eds), Routledge and Kegan Paul (1985).

Ateneo de Manila University Press, for material from *Payson and Revolution: Popular Movements in the Philippines, 1840–1910*, by Reynaldo C. Ileto (1979), © 1979 by Ateneo de Manila.

Bulletin of Concerned Asian Scholars, for "The Transformation of the State in Indonesia", by Richard Robinson, *Bulletin of Concerned Asian Scholars*, 14 / 1 (1982).

Cambridge University Press, for material from "Idealogy and Social Structure in Indonesia", by Joel Kahn, *Comparative Studies in Society and History* (1978).

Centre of Southeast Asian Studies, for material from "An Undeveloped State: The Study of Modern Burma's Politics", by Robert H. Taylor, Working Paper No. 28 (1983).

Croom Helm Ltd, for material from *Multinationals and the Growth of the Singapore Economy*, by Hafiz Mirza (1986) pp. 70–80.

Anan Ganjapan, for material from "Conflicts over Deployment and Control in a Northern Thai Village", unpublished PhD thesis, Cornell University (1985).

The Institute of Development Studies, for "Socialist Transformation of Agriculture and Gender Relations: The Vietnamese Case", by Christian Pelzer-White, *IDS Bulletin*, Vol. 13, No. 4 (1982).

Celia Mather, for material from "Capitalism and Patriarchy in the Industrial Hinterland of West Java", unpublished paper, SOAS, University of London (1981).

National Museum of Ethnology, for material from "Limits of Ideological Domination and the Formation of Social Consciousness', by A. Turton, "Transformations of Iban Social Consciousness" by M. Uchibori; and "Cognition of Time, Change and Social Identity", by E. Magannon in *History and Peasant Consciousness in South East Asia*, A. Turton and S. Tanabe (eds), Senri Ethnological Studies, No. 13 (1984).

Oxford University Press, East Asian Branch, for material from "Dialectics of Akhazan", by L. Alting von Gesau, in *Highlanders of Thailand*, J. McKinnon and W. Bhruksasri (eds), (1983).

Yale University Press, for material from *Weapons of the Weak* by James C. Scott (1986) pp. 169–78.

Every effort has been made to trace all the copyright-holders, but if any have been inadvertently overlooked the publishers will be pleased to make the necessary arrangement at the first opportunity.

Introduction

Analyzing the Southeast Asian region, one soon encounters a paradox. Viewed from any standpoint – economic, social, cultural, political or strategic – the area has a crucial importance. Yet the degree and quality of much of the research on the region often does not enable one to address the most important aspects of its current and future development.

This is apparent when we compare Southeast Asia with other regions dealt with in the "Developing Societies" series. Latin American scholars have produced theories of structure and dependency to explain their continent's place in the world economy. Debates on East African development have raised important issues about the role of the state and its relation to indigenous classes. South Asian scholars have analyzed the development of capitalist relations of production in agriculture and rural differentiation in ways that have produced important insights into current trends in the agricultural sectors of their countries. In contrast, until recently, development studies within and on Southeast Asia have often been overly general, repetitive and descriptive, utilizing theories derived from other developmental experiences rather than generating indigenous explanations of the region and its place in the world economy. Later in the introduction we will try to show how this situation has arisen. For the moment, let us focus on the other side of the paradox – the importance of Southeast Asia for the analysis of development.

The Region

Southeast Asia embraces a vast area, comprising the mainland peninsula countries of Burma, Thailand, Malaysia, Vietnam, Laos and Cambodia (Kampuchea), the Indonesian archipelago, the island state of the Philippines, and the statelets of Singapore and Brunei. While its total land mass is roughly equivalent to that of India, in comparison it covers a greater part of the globe, since it includes thousands of islands, from the massive Borneo to the tiny islands of Eastern Indonesia. If placed on a map of Europe, Southeast Asia's territory would extend from the northernmost tip of Europe to sub-

1

saharan Africa, and from Spain in the west to Eastern Turkey. It is strategically located to the south of China and the east of India, linking the Pacific and Indian oceans.

As a region, Southeast Asia has acquired increasing importance since the end of the Pacific (Second World) War. Economically its role as a provider of crucial raw materials and agricultural commodities has been reinforced by its recent experience of very rapid economic growth in industry and manufacturing; in the 1970s, it grew at a faster rate than any other region in the world economy. Politically it has played an important role in the emergence of influential movements of socialism and non-alignment – notably in Indonesia, Vietnam and the Philippines – while it has also been the site of one of the most important conflicts in the post-war period, the war between the countries of Indochina and the United States. Socially it has undergone one of the most rapid transformations ever seen historically, with the major institutions of most of its constituent countries being changed beyond all recognition in a forty-year period – whether it be in such different directions as the corporatist capitalism of Marcos's Philippines, the state socialism of Vietnam, or the populist national capitalism of Sukarno's Indonesia.

Such changes and events, pushing the region more to the forefront of world affairs, have also served to highlight the characteristics which make it one of the most exciting regions of the developing world for political and sociological analyses. When asked why she was specializing in the study of Southeast Asia, a Masters' student of development recently replied to us that, "well, from a development point of view, its got everything". Her reasons for reaching such a conclusion would probably include the following points, on which we can briefly elaborate, by way of illustration.

Diversity and Transformation

In Southeast Asia we encounter a tremendous variety of different social systems. Long before the entry of Western Europe, social structures varied considerably. The most striking of these were the centralized kingdoms. Mainland Southeast Asia has been dominated for centuries by such societies, which can arguably be better understood in Europe by reference to the nineteenth century concept of the "Asiatic mode of production" (see Marx, 1964) rather than classic notions of European feudalism. They were located in what are now the nation states of Burma, Thailand and Cambodia, and were characterized by centralized state systems, governed by a monarch and his immediate family, whose legitimacy derived from his linking the kingdom to the cosmos. The monarch was viewed as the representative of heaven on earth. This notion was expressed in the Theravada Buddhist religion which, building on existing Hindu beliefs, conceived of the monarch as a repository of spiritual merit, who thereby had sacred status. The monarch governed through a centralized bureacracy strongly influenced by Brahman advisers, and located in the capital city. Regional power was exercised by local governors appointed by the central bureaucracy. The villages which the governors controlled paid tribute – in labor and in the form of crops, local handicrafts or precious artifacts – to the monarch who, in return, provided the means to ensure the continuing reproduction of the agricultural system – by organizing labor to maintain irrigation systems, organizing food storage in preparation for food harvests, and devising annual calendars to regulate the agricultural year.

By the time European colonialism was established in Mainland Southeast Asia in the nineteenth century, the Buddhist kingdoms had been in place for five hundred years or more. In the archipelago region, however, the kingdoms had not been able to survive for as long a period, due largely to the influx of Islam from the thirteenth century and the later entry of the European powers, in the sixteenth century. The centralized kingdoms located in Central and Eastern Java – and particularly the state of Majapahit – had been split into interior and coastal kingdoms, the former retaining the Hindu traditions and the latter succumbing to the Islamic ideologies introduced by Arab traders based in Malacca.

In what is now Vietnam, by contrast, the kingdoms survived into the middle of the nineteenth century. They differed a little from the monarchies of the other mainland and archipelago regions, in that the bureaucracy exercised greater power, and the monarch – or emperor – was seen more as a "mediator" between heaven and earth, whose skill in interpreting the sacred was vital in ensuring a basic standard of living for the people. As such, he was usually a Confucian scholar and teacher, setting a moral example by which he ensured a flow of tribute from his village subjects.

Alongside these kingdoms which for the most part were in the lowland irrigated areas, there existed very different societies inhabiting the hills and mountains of the mainland and hinterland of the archipelago islands. Practising a dry cultivation in which they cleared the forest, harvested it for a few years, and then moved on to new fields, these societies were generally stateless, but organized politically on the basis of kinship networks, sometimes governed by a chief and his extended family. Although some of these societies had periodic contacts with the kingdoms through trade and military incursions, they remained largely isolated and distinct from Buddhist and Hindu cultures. They were based on a variety of ethnic groups speaking a multitude of different languages – from the hill tribes of the Philippines to the village groupings of Eastern Indonesia, and the hill peoples of Burma, Thailand and Vietnam.

In addition to the kingdoms and stateless societies of Southeast Asia, there were also what may be loosely termed riverine or coastal states, located mostly in the western and central regions of the archipelago. The regions surrounding these states were generally unsuited to settlement, being covered with dense rain forest, often mountainous, with heavily leached soils. Communications were only possible by river, and preferably at the headwaters. Consequently, societies developing in these regions generally centered on areas where the river met the sea, and their primary focus and rationale was trade – up-river and with other coastal states. Political power rested on the ability of the ruler to obtain trading concessions with other states, secure trading arrangements with up-river tribes, maintain access to local fishing areas, and so on. In return for these, the ruler was permitted to levy a tribute on trade, and to raise taxes from his subjects. The ruler – variously known as raja or sultan – legitimized his position through membership of a royal lineage, and was supported by a small bureaucracy. Society was clearly stratified on the basis of noble descent or access to an administrative office. The vulnerability of these coastal states to attack or the inability of their rulers to deliver the appropriate trading conditions meant that they were rather fluid, both structurally and geographically. In many, one ruler succeeded another with amazing speed, as a result of attack or internal dissent – an effect which made them particularly vulnerable to the various Western influences entering the region.

Apart from the early Hindu and Buddhist influences shaping the development of the region's kingdoms, the other two major influences on the region have been Islam and Western European colonialism. Both had profound effects on the societies they encountered.

Arriving in the middle of the thirteenth century, Islam began to take root in the coastal areas and – particularly – in the Malay port of Malacca. From the fifteenth century onwards, it spread throughout the region, reaching as far as Mindanao, in what is now the southern part of the Philippines. Its impact, although uneven, was substantial. While it hardly touched the hill tribes of the interior and made few inroads into the Buddhist states of the mainland, it had a marked effect on the coastal states. It strengthened the position of the rulers of these states by broadening their trading networks, justified the importance of trade as a social ethos, and provided support in any conflict with the kingdoms. In Indonesia it sharpened the conflict between the trading states and the declining remnants of the Majapahit kingdom of the interior, the eventual result of which was the emergence of a new empire, Mataram, unifying Java in the early seventeenth century to produce a state whose ruling ideologies syncretized Buddhism, Hinduism and Islam.

The social, political and cultural diversity of Southeast Asian societies was increased further by the European impact. As with Islam, its impact was widespread, but, as distinct from earlier influences, it had a more marked effect on the economies of the region, producing profound changes in systems of cultivation and production. These changes varied, depending upon the period in which colonization occurred.

For example, the Philippines were colonized by Spain in the sixteenth century during the high-point of European feudalism. Consequently, much of its agricultural economy was transformed into large feudal-type estates, ruled by elites of Spanish and Mestizo origin, legitimizing their position through the value-system of a hierarchical and authoritarian Catholicism. This produced a society which was more thoroughly colonized at a much earlier stage than others in the region, and which – as a result – developed some highly distinctive economic features. Its indigenous economy, based on shifting cultivation with land held in common, was utterly transformed into one based on the private ownership of landed estates growing crops primarily for export. An economic hierarchy was created, quite alien to Filipino culture, in which peasant producers, tied by indebtedness to the estate owners, were separated from the wealthy elite, thus producing a highly polarized economic structure.

In contrast, the Dutch, after having colonized most of Indonesia in the eighteenth and early nineteenth centuries, retained much of the rural structure of Java, but exploited it more intensively. Villages were forced to set aside part of their land – usually one third – to cultivate export crops such as coffee, sugar and indigo for sale to the colonial state at fixed prices. As a consequence, the peasantry were left with insufficient land to cultivate crops for domestic consumption; and there emerged an adverse ratio of land to population – a phenomenon which still is evidenced in Java's current economy.

While areas such as the Philippines and Indonesia were colonized during pre-industrial phases of European development, the Malay peninsula came under colonial control by Britain during the second half of the nineteenth century, in the heyday of industrialization. As a result, it was affected profoundly, but in a way that was directed much more specifically to the needs of an industrial economy. Tin mining led to large-scale infrastructural developments, while most of the agricultural sector was converted into plantations cultivating rubber for export. As a result, the village economy was undermined, but, in addition, the British sponsored a migration of India's Tamil population to work on the plantations, and fostered the growth of the Chinese population as a labor force for the mines. The economic gulf between the Tamils and the Malay population, and the exclusion of the Chinese from political power by the British produced increasing antagonisms which have characterized Malay society ever since.

Such examples illustrate the differential impact of European colonialism on Southeast Asian societies. Other cases could have been cited. Politically, for example, while British colonialism maintained a degree of traditional order and autonomy in the Malay states, Spanish colonialism undermined more fundamentally the traditional political system in the Philippines, and French colonialism marginalized village elites without undermining the conditions for their reproduction. Similarly, at the cultural level, while French rule in Indochina placed few restraints on local culture in the regions it occupied, British rule in Burma was less tolerant of indigenous cultures. Furthermore, there were areas such as Siam (Thailand) where colonial rule was never formalized, and others, such as Portuguese (East) Timor where the colonial administration remained confined to the main towns and villages.

Consequently, when we examine the European colonial impact on Southeast Asia, we encounter societies which have been transformed in rather different ways and in differing degrees during different phases of European pre-industrial and industrial development. While in some states and during some periods economic structures and social and cultural systems were transformed, in others they were retained, or continued to reproduce themselves despite attempts at colonial change. A complex variety of combinations of economic, cultural and social forms were thus added to the considerable pre-existing diversity of the societies in the region. Southeast Asia thus provides us with excellent case studies for examining in detail such important issues as the ways in which aspects of pre-colonial society have been transformed or reproduced throughout the colonial and post-colonial periods, the means through which they are reproduced, and — most importantly — the impact they have on current developments. This applies, for example, as much to such micro-phenomena as the mix of wage and non-wage labor in the rural sector as to the more general macro-area of the role of "traditional" political ideologies in the contemporary political systems of developing societies.

"Minorities"

As well as transforming the social systems of the kingdoms and coastal states of Southeast Asia, European colonialism also tried to undermine the autonomy of the hill and hinterland peoples who had hitherto existed on the margins of these systems. Their previous economic and cultural disadvantages in relation to the lowland states were now to be compounded by their incorporation into colonial systems with which they had neither current nor historical affinity. In most cases colonialism failed in this task, and the upland tribes retained their identities. With the advent of independence, however, boundaries drawn by colonial powers became the borders of new nation states. As a result, upland peoples became part of a national unit whose interests they were required to uphold. They found themselves redefined as "minority peoples" within a newly created national community, their ethnic identities questioned by governments who stressed the attainment of goals such as development and political unity solely in national terms.

During the period following the Pacific War, a crucial issue was thus raised for the governments of the region – of how to create new forms of culture or transform existing ones to provide a sense of nationhood without alienating or undermining indigenous ethnic cultures. This was also a vital question for Development Studies in general, for which Southeast Asia has since provided a host of case studies. Unfortunately, almost all of them are negative. In most cases attempts have been made to restrict or eradicate the influence of indigenous cultures. This can be illustrated by reference to many examples: the Karen, Shan and Kachin peoples of Burma, the highland peoples in Thailand and Laos, the Moros of the Philippines and the West Papuans in Indonesia – all these ethnic groups have experienced coercive campaigns of cultural assimilation and economic exploitation by newly-formed national governments.

In contrast to the negative approach of such governments, the positive assertion of ethnic identity and the organization of resistance to incorporation by these peoples has provided us with an extensive knowledge of the ways in which indigenous peoples can counter cultural assimilation. The recent history of Southeast Asia is rich in such experiences, so vital to the field of Development Studies as it increasingly recognizes the fundamental importance of the issue of ethnic identity in the development of the nation state.

Strategies for Economic Development

During the past four decades the economies of the Southeast Asian region have been guided by a range of development strategies, whose impact has provided a wealth of data. There are economies such as Indonesia which have experienced, in turn, Keynesian planning in an open mixed economy, import-substituting industrializ-ation, and monetarist planning under centralized military rule. Thailand exhibits a similar combination. By contrast, the Vietnamese state has overseen the implementation of several development strategies which, although they can be described in the broadest sense possible as socialist, are very different from the conventional models provided by the Soviet Union and China. There are examples of states which have pursued the same development strategy for unusually long periods – two decades of monetarist guided export-led growth in Indonesia, and a slightly longer period of state-directed import-substituting development in Burma. Many of these strategies have occurred at very different times in the development of the world economy during the post-war period, thereby making their assessment all the more important.

Furthermore, during the last two decades Southeast Asia has undergone a period of rapid economic development, as evidenced in the substantial growth in manufacturing output as a percentage of gross domestic product, and the increase in the number of people leaving the rural for the industrial sector. This has resulted primarily from the region's growing involvement in the process of relocation of sectors of production from the industrialized countries of Europe, Japan and the United States, and from its increasing emphasis upon the production of manufactured goods for export. Whatever conclusions one draws from this – whether, for example, one sees it as creating a basis for self-sustaining industrialization, or regards it as establishing islands of growth in a sea of economic underdevelopment – there is little doubt that several economies are going through a profound process of capitalist transformation, whose speed has widespread implications not only for the region but also for a world economy which is itself undergoing a fundamental restructuring.

In selecting these examples, obviously we have not established – in the student's phrase, cited earlier – that Southeast Asia has "got everything". However, we do hope that they have given some idea of the ways in which the region is a crucial area for many of the major issues raised in the sociology and political economy of developing societies.

To turn, then, to the other part of our paradox: How has Southeast Asia been studied as a developing region? During the colonial period, a number of scholars – many of whom were themselves administrators – undertook analyses of aspects of the societies in which they were located. In this, they developed and elaborated a number of concepts which subsequently proved of some use in the study of the region. Most notable of these were Boeke, with his analysis of the "dual economy" in Indonesia, and Furnivall, with his development of the "plural society" framework for analyzing Burma and Indonesia. Of particular importance was the detailed research, notably that undertaken by Dutch and Portuguese ethnographers in Indonesia and East Timor and French in Indochina, which provided knowledge of the peoples of the archipelago. Although these studies produced kinds of knowledge which may still have historical value, they were inevitably constrained in one or another by a power structure and mode of discourse which affected both their choice of material and their treatment of it. This is aptly illustrated by Robert Taylor in his analysis of Furnivall's writing in this volume, or, again, in Sullivan's account (Higgott and Robison, 1985) – of the ways in which colonial historians of Malaya focused on specific areas, such as ruling factions, state ceremony and ideology – and how this influenced the future course of Malay historiography. Such research left a legacy of restricted vision and conceptual underdevelopment. These constraints were reinforced by indigenous scholarship being tied necessarily to the needs of political movements and the growth of nationalist awareness.

Modernization

If the focus of colonial research was rather narrow, the same could hardly be said of the body of theory that came to dominate studies of Southeast Asian development in the post-war period. Founded on the tenets of structural-functionalism, modernization theory claimed to provide a total societal framework in which all the major issues of development – economic, social, political and cultural – could be explained and predicted. Countries were placed on a linear evolutionary continuum from the "traditional" to the "modern" ideal-type, depending on their proximity to the "basic character-istics" of industrial societies. They were to progress via social and cultural differentiation, and increasing adaptation, until they reached their inevitable destiny in the "complex" form of the western industrial nation state. Once they accepted these tenets, planning within the theory became relatively simple. It was a question of what "inputs" one had to make into the various sub-systems of society to promote the changes necessary to progress along the continuum, and of how "disturbances" produced by these inputs could be handled without leading to conflicts which could destabilize the functioning of the structure (see Taylor, 1979).

Wherever one looked in the 1950s and early 1960s, research on the region was permeated with the concepts of modernization – the "bureaucratic polity" in Thailand, the "modernizing elites" in Indonesia and their counterparts in the "entrepreneurial moderni-zers" of the Javanese economy, the "patron-client" relations in the Filipino political system, and so on. In each case, the objective was similar – to discover barriers to development, to locate groups who could be instrumental in promoting development, and to analyze which were the most important changes to be made in the functioning of the social structure to encourage development. Once answers had been produced to these questions, the engineering of the structure could go ahead, with the aid of capital, skills and technology diffused from the relatively more modernized West. Planners, teachers and administrators schooled in modernization theory and its application imbued their students with the finer details of the theory's conceptual labyrinth, so that the next generation of scholars could use its notions with greater clarity and rigour. The theory continues to exert an influence in much routine practice of development planning and administration.

New Trends

Criticisms of modernization theory inevitably emerged, spurred by the impact of the Indochina war in the 1960s which led many academics and scholars to question the role of the West in the development process. The United States government had pursued one of the most destructive and murderous wars against a civilian population in history, unleashing the world's most powerful military machine against peasant societies with limited means of self-defense. Incredibly the American military was defeated, but it left behind devastated countries with almost insoluble problems of reconstruction. The nature of the war and its impact led intellectuals in both "developed" and developing societies to raise fundamental questions as to the desirability of different types of industrialization, and about the very notion of development itself. From this there arose a basic questioning of the structure and concepts of modernization theory – on the inadequacies of the "traditional" model for analyzing the non-capitalist societies of the Southeast Asia region, the failure of "diffusion" to generate a basis for developing the domestic economy, and a questioning of the appropriateness of the characteristics of the "modern" type as a structure enabling successful industrialization. Growing dissatisfaction attracted scholars to alternative paradigms – notably those of Underdevelopment, Dependency, and Structural Marxism. In Southeast Asia, compared with other regions such as Latin America or South Asia, the critique of modernization came relatively late, with the consequence that as developmentalists began to examine their relevance, the theories themselves were already being seriously questioned. Thus, there is a relatively small number of works written from within these perspectives – for example, Mortimer (1973), Nartsupha *et al.* (1978), Arief and Sasono (1980).

Faced with the vagaries of holistic and teleological theories in both the functionalist and alternative approaches to the analysis of development, researchers began to look more directly at the specific features of the area, rather than attempting to fit them into general theories of structural development derived from the experiences of nation states in other regions. The subjects subsequently chosen enabled the particularities of the region, individual countries and "sub-national" regions to be highlighted more clearly than had been the case thus far. They include, first, a concern to analyze the economic and political effects of the region's increasing involvement in export-oriented strategies of growth, with particular reference to the effects of this on class formation (see Higgot and Robison, 1985). Secondly, new attention is being paid to the history and development of popular culture, and popular social and political movements, and on the constraints within which they have their existence (see Turton and Tanabe, 1984). Thirdly, there is an emphasis on the importance of detailed local empirical studies of local processes of agrarian transformation and differentiation (see Hart, Turton and White, 1988). Finally, there is an increasing focus on issues of gender and gender relations, with special attention being given to such aspects as rural household production, migration, income inequality, technology and labor displacement, and industrial work and conditions (see Heyzer, 1986). In the last few years, research in these areas has raised fundamental issues about contemporary Southeast Asia – on the effects of the rapid changes the region is undergoing, and the responses of its constituent societies to these changes. Recent work has critically challenged not only the adequacy of existing knowledge of these processes, but also the assumptions, and the holistic and *a priori* approaches on which such knowledge was based.

The collection of edited readings in this volume is situated at this particular conjuncture of theory and research. The collection is intended to be used as an introductory text. Readers are encouraged to follow up the topics and authors mentioned and to return to the original texts from which selections have been made, many of which have necessarily been abridged. While we have included material on almost all the countries of the region, it was clearly impossible in a volume of this nature to address all the themes of the sections in relation to each country. In many cases, however, the analysis of local situations (for example, dealing with sharecropping, Islamic values concerning women, dilemmas of minorities etc.) are pertinent and suggestive for other localities and countries, and, indeed, that has been one criterion for inclusion. Similarly, the discussion of major themes is not confined to particular sections. Thus political and economic themes recur in all sections and most pieces; gender is also raised in the sections on industrialization and agrarian differentiation; culture and ideology are clearly also aspects of the sections on gender and minorities, and so on. The section introductions, bibliography and index are designed to encourage cross-referencing and further reading. We ask the reader to note that we have here provided references to works in the English language only, and which are likely to be available in university libraries. There is of course a large and relevant literature in other colonial languages of the region (notably French and Dutch) and in Southeast Asian languages. However, bibliographies contained in English language works cited give many references to important sources in these other languages.

The six parts into which the book is divided are intended to highlight issues and areas of current research of particular concern. They offer a range of alternative explanations and approaches to those provided in earlier, but often still prevailing, theories. Most importantly, they are grounded in detailed empirical studies based on prolonged, local-level research by the authors. At the same time, the analysis seeks to link local particularities with wider historical and societal perspectives. This typifies a discernibly new process of investigation, especially by local scholars from within the region, which has grown both in its theoretical rigor and originality, and in its commitment to field research, often carried out despite considerable constraints of authoritarian political control. If this volume had been produced ten or fifteen years ago, it would have most probably contained only the first three sections, since apart from orthodox repetitions of structural-functionalist descriptions, little of analytical worth was being produced on gender relations, popular culture, or ethnic histories in relation to development. Furthermore, a far greater proportion of the contributors would have likely come from outside the region. These changes are symptomatic of a major increase in indigenous scholarship in a relatively short period of time. If the trend towards more concrete analysis of local conditions continues, the Southeast Asian region will begin finally to receive the level of explanation and understanding merited by its increasingly crucial importance for the world, and more particularly for those societies which are currently termed "developing".

Part I

Nation, State and Politics

Introduction

The peoples of the Southeast Asian region have experienced a variety of political systems during the period since the end of the Second World War. During recent years countries such as Indonesia and Thailand have been governed by authoritarian, military dominated states, while, in an earlier period, populist governments have prevailed in Cambodia and Indonesia in the aftermath of the war. Until recently, patriarchal states have dominated Philippine society. In contrast, Burmese society has been guided by a bureaucratic state, loosely based on a mixed economy.

Scholars of the political systems in these societies might well object to these classifications as too vague, overly-general, and perhaps even misleading – and herein lies a fundamental problem. In many cases the diversity and complexity of Southeast Asia's political systems are such that they cannot be described, let alone explained by such concepts. When we try to use them they simply do not "fit". Yet this has not prevented theorists working in western sociological schools of thought from focusing on some aspects of the political system in operation, since they are recognizably "political" within the range of American or European experience. In so doing, however, they grasp only a part of the system they are seeking to explain. Thus, for example, political scientists observing the prevalence of personal rivalry within Thai elites have generalized this unfoundedly to Thai politics as a whole, referring consequently to the political system as being "loosely structured". Similarly, the values of elite Javanese political society are characterized by a patron-client system which commentators, again, have generalized erroneously to society as a whole. In such cases, aspects of the exercise of power which are readily recognizable are highlighted, while the unfamiliar are relegated to the sidelines. Consequently, many theorists – and particularly those of the Modernization and Dependency schools – have overlooked crucial aspects of the control and use of power. Furthermore, they have also tended to ignore the fact that in most cases the newly-formed political systems of

15

Southeast Asia have been produced through the amalgamation of very different political structures. Consequently, the most important issue is often that of the means by which these structures can co-exist. Ideologies were developed for this purpose, and many incorporated western forms. yet these forms have often been peripheral to the system's actual operation – unbeknown to many of the theorists who recognized in them only those aspects compatible with their ready formed concepts.

There is a further problem with many conventional approaches. Since the focus is usually upon the national unit, there is also a marked tendency to overlook the local structures of political power, and the connections between them and the organization of state power. In Godelier's words, there is no attempt to get at the "components of power and domination, beyond the mere functional definitions of power", with the result that local politics is seen simply as a mirror image of the national structure (Godelier, 1986).

Just as there has been a certain conceptual rigidity in the analysis of states in the capitalist societies of Southeast Asia, so too have analyses of socialist states such as Vietnam or Laos been dealt with in terms of their proximity to models derived from the study of Chinese or Russian developments in the twentieth century.

There has also been a marked focus on some countries to the detriment of others. For example, while there is no shortage of works analyzing the Thai or Indonesian states from differing theoretical perspectives, there are few on post-war Burma or Cambodia (Kampuchea).

Despite such problems with many of the existing holistic approaches, the study of the state and politics in the region is crucial because of the state's overwhelming preponderance in the contemporary period, as evidenced in the weakness of civil society, the incorporation of the trade unions, and the systematic control of the political opposition. Whatever the form taken by the state, politics plays a crucial role in economic development – in creating conditions for industrialization, initiating land reform, and setting up external trading and investment links. Similarly, the state has been the vehicle through which nationalism has been propagated in societies with a complex combination of social systems – from dispersed upland peoples largely based on kinship groups to village communities and technologically advanced urban centers, each with their own economic, political and cultural characteristics. Consequently, the state has had to present itself as representing a whole range of interests, while in reality being controlled by relatively small sectional interests, carrying out their own particular projects of economic planning and social engineering in the interests of an illusory or "imagined" national community – to use Anderson's phrase (Anderson, 1983). As such, the state has become the site in which many of the conflicts between classes in Southeast Asian societies has been worked out. Furthermore, political developments within the state have often led to the creation of classes which have come to assume a preponderant social role. For example, in Indonesia and Thailand military rule has created a bureaucratic stratum whose access to the economy has enabled its members to create a dominant role for themselves in the process of development. Similarly, in Vietnam, the control exercised by the party over the state has generated elites whose members can influence significantly developments in both the rural and manufacturing sectors of the economy.

Several of the contemporary approaches to the analysis of the state in Southeast Asia – and notably the theses of relative autonomy and bureaucratic capitalism – are criticized by Lim Mah Hui, who traces the development of different segments of the Malay bourgeoisie. He shows how, replicating the Japanese Meiji state, the growth of state ownership has favored this nascent class. He argues that state ownership, through its favoring the Malay population, has produced a "legitimation crisis" for the Malay bourgeoisie. Firstly, because classes which are important for the longer-term maintenance of state power have been alienated by their status as non-Malay. Secondly, because the actions of the state are producing an alienation of strata of the Malay population itself, notably the petty-bourgeoisie and sections of the working-class and peasantry.

Robert Taylor examines the frameworks in which Burmese state and society have been analysed, with particular reference to the pioneering studies of Furnivall. He notes the absence of any serious studies of the contemporary state, classes and political discourse, and analyzes the reasons for this. He concludes by stressing the importance of the state as a unit of analysis for Burmese society, analyzing its pervasive role in the contemporary social structure.

Richard Robison analyzes the stages in the development of the Indonesian state since the late nineteenth century emergence of capitalist cultivation and production. He argues that the Indonesian state has assumed a capitalist form since that time, establishing the conditions for capital accumulation, and ensuring the social dominance of different fractions of the industrial and financial bourgeoisie. He focuses on the structure of what he terms the "bourgeois alliance" which he argues holds state power in contemporary Indonesia, analyzing its reproduction and its relations with other classes in the social formation. He concludes that the form taken by the state in the coming period will be influenced crucially by the extent to which the process of industrialization can consolidate the social and political power of the domestic bourgeoisie.

Contradictions in the Development of Malay Capital: State, Accumulation and Legitimation

Lim Mah Hui

Economic and political developments in Malaysia since independence are marked by two major and interrelated events – the growing participation of the state in the economy and the rapid growth of the Malay bourgeoisie. By the late 1970s state ownership had become dominant in the banking, plantation and mining sectors of the economy. Scholars who have observed this phenomenon interpret its significance differently. For most, it represents a movement towards a "mixed economy" – a market economy where the state attempts to regulate production and distribution through planning as well as ownership of state enterprises. Within this school, there are those who see state enterprises as indications of socialism (Milne and Mauzy, 1978) and others who see them as instruments of affirmative action for the *Bumiputras* i.e.: as institutions which undertake to correct economic inequality between Malays and non-Malays (Wheelwright, 1966). There are still others who see the significance of state economic participation in terms of the impact on class formation. In particular, Jomo (1977) puts forward the thesis that state enterprises have spawned a new class identified as the bureaucratic bourgeoisie.

In studying the growth of the Malay bourgeoisie, practically all scholars (Popenoe, 1970; Charlesworth, 1974; Abdul, 1977; Chee *et al.* 1979) have concentrated on the growth of the Malay petite bourgeoisie. Little attention has been given to studying the different segments of the Malay bourgeoisie: how each has different origins, political and economic resources and interests, and how they relate to one another – either in co-operation or in conflict.

In this article I attempt to relate the increasing economic participation of the state to the development of the different segments of the Malay bourgeoisie. I argue that though state ownership of the economy in Malaysia has grown tremendously during the 1970s, this does not warrant the state to be termed a state capitalist regime; neither has the state spawned a new bureaucratic bourgeoisie with identifiable interests that are separate from those of the bourgeoisie. State ownership does not automatically transform a capitalist state into state capitalism. In the case of Malaysia, even when the state is owning and controlling enterprises, it is acting on behalf of the nascent Malay bourgeoisie and it did not develop its own autonomy. This situation is neither unique nor new; in fact, it was modelled after the Japanese Meiji state which established and controlled productive enterprises that were subsequently divested to the nascent Japanese bourgeoisie.

If state capital accumulation in Malaysia has not led to the development of state capitalism or a bureaucratic bourgeoisie, it has brought about other effects – the most significant of which is its own legitimation crisis and consequently an increase in the level of coercion in society. The 1970s in Malaysia witnessed a growth in protest movements and concomitantly a rise in the level of political coercion. Part of this is a result of the export-oriented industrial-ization strategy, promoted by the state, which requires a lowly paid and highly controlled labor force. But a second set of factors which account for the rise of political coercion is related to the increasing contradiction between the accumulation and legitimation functions of the state. When the state is directly involved in capital accumula-tion, it undermines its legitimation function. This decline in the legitimacy of the state is reflected in the mounting protests among peasants and labor who are directly dependent on the state for employment or price support. These protests in turn forced the state to respond with policies of co-optation and/or repression. Legitimation crisis also emerges when the state is viewed as disproportionately favoring certain classes or ethnic groups. Expres-sions of such discontent have traditionally been registered among the non-Malay population; but what is significant today is they are also increasingly found within the Malay population.

Material Base of the Dominant Classes Before Independence

On the eve of independence, there were three segments in the dominant class in Malaya: a metropolitan (British) bourgeoisie still in firm control of the economy, a local non-Malay (predominantly Chinese and some Indian) bourgeoisie, economically subservient to British capital but stronger than Malay capital, and finally a Malay dominant class, consisting of Malay bureaucrats and aristocrats who enjoyed political and administrative advantages but without economic power. The subordinate classes were likewise economically and ethnically divided: the majority of Malays were peasants, the Chinese mainly urban proletarians, and the Indians rural proletarians. There was, of course, representation from all communities in the professional and middle classes.

The position of the Malay dominant class which was characterized by political strength but economic weakness can be traced to its historical roots. Even in the pre-colonial era, the Malay aristocratic ruling class was not economically active; the production of tin, pepper and other agricultural goods in Malaya was undertaken mainly by Chinese miners and planters. The income of the Malay rulers came primarily from taxation levied on trade and economic production. British colonial rule displaced the Malay ruling class politically and Chinese capital economically to second place. The colonial state stripped the Malay rulers of effective political power and provided them with fixed stipends. They also trained children of Malay aristocrats to become junior administators in the colonial bureaucracy. On the other hand, through a set of policies which favored British capital, Chinese capital was discriminated against and eventually became subservient to the former. The colonial state also adopted a "protectionist" policy towards the Malays: Malays were regarded as native dwellers who received certain political and economic rights which were not available to non-Malays. Therefore the seeds of economic and political inequalities among Malays and non-Malays were reinforced during the colonial period and continued into the post-colonial period.

The Development of Malay Capital

Although the dominant Malay class succeeded in wresting from non-Malays and the British a legal recognition of the need to develop its economic position after independence, it was constrained in its initial attempts by its economic and administrative weaknesses. For example, attempts were made to develop a Malay industrial and commercial bourgeoisie. Three major strategies were used: (a) Protection: Malay quotas were imposed on business licences, employment and education; (b) Assistance: facilities were provided in the forms of credit, training and business premises; (c) Acquisition: Malay ownership of the corporate economy was expanded. In general these were unsuccessful, and their lack of success led to loud protests articulated in two major conferences – the First and the Second Bumiputra Economic Congresses in 1965 and 1968. The leaders of the conferences were mainly Malay businessmen, politicians and bureaucrats. Complaints were directed not only at non-Malays but also their own leaders who had not distributed the spoils fairly. At the Second Congress, the Selangor Malay Chambers of Commerce criticized the small number of Malays who monopolized the directorships of large corporations and suggested that a board be set up to allocate these directorships to benefit more people. The participants were aware that thus far *laissez-faire* capitalism had worked towards their disadvantage and called for a reorganization of the economic system modelled along the early Japanese industrial period where the state would participate more actively in capital accumulation on behalf of a weak indigenous bourgeoisie and then transfer the resources to them at a later date.

The Congress cited at length the Meiji State and how it started enterprises which were then resold to private entrepreneurs, providing special credits and contracts for private business. The Congress can be identified as the watershed which laid the foundation for the post 1970 New Economic Policy.

Finally the Congress contained not only statements of complaint and recommendation but also of warning to the effect that if Bumiputras were not given a stake in the economy, there would be no guarantee of peace and security, a prophecy that was tragically fulfilled in the racial riots of May 1969.

Non-Malay Discontent

In contrast to the dissatisfaction that the Malay bourgeoisie felt and expressed in the congresses, the reaction of foreign and Chinese capital to the role the state played in the development of Malay capital was rather mild. There were a few instances when Chinese capital, threatened with elimination, fought back, but on the whole, foreign and Chinese bourgeoisie remained relatively calm; non-Malay bourgeoisie were unhappy with the Malay Special Rights provisions, but they were not drastically hurt either. Behind the impressive statistics showing the fulfilment of Malay quotas, many of the Malays who received these business licences simply resold them to non-Malays or allowed the latter to run the business for a fee which they collected.

If the foreign and Chinese bourgeoisie were not badly affected, the same cannot be said for the non-Malay petite bourgeoisie and working class. The implementation of the Malay Special Rights program was more effective in the public employment and educational sectors. Under this program, the employment ratio of Malays to non-Malays in the public sector was 4:1. As an example of its implementation, the percentage of Malays in the Malayan Civil

Service rose from 35% to 87% between 1957–70, while the percentage for non-Malays increased from 4% to 13%. (Puthucheary, 1960:54). In the field of education as the position and status of Malay education and Malay school teachers grew, particularly after the Razak Education Report, that of the Chinese teachers and education gradually whittled and then declined precipitously with the Talib Educational report which recommended government subsidies to Chinese secondary schools be stopped. This no doubt generated intense resentment among the Chinese and resulted in widespread disturbances especially in Penang.

Between 1962–8, the number of students in Malay secondary schools rose from 13,000 to 136,000 while the number of students in Chinese secondary schools dropped from 34,000 to 20,000 and that in English secondary schools doubled from 152,000 to 334,000. The educational policy was further affected in 1967 when the National Language Act was passed designating Malay to be the sole official language and then three years later, English medium schools were converted to the Malay medium, beginning with grade one. This closed the avenue of social and economic mobility for many of the non-Malays who had sent their children to English medium schools. At the tertiary level, the dominant position of non-Malays in the University of Malaya declined from 80% to 60% between 1963–70 (Snodgrass, 1980: 246, 248, 250).

It is hardly surprising that the grievances of the Chinese were articulated not so much by the Chinese bourgeoisie but by the middle- and lower-class Chinese whose employment and education opportunities were restricted. They were expressed in fields of culture and education.

Distressed by the educational policies, they demanded economic equality, the preservation of Chinese culture and the allocation of more seats in the coming elections; but in this tussle, not having the full support of the Party, they lost and conceded to UMNO in the end. The National Language Act of 1967 also invited hostile reactions particularly from the Chinese Teachers Associations who then proposed to establish a Chinese University. The ineffectiveness of the MCA to represent adequately the interests and aspirations of the middle- and lower-class Chinese led to an erosion of their credibility among the Chinese. Even at the peak of its performance in 1964, MCA obtained less than 50% of the non-Malay votes. In 1969 MCA suffered a disaster; it won only 13 of 33 parliamentary seats it fielded and performed worst in Chinese-dominated states.

In the pre-1969 period, even though the state did not engage itself directly in capital accumulation, it was unable to gain adequate legitimacy from the different communities. In the eyes of non-Malays, its impartiality was undermined by the preference shown to Malays; yet this did not endear them fully to the Malays. The Malays too were unhappy with the policy of *laissez-faire* which served to benefit more the non-Malays. This crisis of legitimacy was finally expressed in the general elections of 1969 when support for the Alliance Party was seriously eroded, though it won the general elections. The greatest threat was posed by the non-Malay opposition parties that won enough votes to form the state governments in four major states. This political challenge coming on the heels of the economic threat, resulted in the communal riots a day after the elections.

Post-1970 New Economic Policy: State Accumulation

With its legitimacy severely questioned, the Malay dominant class set about to change its political and economic strategy. Economically the most important change was the step up in the acquisition of share ownership and the participation of the state in this process. Public development expenditure allocated for commerce and industry jumped from less than 3% to 13%. The major vehicles for capital accumulation were the state corporations which mushroomed overnight. In 1957 there were only 10 public enterprises, by the end of 1974 the number was 82 with 65 subsidiaries and 185 joint-ventures. Between 1971–80, Malay ownership of equity in the corporate sector grew from 4% to 12.4%, at an annual rate of 31.4%. However, most of this growth was accounted for by the public sector which owned 8.1% of the equity. By 1980, the state owned 77.4% of the local banking industry and 50% of the total banking industry. In insurance, out of a total of 36 companies, Malays have interest in 32; with more than 51% equity in seven and more than 10% in 11 companies.

In the tin and plantation industries, once the domain of foreign capital, state penetration has been nothing less than dramatic since 1975. In a period of seven years, the state has taken ownership and control of almost all the large plantations: Sime Darby, Guthries, Boustead, Highland and Lowlands, Barlow, and Harrisons and Crosfield, (*Far Eastern Economic Review* 8 August 1980; 9 October 1981; 27 February 1981; *New Straits Times* 9 September 1981; 11 June 1982). In tin, PERNAS, in partnership with Chartered Consolidated took control of London Tin Corporation and merged to form Malaysian Mining Corporation which later merged with

Malayan Tin Dredging, assuring control of more than 30 per cent of the tin output in Malaysia.

Opposition of Non-Malay Bourgeoisie

In short, the state has come to control the mining, plantation and financial sectors of the economy, a process that has not been without conflict. Prior to 1970, Malay and state acquisition of corporate equity was minimal and hardly any feathers were ruffled. But when the process gathered momentum, the reactions of the foreign and Chinese bourgeoisie were less calm.

The penetration of Malay capital into the corporate sector was distinguished not only by its speed but also by its organizational method. Giant corporations capitalized at hundreds of millions of dollars were established to foray the market; most of these represented state capital, but some came from private Malay capital mobilized through co-operatives and religious institutions. Chinese capitals, most of which are small- and medium-sized became aware of their handicap and started to emulate the Malay strategy, organizing economic conferences and establishing co-operatives to mobilize capital from the rank and file. The passage of the ICA precipitated the MCA into action; it held a seminar which arrived at a five-point program to consolidate the position of the Chinese: the establishment of Tunku Abdul Rahman College, a new MCA headquarters, a Chinese cultural society, a membership drive to widen its base and the formulation of Multi-Purpose Holding (MPH).

MPH was incorporated in August 1975 but its first public issue of 29.8 million shares was made in 1977 which resulted in Malaysian Multi-Purpose Co-operative Society known by its Malay-language initials KSM) holding 10% of the shares. The basic rationale of MPH was to pool resources from individuals and to modernize the traditional Chinese family enterprise. Between 1980–2, its share capital increased six-fold from 75 million to 450 million shares, making it the biggest company on the Kuala Lumpur Stock Exchange in terms of paid-up capital. Ostensibly MPH is a non-partisan public company with 32,000 shareholders; but its political affiliation is undeniable. All its top officials are leading MCA politicians and KSM owns 52% of the shares. Flushed with funds, MPH embarked on a buying spree and acquired a string of corporations including Magnum Bhd. in 1977, Malaysian Planta-tions (1978), United Malayan Banking Corporation (1981), Guthrie Bhd. (1981), Kuala Lumpur-Kepong (1981), Dunlop Estate (1981).

The group's assets leapt spectacularly from $30 million to more than $800 million between 1977–82.

The concept appealed to the Chinese enough that MCA state branches were able to induce the community to part with $200 to $300 million of funds for investment. For example, Johore MCA collected some $50 million and owns Matang Holdings with $10 million capital; Perak MCA runs Peak Hua Holdings with $20 million capital.

These acquisitions have brought MPH into conflict with segments of the Malay dominant class who view it as another attempt by Chinese to thwart the development of Malay capital. In 1976 Pernas bought 30% of United Malayan Banking Corporation, the third largest bank in Malaysia, which however, was still controlled by Chang Ming Thien. In 1980 Chang agreed to sell 50.2% of UMBC's shares to MPH causing a big controversy within UMNO which required the attention of the Prime Minister. A compromise was finally reached in which UMBC's capital would be enlarged and MPH and Pernas would each own 40% of the capital with the rest held by Chang. A similar outcry accompanied the acquisition of Guthries Bhd., the trading arm of Guthries Corporation; this time a deal which involved British, Chinese and Malay capital. By the late 1970s, the government had shifted into full gear buying some of the largest plantations. A few companies, such as Guthries and Harrisons & Crosfield, continued to hold out causing irritation to the state. To aggravate matters, Guthries Corporation in London sold off its subsidiary Guthries Bhd. to MPH and began to diversify its operations outside Malaysia. This prompted PNB (Perbadanan Nasional Bhd.) to make a lightning purchase of Guthries Corporation on the London Stock Market in September 1981. This episode offended British capital who accused the Malaysian government of 'back door nationalization' and worked hastily to amend the City of London Takeover Code to prevent future takeovers.

Malay Petite Bourgeoisie

While most of the state's resources were poured into public enterprise, it was not possible, for political expediency, to ignore the position of the Malay petite bourgeoisie who felt economically overwhelmed in the Chinese-dominated urban centres.

Prior to 1970, the major part of the state's efforts had been directed to the creation of such a petite bourgeoisie class, but the results had been disappointing. Licences were issued to them but the pressing problem they faced was credit; yet only £70 million loans were given to them by MARA between 1951–70 (Malaysia, 1976: 192), and in 1968 only 4% of the total commercial bank loans were for Malays (Treasury, 1975/76: Appdx 9.2; 1979/80: Appdx 6.2). Obviously this imbalance had to be redressed. In 1972, the state directed banks to lend a portion of their loans to small businesses. Under this scheme 60% of the loans would be guaranteed by the Credit Guarantee Corporation (CGC). The quota was raised to 12% in August 1974 and eventually 20% in October 1976. By December 1977, CGC had guaranteed 54,591 loans worth $480 million with 67% of the number of loans and 42% of the value going to Bumiputras. As a result of these measures bank credit to Bumiputras reached 20% totalling $4780 million in 1980. Under the Fourth Malaysia Plan, $50 million was allocated to the Petty Traders Program for small businesses.

Despite the assistance given, it is generally regarded that state policies have favored big business more than small ones. A study of small Malay business remarked that government fiscal incentives favored capital intensive industries; provisions of industrial sites by the state benefited the larger firms; commercial bank credits are more inclined to large establishments; estate duties, social benefits and welfare legislations all place a heavier burden on small businessmen. Furthermore, larger firms are more likely to get contracts and tenders from government.

The Malay petite bourgeoisie are confronted with serious obstacles to capital accumulation: inadequate capital, skilled labor shortage, market limitations and stiff competition. Charlesworth has pointed out that 70% of his sample of Malay small businesses started with their own capital and 90% of them have less than $10,000 capital outlay (Charlesworth, 1974). The turnover and profits of these establishments are low and consequently, a majority are unable to reinvest. Eighty-two per cent of Malay small businesses do not have skilled labor; do not use machines; 95% cater only to local market and the majority face stiff competition not only from Chinese businessmen but also the state enterprises. . .

The Malay Chambers of Commerce at the state level have been vocal in articulating the demands of the Malay petite bourgeoisie. Although such demands have arisen, the state has, hitherto, been successful in bringing them under control principally by encouraging the formation of economic organizations under the patronage of prominent Malay politicians.

More serious and disturbing, however, is the competition that has been exacerbated between the Malay and Chinese petite bourgeoisie.

The growth rate of Malay small business establishments (sole proprietorships and partnerships) has been twice that of the Chinese. In 1974 Malay small establishments accounted for 18.2% of the total; this increased to 23.2% by 1979. Among the sectors in which the Malay petite bourgeoisie have made the most inroads are the construction, transport and trading sectors, once the domain of Chinese capital. Between 1970 and 1980, the percentage of Bumiputra contractors registered with the Ministry of Works and Utilities rose from less than 30 to 63%. Ninety-four % of them, however, were concentrated in the small establishments (categories D-F), as compared to 70% for the non-Bumiputras. More revealing is that the number of non-Bumiputra small contractors dropped from 3138 to 2494 while the number for the Bumiputras increased from 1874 to 5673. This displacement of non-Malay contractors has caused resentment among Chinese capitalists who have either increased the prices or reduced the supplies of raw materials. This problem has been raised at different Bumiputra economic seminars and some have recommended that Pernas be appointed sole distribution agency or 30% of the distribution be reserved for Bumiputras.

Malay Bourgeoisie

The third component of the development of Malay capital is the creation of the Malay bourgeoisie. Until the mid-1970s, prominent Malay bourgeois were primarily directors of large corporations, and most of them did not own the companies on which they sat. They could not be identified as a dynamic segment of the Malay bourgeoisie. Events changed by the late 1970s; the number of Malay millionaires began to escalate significantly and their wealth and activities were occasionally revealed in the public media. . . .

What is the nature of this new breed of Malay bourgeoisie? The first striking pact is most of them are either politicians or aristocrats or have close connections with such people. It is true that a few have humble origins, but their development hardly resembles the tale of a bourgeoisie who slowly made it from rags to riches without state assistance. Practically all the prominent Malay bourgeoisie have made a dramatic leap into a corporate world through an initial windfall obtained from state concessions. Timber, construction and mining concessions are the most common entry points, and increasingly the purchase of shares is the important avenue for upward mobility. Without political connections and state patronage it is unlikely they could have succeeded today.

Lacking capital, know-how and market connections, all invariably end up in joint partnerships with either foreign and/or Chinese capital, crating a symbiotic relationship between Malay and non-Malay bourgeoisie. . . .

It has been argued by Jomo (1977) that state participation in the economy and state assistance in the development of the Malay bourgeoisie has resulted in a new class fraction called "the bureaucratic bourgeoisie". His thesis is based on Shivji's concept of the bureaucratic bourgeoisie in Tanzania. The Malay bourgoisie, however, differs from the Tanzanian bureaucratic bourgeoisie in a number of crucial ways. In Tanzania state ownership is more extensive and private capital is limited to small-scale businesses. Furthermore, state officials are not allowed to engage in private capital accumulation. These conditions do not apply to Malaysia.

The Malay bourgeoisie should also be distinguished from the military-bureaucratic bourgeoisie of Indonesia. According to Robison (1978), the Indonesian military-bureaucratic bourgeoisie are not involved in production; they derive their income from "tributes" paid by their Chinese and foreign capitalist partners who own and run the enterprises. Furthermore, the income of the military-bureaucratic bourgeoisie is used not for capital accumulation but for conspicuous consumption and for the purchase of military and political support from lower echelon officials. Under such circumstances, the existence of the military-bureaucratic bourgeoisie is precarious and transitional. Committed not to rational accumulation, this group engages in rapacious exploitation, contributing to economic and political instability as well as corruption on a scale difficult to surpass.

In Malaysia, neither the military nor the bureaucrats have developed enough muscle to fully control politics and economics simultaneously. Bourgeois parliamentary state form and private enterprises are still the dominant mode of political and economic organizations in society. There is no sign that state capitalism is on the rise or that it has spawned a new class or class fraction with different interests.

The proliferation of state enterprises should not be equated with the elimination of the private sector. It was noted in the First Bumiputra Economic Congress that the eventual goal of state capital accumulation was the transfer of assets to the Malay bourgeoisie and not the creation of a rival class fraction. By 1978 it appeared that the growth of state enterprises seemed overwhelming and would come into conflict with Malay private capital. A year later, the Prime Minister and the Finance Minister announced a scheme to divest the shares of state enterprises to Malay individuals.

In the late 1970s the Bumiputra Investment Foundation and its investment arm Permodalan National Bhd. (PNB) were set up and $1.5 billion was allocated to PNB under the Fourth Malaysia Plan. PNB buys shares for Bumiputras in corporations, then resells them to Bumiputras in the form of unit trusts. In 1981 the government offered 31% or $1.5 billion of its total shares for sale to private Bumiputras through the PNB. It was estimated that as many as 850,272 Bumiputras participated in this scheme.

What began as a political strategy of divestment is now gaining further momentum because of economic necessity. It was conservatively estimated that $1 billion is required annually, between 1976–1990, for Malays to achieve 30% ownership of the corporate economy, a sum which the state is presently finding difficult to provide. Since 1981 export earnings, and consequently government revenues, particularly from petroleum, have tumbled.

Desperately strapped for funds, the state adopted the following strategies to meet the problem: a drastic reduction in public expenditures, including funds allocated to state enterprises, and a heavy reliance on foreign borrowings.

Under the Third Malaysia Plan private investment fell below the government's target, despite the concessions it had made to private capital through amending the PDAA and ICA. Based on this experience the state toned down its strategy for the acquisition of private companies. Faced with a shrinking purse and a cautious private sector, the state launched a new scheme – Malaysia Incorporated – in early 1983 (*NST*, 7 March 1983). This idea emulates the Japanese model, and aims to bring the private and public sector to work more closely together. . . .

Contradictions in Capital Accumulation and Legitimation

In Malaysia, the role of the state in capital accumulation has generated problems of legitimacy which have become more apparent in the post-1970 period. The direct identification of the state with the interests of one segment of society, i.e.: the Malays, has undermined its legitimacy in the eyes of other ethnic communities. But this loss of legitimacy has not been overly disconcerting to the state since the bulk of its political support comes from the Malay community. Discontent expressed by non-Malay subordinate classes is often branded as communal disturbance and is easily repressed. But protests by non-Malay and foreign capital have, as we have seen, forced the state to temper its policies.

But even as the state has directly sided with Malays, it has not been able to gain the full loyalty of that community. We have observed the dissatisfaction voiced by the Malay petite bourgeoisie over the competition they face from state enterprises. This intra-Malay protest compelled the state to trim back the role of state enterprises, moving away from competitive industries, to focus on heavy industries, and finally divesting ownership of state enterprises to Malay individuals.

More disconcerting to the state are the frequent strikes and mass protests that have been directed at the state. In 1974, when rubber prices fell, tens of thousands of Malay peasants, supported by students, took to the streets. This was one of the first occasions Malay peasants demonstrated against the Malay-dominated government. The issues surrounding this protest galvanised Malay and non-Malay students into taking class action which transcended ethnic divisions.

In the urban areas, discontent also simmered among state employees. In January 1979 4000 workers in the Malaysian Airline system (a state-owned airline) staged a work to rule campaign, disrupting the airline schedules, and gained the support of other national and international unions. This demonstration by the state employees invited stern measures from the state: the internment of union members, the de-registration of the union, and the amendment of labor laws which would make it almost impossible for state workers to strike or to have contact with other organizations.

Even the middle classes have not remained unaffected. The sympathy some academics displayed to the plight of the peasantry and the criticisms that many have directed against the development efforts of the state were dealt with by the state using the carrot and stick approach. On the one hand, it sought to mollify the middle classes by offering handsome increases in salaries for civil servants, ranging from tens of dollars for the lowest ranking employees to thousands of dollars for the high-ranking officials. On the other hand it instituted staff disciplinary orders which prohibited civil servants, including academics, from participating in politics.

As the channels for articulating disagreements are reduced through legislation, alternative avenues of protest through religious, economic and social organizations became more salient. Among the most prominent movements are Islamic revivalist movements (e.g., ABIM), consumer movements, environmental movements, and the thousands of Chinese guilds and associations which exist. The reaction of the state to these organizations and their activities was predictable. The Societies Act was amended to ban all societies save political parties from political activities. . . .

In sum, since the second half of the 1970s, we have witnessed a heightened activity on the part of the state to depoliticize all segments of the population – from priests to peasants, proletariat to petite bourgeoisie – at a time when the increasing direct participation of the state in capital accumulation is undermining its legitimation function.

Class discontent is not necessarily revealed in class forms; it can be expressed as religious or ethnic conflicts. Such has been the case in Malaysia where economic divisions coincide with ethnic and religious differences. However, the degree of ethnic stratification has declined over the last decade. The percentage of the Malay proletariat in the urban areas has grown steadily from 34% to 45% between 1970–80. In certain sectors, such as the pioneer industries, Malays accounted for 50.6% of the workforce in 1974. This has sometimes given undue hope to some that the increasing proletarianization of the Malays would automatically be accompanied by greater class consciousness and unity between Malay and non-Malay workers. As I have argued elsewhere, if the development of a Malay proletariat is not accompanied by the concomitant development of a Malay bourgeoisie, such a situation would instead of furnishing the objective conditions for class consciousness, sow the seeds for further ethnic consciousness and conflict. A Malay proletariat confronted with non-Malay capital is more likely to view the problem of economic inequality in its most obvious form, i.e., as ethnic inequality. Thus the development of a Malay bourgeoisie as outlined in this paper is one factor that would allow for the development of class forces to proceed with fewer interruptions.

An Undeveloped State: The Study of Modern Burma's Politics

Robert H. Taylor

When Burma regained political independence in 1948, English-language studies of the country's politics in a social, economic and international context were more advanced and sophisticated than those of most other areas of Southeast Asia. Modern Burma studies had been founded by a generation of scholar-officials and academics who had lived and worked in the country during the latter years of British rule; and the most illustrious of these, men like J. S. Furnivall (1948) G. E. Harvey (1946) and D. G. E. Hall (1932; 1945; 1950; 1955) were the early giants of English Southeast Asian political and historical scholarship. Building on their solid foundations, studies of Burma's politics slowly grew over the next 18 years, though few later scholars could match the pioneers' depth of experience or breadth of knowledge. The research of the 1950s and early 1960s had a greater political immediacy to it and so turned much more to a careful chronicling of current developments and passing phenomena than did the imposing works published before 1948.

Since 1966 there have been published only two monographs on the nature of Burma's politics based on research conducted since 1962, the useful works of Josef Silverstein (1977) and David I. Steinberg (1981). Among the handful of works by foreign scholars who worked in the country between independence and the coming to power of the Revolutionary Council in 1962, one finds few guides to post-coup politics. The frequent claim by seven-day visitors to Rangoon that time has stood still in Burma is truer of Burma studies themselves than of Burma's politics.

An examination of the major political histories and studies of modern Burma reveals that most of the work has been done by Americans (Butwell, 1969; Cady, 1958; Moscott, 1974; Pye, 1962; Silverstein, 1977, 1980; Smith, 1965; Steinberg, 1981; Trager, 1966) supplemented by two British scholars (Tinker, 1967; Donnison, 1953; 1970) and several other foreign authors (Chakravarti, 1971; Sarkisyang, 1965; Yegar, 1972) as well as two Burmese writing in English (Maung Maung [Dr.], 1961; Maung Maung [Brig. Rtd.] 1980). Often, however, more revealing insights into the nature of

Burma's politics are found in the work of scholars in disciplines other than political science and history. Anthropological studies (Mendelson, 1975; Nash, 1965; Spiro, 1970; Lehman, 1967; Maran La Raw, 1967; Leach, 1960, 1965) and economics and economic histories (Adas, 1974; Walinsky, 1962; Cheng, 1968) are especially helpful. The bulk of the recent work done by political scientists, like that of historians, has been descriptive, and interpretation has been achieved through the selection of "national-level" topics and the emphasis given to various aspects of the "story of Burma" in this century.

The personal interests or official and semi-official roles that some scholars once played in Burma provide us with some evidence as to why Burma studies have developed as they have. It is clear that compared for example with Thai or Indonesian studies, there has not developed a cadre of academic students of modern Burma. This has led to Burmese studies being undeveloped both in terms of the quantity written and the interpretative arguments advanced. The easy reason often given for this situation is that since the coup of 1962 it has been almost impossible to do research in the country. This has certainly been a factor, but even when the country was "open" to Western scholars, little progress was made in advancing interpretative paradigms beyond the assumptions, patterns and methods used by colonial officials-cum-scholars in the British era. Probably the major effect of "closing" Burma to foreign scholarship has been to reduce the number of new recruits to the group that made the study of the country a career. Burma's closure, however, cannot be the only reason for the failure to train a new generation of scholars. The study of China's and Vietnam's politics, after all, continued to grow in the 1960s and 1970s despite the difficulty of access to these countries.

A major factor that has inhibited the growth of Burma studies is the absence of an external institutional infrastructure for research because the country is of relatively little strategic or economic importance to the United States and other major western countries. There is no major center devoted to Burma studies and offering integral language training in the West. Elementary research aides, such as an up-to-date Burmese-English dictionary, have not been funded by governments or foundations and therefore access to modern Burmese literature for foreign scholars and government officials has been severely restricted. With the demise of the Burma Research Society there is no longer any journal published in English devoted to scholarly research on Burma's history and society. This situation stands in marked contrast to the conditions of the study of all other major Southeast Asian countries.

However, in the 1950s Burma studies seemed well served by the fact that so much was published in English about the country during the colonial period. The colonial dual language pattern continued for the first 14 years after independence through the publication of most government documents in English as well as Burmese and in the existence of several independent conservative English-language newspapers in Rangoon. As the first generation of post-independence elite politicians and civil servants were also fluent in English, interviewing was an easy and enjoyable research method. It therefore seemed possible during the 1950s to be a Burma specialist without learning the language well enough to use it as a research tool. In Southeast Asia, probably only the study of Philippine politics has been as monolingual. . . .

If one surveys the scholarly terrain of modern Burma political studies, one author's works stand out clearly, giving some order and sense to the apparent randomness of history. That author, of course, is Furnivall, for not only was he the major authority on modern Burma writing in English who used Burmese sources but also his theory of the plural society and the economic determination of Burma's political condition up to independence has shaped almost all later interpretations. From being a British colonial servant to an advisor to U Nu's government in the 1950s, he had access to greater and more varied sources of information than any other writer. In large measure, the standard interpretation of modern Burma is Furnivall's and thus the assumptions of most other writers flow from Furnivall's beliefs. From being a severe critic of the state and its spokesmen in the 1920s, he had become by the 1950s the bulwark of conservative orthodoxy.

Like all pioneers who become guides for those who follow, Furnivall opened up trails which he did not have time to develop into broader and better marked paths. His primary concerns were economic, especially the economic conditions of the Burmese peasant population. He saw the major fault of British rule in Burma as the unwillingness of the colonial state to dominate and direct the economic forces that European capitalism had unleashed on an unsuspecting and defenseless peasantry. The future of Burma, if it was to be peaceful and prosperous, and if the indigenous population was to benefit from peace and prosperity, required that politics come to dominate economics. Furnivall taught this lesson in many ways and the evolution of government policy after independence suggests that it was well learned by the many Burmese who came into contact, directly or indirectly, with his ideas. . . .

Imperialism, Tradition and Nationalism

. . .The general conclusion drawn by Western writers has been that even if the coming of British rule was the result of nefarious British imperialist intrigues, by and large, it was no bad thing. Old Burma was stagnant and unjust and British dynamism and fairness dragged it unwillingly into the modern age. This was historically inevitable and no alternative path for Burma was considered possible, even though the contrasting patterns of change in Thailand and Java, as Furnivall himself examined, lay close at hand. The imposition of British rule led to the consequences that it did because of the nature of the modern state, the laws of economics and the nature of "world society", and one could not have expected it to have been otherwise. The "common sense" of the Western imperialist state faced the social stagnation of the East in Burma and the outcome was a foregone conclusion. In the economic determinism of Furnivall and those who followed him, including Burmese Marxists, there was nothing to be gained by thinking much about the past other than perhaps to lament its long-lost romantic qualities. The only really bad and not inevitable aspect of British rule in Burma was that it had not made the people fit for self-government even after the Second World War. Only when this was made academic after independence was the question of "fitness" dropped from most works.

It may seem unnecessary to discuss these points even briefly in an essay primarily concerned with the writing of twentieth-century political history, but the generally negative attitude toward Burma's pre-colonial political and social traditions has been most important in shaping assumptions and arguments about what was reasonable and unreasonable behavior during and after the colonial period. Even now it is not unusual to read judgements of the present government's policies that are very similar to those expressed by the earliest imperialist historians. The claim is made today just as it was about the pre-colonial period that one of the reasons why Burma is not as economically "developed" as some think it ought to be is because the government has "made absurd rules that interfered with trade" (Cocks, 192?: 15). Then as now foreign observers have made little attempt to understand the internal and external structural constraints on state action nor have they considered carefully the reasons for government policies.

In the literature when the image of pre-colonial economic stagnation, village cohesion but political disorder is juxtaposed against the image of politics in the colonial period, a slightly different Burma begins to emerge. From the beginning of British rule Burmese society is thrown into a vortex of change. Pre-colonial political chaos is intensified by rapid social disintegration. Unlike in the study of twentieth-century Thailand where the search for continuities has been the dominant theme until recently, Burma studies have quite correctly evoked an image of a society undergoing continuous and radical stress and transformation. Looked at from the perspectives of peasant rebellions, nationalist movements, colonial government policies, war and revolution, politics was in constant flux. While it would be an exaggeration to say that the major writers have ignored the underlying continuities and stability of Burmese society, none has ever emphasized them. And yet we know from the study of other societies which have undergone equally traumatic and rapid political and social change, such as Russia and Japan, that political traditions and attitudes change very slowly even in radically altered circumstances.

Where continuity has been seen, it has usually been noted in the ongoing activities of the Buddhist sangha and the values it has perpetuated. In terms of politics, these continuities have almost uniformly been judged as bad, for they clashed with the liberal values of Western writers. Few scholars have attempted a serious study of the power of Buddhist tradition on Burmese political behavior. Even those students of politics such as E. Sarkisyanz who have sympathetically and from Burmese Buddhist sources attempted to study the sangha and its political role have concentrated their attention on the minority of the monkhood labeled "Buddhist modernists", (Sarkisyanz, 1978: 91). Most share Furnivall's judgement that nationalism definitely progressed only when lay politicians began to break their contacts with sangha leaders. The exceptions to this generalization, Smith's *Religion and Politics in Burma* and Mendelson *Sangha and State in Burma*, have most effectively advanced our understanding for they have not seen the sangha's political function in the colonial period, or since, as somehow unusual or just a passing phase.

In writing about the high colonial period between 1920 and 1940 the primary explanatory variable used by most writers has been nationalism, but the concept is without definition, form or content. As with the generally negative definition of Burma's past, modern

Burma's nationalism was also seen as essentially a negative manifestation of a retrograde character. Even when it was seen to be a positive, healthy development, Burmese nationalism was still often considered to be ineffectual politically, although it had an important role to play in reform.

For Furnivall, nationalism was a force to re-integrate society and was thus juxtasposed against the disintegrating consequences of capitalism. Beyond this, nationalism was not defined and as Furnivall developed the idea, was incapable of victory against the laws of economics. In a contradictory manner, Furnivall thought that a politically united people could combat the economic determinism that had created the dominant capitalist world society, but of course this could only be done, as he also recognized, when they had regained their independence; but the latter he did not think they were yet capable of managing. His was a voice of pessimism.

For other historians, less consciously aware of economic forces, the failure of the Burmese to form themselves into a cohesive force against the British was indicative of the weaknesses of character and social structure that had allowed the initial conquest of Burma by the British. Though Cady recognized the economic and social causes of Burmese disunity, the thrust of his argument was to attribute the repeated factionalism of Burmese nationalism during the 1920s and 1930s to defects in the character of leaders who were too open to bribery, corruption, and the spoils of office. Others follow, noting the destruction of social solidarity due to a century of turmoil. All of these attempts at explanation are essentially apolitical for none of them addresses the question of social structure and the distribution of wealth and power within colonial Burma.

War, Revolution and Communism

Burma has been a one-party socialist state formally only since the introduction of the new constitution in 1974, but Marxism has been a major factor in political debate and organization in the country since the late 1930s. Except for Vietnam, Burma is the only socialist state in Southeast Asia which has been created as a result of essentially internal factors. It also has the longest running communist-led insurgency in the region. Yet, almost no writing on Burma's modern politics considers Marxism as a serious intellectual current. This situation is even more astounding when it is recalled that for four years after independence the country was involved in a civil war between an avowed socialist government and a major communist movement. But one searches long and hard to find even a reference in the literature to the fact that Marxism has influenced anybody other than the Rangoon political elite. . . .

The standard thesis on the role of Marxism in Burma is retailed by John Seabury Thomson in his essay *Marxism in Burma* (1959; see also Badgley, 1969, 1974). This essay, like the works upon which it is based, and those that have followed it, argues that Marxism in its communist version is essentially irrelevant for an understanding of Burma's politics. Working within the standard Cold War framework of the 1950s, Thomson juxtaposes communism to nationalism and argues that the former defeated the latter in Burma. Despite evidence to the contrary, it is generally conceded that the Marxism of the Thakins in the late 1930s was just a passing youthful fancy that "infected" only two or three students. Aung San's role as a founder of the first communist cell in Burma is played down and it is generally accepted that the Tahkins had no fixed ideological goals. The basis for this and other claims about the unimportance of Marxist ideology in Burmese nationalism is Furnivall's translation of U Nu's wartime memoirs, *Burma Under the Japanese* [The original version of this chapter contains a critique of this translation – Eds.], but this work systematically excludes any discussion of the place of Marxism in the resistance movement.

The larger question of the role of the communists in the anti-Japanese resistance and the immediate post-war anti-British movement is one about which the standard authorities tend to differ and even contradict themselves. Furnivall, for example, writes in one place that by "taking the lead in national resistance to the Japanese, they taught the troops, the militia, the under-ground army, and the common man to identify nationalism with communism" (1950: 13). In other places he ignores the role of the Communists and attributes formation of the resistance and its major institution, the Anti-Fascist People's Freedom League (AFPFL) to Aung San and various other organizations, especially the socialists. Thomson also plays loose with the facts. He writes at one point that it was "clear that, although the largest single organization in the AFPFL was the Socialist party, the best organized element was the Communist party...." (1959: 30). In fact, of course, in 1945–6 neither organization was terribly well organized but clearly the Communist Party was the largest political group in the country except for the army and later the PVO. At that time the socialists did not even refer to themselves as a party (*pati*) but as an *ahpwe* or group. Though it is generally conceded that the general strike, coupled with the anti-tax/anti-rent campaigns against the government, in

1946, was the catalyst that finally forced the British to negotiate independence more rapidly, and that the communists were responsible for organizing these, the credit for the speedy hand-over of power to a national government is almost always given to Aung San and the non-communist AFPFL leadership.

In criticizing the communists and blaming them for starting the civil war of 1948–52, the standard interpretation has relied heavily on an argument that their differences with the non- or anti-communist nationalists was at base irrational. Policy differences and ideas about the proper organization of the state did not, in this view, enter into the dispute. . . .

There has yet to be written a thorough study of the politics of Burma between 1945 and 1948. The rift between the communists and the socialists in the nationalist movement has been interpreted almost entirely from the perspectives and sources of the socialists and the government. For example, that there was any justice in the communists' claim that the independence negotiated by Aung San and Nu was less than complete is never considered, but an examination of the post-independence financial settlement and the Let Ya-Freeman agreement on the British military mission to Burma might suggest that there were strings attached to independence which an alternative leadership might well have found unacceptable. Moreover, the writing on this period conveys the general impression that the choice of a form of liberal democratic government and initial ties to the West were a foregone conclusion which domestic politics should or could not have altered. That ideology or interest could have played a role in these processes is effectively ignored in favor of a concentration on personality and the alleged inability of Burmese to organize coherent political organizations.

Thomson's work like others fails to mention even such rudimentary facts as that the government, in the form of Home Minister U Kyaw Nyein, had ordered the arrest of the major communist leaders on the eve of the day they went underground, clearly denying them the opportunity to continue to pursue constitutional and open political organization. Almost nowhere in the literature is there even a hint of the fact that the Communists were at least as powerful or popular as the anti-communist political groups. Yet how else can the civil war of 1948–52 be explained except in terms of the widespread support the communists received at the time?

The State After Independence

Two largely unquestioned assumptions in most studies of post-independence politics have been that the state and the group that initially controlled it were viewed as legitimate by most of the Burmese population and that the constitutional structure and political format of the 1950s were consonant with the ethnic and ideological, as well as the power problems of the state. If these assumptions are questioned and found to be false or misleading, then it is necessary to rethink the post-independence period as well as the politics of the nationalist movement during the 1940s. The question involves the problem of whether the weakened post-colonial state in Burma could survive if organized as a representative or plebiscitary institution or whether its continuance did not depend upon its functioning, in an altered guise, much like the colonial bureaucratic and armed state.

This question raises the vexing problem of legitimacy. Most political analysts most of the time accept the legitimacy of whatever state (and the government or group that controls it) they are studying. However, this is not always appropriate as the now generally irrelevant studies of South Vietnam's politics demonstrate. Even anti-colonial writers generally conceded that internationally the imperialist colonial regimes were legitimate at the time and that internal armed opponents were rebels against constituted authority. Certainly the officials and scholars of colonial Burma did not seriously doubt their own legitimacy until after the Second World War when they found it impossible to continue to operate "normally". For independent states and governments, and their students, however, the problem of legitimacy is much more crucial, for genuinely independent regimes cannot trust outside powers to keep them in place for long against a population which has violently withdrawn its consent or not been cowed into submission.

In the case of Burma at independence, the easy assumption made in most studies of the legitimacy of the state bequeathed by the British, and the AFPFL government which controlled it, seems unwarranted. In terms of the state itself, had not peasant protests and rebellions since the 1880s been directed against the British state and its exactions? In terms of the government, had not the AFPFL become divided by ideology before independence so that by 1948 it was a mere shadow of the original national front? Had not some minority leaders withdrawn their cooperation from the AFPFL? Certainly after the death of Aung San, if not before, the overwhelming support which the AFPFL had received in 1945–46 had disappeared.

One need only look at the 1948–52 civil war when the government at times barely controlled more than central Rangoon to recognize that the AFPFL government of post-independence Burma was far from being considered legitimate by a sizeable portion of the population. However, only one unpublished Burmese author to my knowledge has acknowledged the 1950s politicians' doubts about their legitimacy. Only by denying the importance of the civil war and its causes can it be concluded that the post-colonial state and the AFPFL government, a minority government led by men who doubted their own positions, were viewed as legitimate by the bulk of the population.

When we turn from the legitimacy of the post-independence regime to examine the 1947 constitutional structure that it created to serve its purpose, it becomes apparent that the divisions that gave rise to questions about the regime's legitimacy also reappear. Since, as is generally conceded, the 1947 constitution owed more to "British tradition and practice" than to Marxism, then problems arise about the legitimacy of the constitution itself, certainly in the eyes of that large proportion of the population that rallied to the left socialists and communists during and after the civil war. While it would be wrong to say that the 1947 constitution contained no socialist inspiration, as Furnivall points out, the contradiction between the views of the liberal authors of the document and of the revolutionary nationalists meant that the constitution was one which only contained "socialist aspirations".

The problem of the legitimacy of the post-independence regime in relationship to the ethnic minorities poses other difficult issues. The original basis of support for the AFPFL amongst the minorities, especially the Shans and the Karens, came from youth groups led by men and women who had contact with student and Thakin leaders in Rangoon before and during the period of the Japanese occupation. Their views and interests were very similar to those of the radical leaders of the League but when, in order to speed up the handing over of power from the British, the League's leaders made compromises with the more traditional and less popular minority leaders who had been supported by the British, they withdrew their cooperation. This meant that while the Shan traditional leaders, the Sawbwas, were able to extract compromises resulting in a guarantee of their power and influence in the Shan states for another ten years, the Karens became divided, some accepting the promises offered, some rejecting them. The result was to weaken the control of the central state and its leaders' "natural" allies in the principal minority regions.

Furnivall conceded, to a degree that most other post-independence analysts have not, that the constitutional structures of the 1950s made stable and progressive government, and therefore by implication a strong state, almost impossible. The contradiction between what that state could afford to provide in the way of social services and development goals as opposed to what it had to pay out for political reasons meant that the task of reintegrating Burma's society could not be achieved by a state and government that had much less power than its pre-war predecessor. While Furnivall never explicitly indicates this, his analysis of the consequences of liberal democratic politics in Burma during the 1920s and 1930s and during the 1950s are essentially the same. The 1923, 1935 and 1947 constitutions were essentially British constitutions. In both local and national government, Furnivall had long recognized that principles of rule appropriate for Britain or America were inappropriate for Burma. In Burma, Furnivall argued, the government and its officials had to work to guide the short-sighted populace rather than giving it what it wanted because what it might want in the short term was not necessarily in the society's or the state's interest in the long term. After independence, when nationalism had caputred the state, then reform would be possible, but since he had lost sight of the politics of the state, the requirements of competitive parties and the imperatives of those who lead them, Furnivall's analysis became less and less cogent.

Liberal democracy in Burma's plural society was not appropriate for social reintegration, for it led to increased ethnic, party and class conflict. During the 1950s the AFPFL became the body which controlled the government rather than the Chamber of Deputies. While there is yet no thorough study of how the League operated, it would seem that on the whole the AFPFL and its leaders had to devote most of their attention to meeting the demands of their local supporters for such things as loans, contracts and small development projects, with little possibility, because of the threat of the next election, of building mechanisms for loan repayments, tax collection and increased production with which to enrich and strengthen the state and to provide capital for investment. But the inability of the AFPFL government to fulfill all the demands made upon it led to the decline in its proportion of the vote in the 1956 elections. With programs nearer to those of the New Deal than to Marxism, the patronage system of the League, using the inadequate resources of the state, was insufficient to buy support from all the segments that demanded attention and failed to touch the ideological and programatic interests of many peasants and workers who were mobilized to vote for the leftist alternative at that time.

The second constitutional issue of the 1950s that requires discussion here is that of ethnicity and federalism. As in many other aspects of politics, perceptions of ethnicity and federalism in Burma have shaped to a large degree political and state action, and there has been a great change in views from the colonial and immediate post-colonial period to the present. Overwhelmingly the literature on Burma's politics has favoured the established leaders of the minorities and their own perceptions of ethnicity and federalism. Cady's *History of Modern Burma* devotes a large proportion of space to the politics of the Karens. Most recently Silverstein's *Burmese Politics, the Dilemma of National Unity* has criticized both the AFPFl and Burma Socialist Programme Party governments for their policies toward the hill peoples. One searches in vain in the English-language literature to find the views of the local anti-feudal, anti-traditional movements in the Shan States that is found, for example, in works such as San Aung's *Nyinyatyēi Ayēitawbon*. The general Western, particularly American, bias towards federalism and pluralism has effectively blurred foreign perceptions of the political situation in the hill areas of Burma.

Might not the whole issue of the cultural/political aspects of ethnicity in Burma, usually posed as alternatives between assimilation and cultural pluralism, be a false one in terms of Burma's cultural history? Is not Burma's culture itself an amalgam of cultural adaptations, borrowings, enrichments and convolutions? Might not the question be put more appropriately as one of the relationship of a central culture and ecological system which has received the most varied inputs and a variety of peripheries each with greater cultural homogeneity but fewer adaptive capabilities? By raising such questions, one is forced to reconsider whether a federal state is a viable "solution" to what is mistakenly defined as a problem rather than as a constantly evolving cultural synthesis.

Behind many issues in the Western understanding of Burma's politics lies a complex of judgements about the relative value of the alleged democratic socialism of the 1950s and the socialist democracy of 1962 onwards. These judgements are intimately connected with the relatively positive assessment of U Nu and the politicians of the 1950s against a relatively negative assessment of U Ne Win and the politicians of the 1960s and 1970s. These judgements are further complicated by the relatively easy access to information available to scholars in the 1950s and the subsequent limitations which have been placed on them in terms of contact and personal rapport.. . . .

. . .Contemporary contrasting judgements of U Nu and U Ne

Win and their colleagues have their precedents in the earlier and widely accepted contrasts drawn between Mindon Min and Thibaw Min. Perhaps because both Thibaw and Ne Win seemed to frustrate or ignore the values and interests of the West to a degree that Mindon and Nu appeared not to have done (the facts aside), Western judgements about the sagacity and appropriateness of Thibaw's and Ne Win's regimes in terms of Burma's condition have been made with more than a small degree of animus.

More fundamentally, however, these contrasting judgements stem from a failure to take into account the moral ambiguities of politics and government, either in our own culture or in Burma's. Judgements about character and purpose tend to be formed by western scholars as well as people generally in good and bad terms, hence our intolerance of politicians who do not fit with our own values. In Burma, however, it can be argued, the culture is more tolerant of rulers perhaps because they are seen less as reflections of the governed than as necessary limitations on human evil and greed – the great excesses in Burmese thought. Either of these cultural perceptions poses serious problems for those who control the state, but in Burma there is a general appreciation, even among opponents of the present regime who have been jailed, not only of the dilemma that the ruler faces in maintaining order, but an acceptance that he exercise the burdens of power while suffering the moral odium of authority. Furthermore, as Hobbes made us aware through *The Leviathan*, societies that have recently experienced a civil war often submit to strong rule for fear of the consequences of its absence. Thus the oft repeated statement in Burma that after Ne Win, things will get worse in the sense that disorder will return.

The Search for Explanations

Most Western writing on modern Burma's politics has not self-consciously searched for explanations of behavior. Where such efforts have been made, explanations have generally been sought in the all-embracing categories of culture, identity and personality. The absence of sociological studies looking at class, interest and patron-client relations, so replete in the study of Indonesian and Thai politics, is striking. From the earliest imperialist historians through to the more recent studies by Western social scientists, indivi-dualism has been given as the main reason for the absence of either unity or effective long-term action on the part of Burmese politicians.

Pye's *Politics, Personality and Nation Building*, while rarely cited by serious students of Burma, is in the wider community of Western social science probably the best known book on Burma's politics. The book is flawed by a number of methodological problems and by an absence of historical accuracy. In essaying what he saw as a clash of backgrounds and roles between the administrators and politicians of Burma in the 1950s, Pye ignored the actual similarity in their social origins and backgrounds. What was in fact a clash of interests between those using the state as a static instrument to ensure their interests and positions and those using the state to ensure their re-election and the strength of their political organizations was overlooked in pursuit of an explanation based upon personality types. Pye went on from his study of a handful of English-speaking administrators and politicians to draw conclusions not only about Burmese "national character", but also Burma's chances of "modernization". Because he did not undertake a complete examination of the actual conditions of the polity and economy of Burma, his overwhelmingly negative judgements have largely been ignored.

Remarkably absent from the literature on Burma's politics are studies of class. In part, this is explained by the widely held belief that Burma at independence was "essentially . . . a class-less or single-class society" (Thomson, 1959: 37): One searches in vain in English-language writings for a discussion of the role of what Burmese writers call the "immature national capitalists" of the colonial period or of the 1950s. The continued immaturity of Burmese capitalists during the 1950s made the group dependent upon the state and thus not a fully autonomous class. Nevertheless, they flourished during the first decade after independence and had an impact on policy-making. Their exclusion from government after 1962 and the consequent radical socialist policies of the ensuing period makes this clear.

Another neglected area of study is the role of the alien, primarily Indian, middle class in colonial or independence politics. There are now in Burmese a wide variety of reports on the workers' movement, peasants' movement and class generally which have yet to be assimilated into the Western understanding of modern Burma's politics. When they have been, there will be revealed aspects of the character of the nationalist movement and of post-independence politics that have been obscure to now. The degree of collaboration that existed within classes across ethnic divides has up till now been obscured by the undue emphasis given to ethnicity alone as the key determinant of political groupings.

There are two other notable absences in the study of modern Burma's politics. One is the absence of some effort to come to terms with the intellectual and conceptual transformations in Burmese political discourse during this century. The standard histories by omission present the impression that Burma's politics have existed in an intellectual void. Where references are made to the ideas of Burmese politicians, it is generally to dismiss them as irrelevant or too muddled to be of use as indicators to action. Thus Western students of Burma have been unable to understand the conceptual framework of political action, requiring analysis to fall back on personality rather than interest or ideology as the well-spring of action.

The other major void in the study of modern Burma is any serious discussion of the state, either as an institution or as an idea, as has been suggested in several places above. Studies of the colonial period of necessity discuss the opposition of the Burmese to British rule, but they fail to attempt to assess the content of that resistance. It was more than opposition to foreign domination; it was resistance to the demands of Leviathan on personal choice. The calls to boycott the government from the "*bu athin/wunthanu*" movement of the 1920s to the Red Flag Communists of the 1940s have a similarity which is not at first apparent until seen in the light of the contrasting interests of the state and of those it attempted to control. The failure to apprehend the needs of the central state, regardless of who dominates it, in relation to the question of ethnic and ecological variety stems from the same deficiency.

Burma's political history for the past one hundred years, when looked at from the perspective of the development of the state, begins to have a coherence that up to now has been lacking. Furnivall pointed to this once but then went on to other work. Perhaps if we begin to retrace Furnivall's path, the study of the Burmese state will reveal a much clearer picture of the nature of modern Burma's politics than we have been able to form up to now.

The Transformation of the State in Indonesia

Richard Robison

Introduction

The recent revival of interest in the state in post-colonial societies is, in large part, a consequence of the decline of dependency theory as a general tool for the analysis of society and economy in the Third World and a move towards an approach based upon the concepts of mode of production and social formation. The focus of analysis has consequently moved from global structures of capital circulation to class struggle within specific peripheral social formations.

The Indonesian social formation, as it has developed over the past century, embraces a complex configuration of petty commodity production (under which I include landlord/tenant and small-holder production as well as household commodity production) and various levels of commercial and capitalist production. The process of capitalist revolution and industrialization proceeds at a snail's pace. Indonesia is not yet a society of bourgeois and proletariat but remains largely one of landlord and tenant, petty commodity producers and state officials, landless and unemployed.

Nevertheless, the Indonesian state for the past century has been a capitalist state, providing the conditions for capital accumulation and securing the social dominance of the various fractions of bourgeoisie. However, it has passed through several distinct stages of development related to major transformations in class structure, level of capitalist production and political conflict. It is only within the context of these specific stages that transformations in the form and function of the Indonesian state can be understood. The crucial periods are:

1. (1870–1940): The period of enclave export commodity production (largely sugar on Java, rubber and coffee on Sumatra) during which time the state primarily constituted the interests of Dutch capital.

2. (1941–58): The period of decline of the enclave export commodity economy due both to global economic factors and the weakening of Dutch capital investment and the capacity of the

Dutch bourgeoisie to dominate the state apparatus. The new republican state operated in a vacuum of social power due to weakness and fragmentation of class forces.

3. (1958–65): State implementation of the nationalization of the decaying colonial economy and mediation of the intensifying struggle between social and political alliances increasingly committed to social revolution or to reconstitution of capitalism. This period closes with the victory of the forces of capitalist rather than socialist revolution.

4. (1965–81): The military-dominated New Order State consolidates power upon the basis of an alliance of foreign, Chinese and larger indigenous capitals and a system of capitalist production generated by US and Japanese investment in resources and energy and increasingly, in industrial production for both import-substitution and export. Accelerated transformation to capitalist relations of production entrenches the social and economic power of the bourgeoisie and the position of the military-bureaucratic oligarchy.

The Legacy of Colonialism

We cannot really talk of a capitalist state in Indonesia until the latter part of the nineteenth century. Under both the Dutch East Indies Company (V.O.C.) and the Dutch government during the period of the Culture System (approx. 1830–70) the function of the colonial state was to enforce the provision of labor on state plantations to collect the produce of this labor and to operate or subcontract a variety of trade monopolies.

During the second half of the nineteenth century the Dutch bourgeoisie began to press for the abolition of this state monopoly and the opening of the colony for private investment. In 1870 new land legislation made it possible for Dutch capitalists to lease large areas of "unused" land for purposes of plantation agriculture and to supplement these with short-term leases (21 years) of village land. The state no longer directly intervened in the production process to coerce labor and ensure the delivery of crops but instead secured the general conditions of existence for the reproduction of the colonial plantation economy.

Apart from providing the legal basis for private land ownership, the state administered labor laws and the leasing of village land to the sugar mills. When the world market faltered it negotiated international commodity pricing agreements and protected the besieged plantation sector against competition from indigenous small-holder producers. At the same time the form of the state apparatus began to change. Officials had previously been paid percentages on enforced crop deliveries or provided with appanage lands from which they could collect tribute. These forms of remuneration were gradually replaced with salaries.

In the early decades of the twentieth century, investment in manufacture began to penetrate the colonial plantation economy. Dutch, and to a lesser extent, Chinese and indigenous bourgeoisie began to manufacture commodities which had previously been either imported or produced by petty commodity production. The state moved to secure this capitalist import substitution industrialization by providing more extensive and complex infrastructures, especially Japanese.

When power passed from the Dutch to the Indonesians in 1949, the new republican state found itself unable to do anything other than continue to provide the general conditions of existence for the colonial enclave commodity production sector. This was essentially because the whole social structure and accumulation process was predicated upon enclave commodity production, of which the Javanese sugar mill was the primary symbol. Dutch finance capital in the form of the culture banks and the major trading conglomerates remained the dominant economic force and the lynchpin of the accumulation process. Within the cocoon of the colonial social formation, indigenous classes constituted a weakly developed and fragmented basis for political challenge to the colonial export economy.

Perhaps the most cohesive and clearly defined domestic class were the Chinese traders. Until the mid-nineteenth century they had been used by both traditional and colonial rulers as tax farmers and operators of state trading monopolies. With the development of estate and small-holder commercial production and the generalization of commodity production they began to establish domestic trade and credit networks dealing in rice and small-holder produce, retailing, moneylending and small-scale processing of agricultural produce such as rice hulling and sugar milling. With the lifting of residence restrictions in 1908 they began to spread into the countryside, replacing the small Javanese and Sumatran traders at the village level. By the end of the colonial period they clearly dominated domestic trading and credit networks, although it is important to remember that they remained essentially a merchant and petty bourgeoisie focused around the extended family. Despite their economic power, the Chinese have been unable to secure political dominance in the post-colonial period because the social hostility of the indigenous population precluded them from the public exercise of political power. In any case, the economic position of the Chinese was firmly embedded in the existing colonial export economy.

Neither did indigenous bourgeoisie constitute a social basis for a political transformation of the colonial economic and social order. The bulk of indigenous businessmen were petty commodity producers and small scale traders in small-holder crops. By 1950, only a handful had expanded their activities to trade on a national level or to factory production, employing wage and piece labor and replacing land with mechanical production processes. Political and economic organization of the indigenous bourgeoisie beginning from the formation of the Sarekat Dagang Islam in 1911 attempted to meet the Chinese challenge by securing control of trade, especially in the batik and textile industries. By the early 1930s the surge had exhausted itself, not only because they failed to seize control of trade from the Chinese, but because the basis of economic power was increasingly one of capital accumulation. In traditional areas of indigenous manufacture, (*kretek* cigarettes, textiles, batik, beverages and foodstuffs), the indigenous producers found themselves increasingly outweighed by the superior capital accumulation of the Dutch and Chinese.

This social and economic weakness of the indigenous bourgeoisie reflected itself in its demise as the core of a national political movement in the 1920s. The nationalist movement of the 1930s was dominated not by any class-based party but by Dutch-educated urban intelligentsia and officials of the Dutch colonial administration. Together with the Indonesian military leaders of the revolutionary period, they constituted the most strategically important political force in post-colonial Indonesia.

Neither did a powerful indigenous landowning class emerge. Precolonial Javanese society (which was the most heavily concentrated area of peasant cultivation) was not a feudal society dominated by a hereditary landowning aristocracy but by a ruling class defined by access to the rights to collect the peasant surplus allocated within personal networks of patronage dominated by the king. With the development of commercial agriculture in the mid- to late-nineteenth century this class chose to become salaried officials of the colonial state.

Although private land title and increasing commercialization of agricultural production were established under colonialism after the mid-nineteenth century, no politically cohesive, economically dominant land-owning class emerged. There was no clear polarization of landless tenants and laborers on the one hand and landlords on the other. Land ownership was fragmented and confused while politics at the village level was not defined by rival camps of landed and landless but by complex patron-client networks which mediated the conflicting social interests of different classes. The real process of class development in rural society was to come after independence and only accelerate in the 1960s and 1970s. At the same time, small-holder producers, mainly on Sumatra, were hard hit by depression and government restriction and remained a relatively fragmented and powerless socio-economic force. Colonialism in Indonesia had produced neither an indigenous hacienda nor an indigenous kulak class.

The Republican State in the Colonial Social Formation: 1949–58

For the first decade of its existence, political power in the new republic was vested in fragile and shifting coalitions of political parties dominated by Dutch-educated urban intelligentsia. None of the parties rested upon a basis of cohesive social power, and political conflict tended to take the form of factional squabbles over political office. The new state held a precarious authority over the military and was faced with major regional challenges to its authority.

As leaders of the nationalist movement in the 1930s and 1940s, the new party leaders had universally espoused opposition to imperialist forms of capitalism and had promised moves towards a national and, although vaguely defined, socialist economy. However, upon seizing power, they were immediately confronted with the enormous difficulties of interfering with the colonial economy. State revenue and the existing social order was predicated upon production of agricultural and mineral exports financed and managed by Dutch and Chinese bourgeoisie. No indigenous class of accumulators was capable of stepping into the shoes of the Dutch or Chinese or of providing an alternative economic system other than regression to petty commodity production. Neither did an indigenous class of accumulators ever command the political power to force the state to act systematically in their interests. No political party had the ideological coherence or base of social power necessary to mount a cohesive move towards some fundamental change to the colonial economy. The immobility of the state was largely the consequence of the vacuum of social power.

However, social and economic interests soon began to emerge and to manifest themselves politically as the struggle to appropriate the colonial economy took shape.

The most powerful of these new politico-economic forces were the politico-bureaucrats (hereafter P-B) who dominated offices of power and authority in the party and state apparatus. A crucial feature of the new P-B was the fusion of political power and bureaucratic authority—the appropriation of the state apparatus by a relatively small group of party leaders. The vehicles for this appropriation were the political parties and factions which secured control of strategic sectors of the state apparatus as the spoils of victory, dividing among themselves departments controlling trade and economic policy, state banks and corporations. Economically strategic offices were filled with party and military officials, political clients and relatives for the purpose of financing the political operations of the factions and providing a basis for building the personal wealth of individual power-holders. Using the appropriated power to dispense licenses, concessions, credit and contracts, the P-B were able to secure monopoly positions in the import sector as distributors of commodities or simply as purveyors of licenses.

The traditional indigenous trading and commodity-producing bourgeoisie and petty bourgeoisie also sought to step into the shoes of the Dutch. However, they were never able to either gain access to the political means of appropriating the Dutch, i.e. the control of licenses, concessions and contracts, or to expand beyond petty trade and commodity production on a basis of capital accumulation. During the 1950s a long history of struggle between the P-B and indigenous bourgeoisie and petty bourgeoisie was commenced, manifesting itself in the struggle for import licenses distributed under the Benteng program and the conflict over fiscal policies of the central government which caused such damage to outer island producers and contributed to the regional revolts against Jakarta in the late 1950s.

A third force was that constituted by the left wing of the PNI and the PKI and its labor and peasant organizations. These groups aimed not only at appropriation of Dutch interests but at a radical restructuring of the existing social and economic order involving the creation of a national industrial economy based upon state corporate capital and a fundamental reordering of landownership in the countryside.

**The Nationalist Challenge to the Colonial Economy:
(1958–65)**

The appropriation of the colonial economy began in 1957 with the attempt by labor unions unilaterally to establish control over Dutch enterprises. Alarmed by this development, the military moved in to take control of the Dutch companies and to assume dominance over the state corporate sector which emerged from the confiscated Dutch interests.

Against a background of nationalization and challenge from regional rebellions, President Sukarno abolished party government and established a populist, authoritarian form of rule by a fragile and uneasy coalition of nationalist forces, including both the PKI and the military, together with indigenous bourgeoisie who hoped to step into the shoes of the Dutch. Economic nationalism was, however, to take the form of state capitalism.

To a certain extent, the economic policies collectively known as "Guided Economy" did provide opportunities for the development of national industrial capital, both state and private. Attempts were made to force domestic investment out of imports and into industry. Imports of commodities which could potentially be manufactured in Indonesia were restricted. Large-scale programs of overseas borrowing were undertaken to create national industries in steel and shipbuilding. With state credit, contracts and monopolies, several private indigenous business groups and state corporations were able to move effectively into manufacture.

However, Sukarno's experiment in creating a national industrial economy failed for a variety of reasons, most important of which was the absence of a national bourgeoisie (either indigenous or Chinese) able to provide the basis for accumulation, corporate organization, management and technical expertise. Neither did Sukarno command a party structure with sufficient ideological coherence and cohesion or political discipline and organization at the mass level to sustain a complex and long-term exercise in social organization, economic planning and management necessary for such a fundamental transformation. Instead he was forced to allocate control of state capitalism to civil and military officials who saw the new state trading companies and the state authorities for coordinating trade and industry as primarily a more effective means of gaining control of the distribution system. . . .

Without either a state apparatus or a national bourgeoisie able to provide a basis of accumulation and management to replace the Dutch, the economy began to disintegrate. This had been evident as early as 1963 when the state began to mediate a withdrawal from the more rigid objectives of the state-dominated and planned economy. However the process of disintegration was irrevocably advanced. Inflation escalated to over 600%, the flow of imported consumer goods and spare parts ground to a halt and the economic infrastructure fell into increasing disrepair and disarray. Export earnings from plantation agriculture declined as production on the estates was affected by lack of maintenance and reinvestment and poor management.

The dislocation affected with greater intensity those elements of society most fully integrated with the previously Dutch-dominated structures of enclave commodity production and commodity import: the state officials, the urban middle classes and the domestic merchant bourgeoisie. For these people and for the military, the solution appeared increasingly to lie in the reconstruction of the capitalist economy and the re-entry of foreign capital as the primary basis for accumulation.

The destruction of the Sukarnoist-state and the return to the world capitalist economy was made even more urgent for the military, the state officials, the merchant bourgeoisie and the urban middle classes because of the social and political contradictions which emerged during this period. Essentially this threat was constituted by the PKI and its labor and peasant organizations. The popular forces in the shaky nationalist alliance saw fundamental social change as a necessary component of economic nationalism and had begun to engage in direct social and political action. In the countryside, the struggle over land was posing an increasing threat to the predominantly Muslim landowning classes. After the military coup in 1975, the New Order state, constituting the interests of an alliance of military, students, urban middle classes, indigenous merchant bourgeoisie and landlords, set about the task of eliminating the social and political basis of resistance to counter-revolution. The political weaknesses of Sukarno, the PKI and the other forces supporting economic nationalism was revealed by the lack of organized resistance to the massacres, purges and imprisonment which decimated their ranks in 1965 and 1966.

The New Order State, 1965–81: The Reconstruction of Political Power

Although Sukarno's Guided Democracy had been populist in the sense that the policies and rhetoric of Sukarno were designed for a mass audience and the approval of the masses was seen as necessary to the legitimacy of the state, it was at the same time authoritarian. The institutions of cabinet government, party politics and elected parliaments were replaced with presidential authority and appointed parliaments. Political participation was channelled through state-sponsored and -controlled organizations representing the "functional" groupings of society.

Apart from the move to authoritarian populism, the most important political development of the Guided Democracy period was the rise of the military, which secured positions of authority within the state apparatus. This power was underpinned by control of strategic economic terminals within the state apparatus (most notably the state trading companies and the state oil companies) which afforded sources of finance independent of the regular state budget and provided the basis for economic alliances with foreign and Chinese bourgeoisie.

With the establishment of the New Order in late-1965 political power was firmly secured by the military, or, more specifically, by the factions attached to General Suharto. The lower *priyayi*, central Javanese background of the new military rulers contrasted with that of the Dutch-educated urban intelligentsia which had dominated earlier party governments. The military soon took over the crucial positions of power in the state apparatus: the presidency, the politically and economically strategic ministries, as well as key positions in the regional and central bureaucracies.

It was soon clear that its allies in the struggle against the revolutionary nationalist alliance in 1965 and 1966 were to be given no greater access to political power than under Sukarno. The major corporatist features of Guided Democracy were retained including the authority of the president over parliament and the channeling of the political activities of trade unions, business associations and other groups into state-sponsored and -controlled organizations. The authority of the state has been further entrenched by the development of complex apparatus designed to mobilize popular support (Golkar) or to repress opposition (Kopkamtib, Bakin).

If the Sukarno regime justified its authoritarian form as most effectively crystallizing the consensus of the masses, the New Order justified its refinement of the same authoritarian features as crystallizing the real will of the masses as revealed by scientists and technocrats. The New Order may be described as technocratic authoritarianism in comparison to the populist authoritarianism of the Sukarno regime. The ideological basis of technocratic authoritarianism derives from the assumption that development may be planned and administered in a scientific and objective manner by officials of the state. With obvious debts to North American social science of the 1950s and 1960s, political struggle and political ideology is considered to be outmoded by the new scientific knowledge. The function of the state is properly regarded as that of providing scientific strategies for economic growth and at the same time imposing political control and social stability in the long-term interests of development. Economic development therefore becomes the ideological possession and the legitimizing factor of the authoritarian technocratic state just as it becomes the justification for depoliticization and repression. . . .

The Reconstitution of Capitalism

A central aspect of the debate over the function of the post-colonial state has been concerned with the degree to which metropolitan bourgeoisies dominate the process of capitalist reproduction in the Third World and the degree to which the state serves the interests of the metropolitan bourgeoisie or constitutes the cutting edge of national capital. . . . To a large extent the attempt is not a fruitful exercise. . . . Capital ownership in any social formation will usually comprise *both* national and foreign bourgeoisie. The national component will depend on the existing capital base of national bourgeoisie relative to other capitals but also to the specific type of capital investment. Foreign capital will tend to dominate in high technology, capital-intensive sectors such as oil, mining and the more complex industrial sectors. National capital will generally wish to integrate with foreign capital in these sectors but will secure state protection and subsidy to replace foreign capital where their capital base and technological resources enable them to operate alone. . . .

In the case of Indonesia, national capital – both state and private – was able neither to generate the capital necessary to sustain an independent capitalist economy nor to secure politically the national bourgeoisie as a ruling class. This situation was rectified after 1965 by the establishment of an authoritarian military state dominated by a military-bureaucratic oligarchy and by the infusion of foreign capital to supplement the process of accumulation.

A crucial element has been the re-negotiation of credit arrangements with western capitalist nations and international finance institutions such as the World Bank and the International Monetary Fund (IMF). . . .

Foreign capital has quickly re-assumed a dominant role in the economy, constituting over half the investments made under the new investment laws (both foreign and domestic) without taking into account investments in oil, banking, the foreign loan components in domestic equity and the informal Singapore and Hong Kong component in nominally domestic Chinese investment. . . .

The economic planners of the New Order generally adhere to an economic philosophy which sees foreign capital infusion spontaneously generating domestic capital accumulation. However, pressures from domestic business have forced them to take more direct steps to ensure domestic participation. In 1968, a domestic investment law was introduced, extending to domestic bourgeoisie the same benefits extended to foreign investors eighteen months earlier. State credit is available for investors under the domestic investment program (PMDN). More recently, the state has restricted the entry of further foreign capital into sectors of investment which it considers either fully catered for or able to be developed by domestic capital. Such restrictions affect investment in forestry, pharmaceuticals, construction and banking.

Business groups in Indonesia also find that the State is able to assist them, as individual companies, with state credit, contracts, monopolies, concessions and licenses. The process operates as follows: military commands, P-B factions or individuals within the P-B secure control over the allocation of state concessions, contracts and monopolies – these may be either sold for cash or used to form the basis of a joint venture between the concession-holder and specific foreign, Chinese or indigenous business groups in which the concession is exchanged for equity. For the latter purpose, the P-B establish their own business groups which may be owned by military commands or political factions and used as sources of revenue for the political needs of the faction, or they may be owned by individuals and families from within the P-B and used as a basis for the accumulation of wealth. Whatever the case, they constitute a particular means of channelling state power into the process of capital accumulation.

The state also directs its resources and power into the accumulation process by means of state-owned corporations which are nominally controlled by a minister and financially accountable to the state.

While state corporations provide revenue for the state and are plundered by the P-B, they also perform a crucial role in the accumulation process in the absence of a strong national bourgeoisie. In part the state corporate structure continues the Guided Economy objective of securing national ownership and control of strategic sectors of the economy. But, as a reflection of the strengthening economic and political power of the various bourgeoisie in New Order Indonesia, it may be increasingly seen as establishing the preconditions for private capital accumulation.

The State and the Structure of the Bourgeois Alliance

Domestic capital ownership in Indonesia falls into five major categories:
1. State capital
2. Chinese capital operating in the medium and large scale sectors
3. Indigenous capital operating in the medium- and large-scale sectors.
4. Chinese capital operating in the sector of petty trade, manufacturing and service sector
5. Indigenous capital operating in the sector of petty trade, manufacturing and service sector.

The conflict between domestic and foreign capital is as yet weakly developed. Certainly there are liberal intellectuals who despair of the degree of foreign economic dominance, but their capacity for effective political action is limited. A more interesting critique of foreign capital comes from the CSIS group (a research and intelligence component of the late General Ali Murtopo's political faction) which argues that national capital is unable to develop effectively within the present structures. They argue for systematic state protection and co-ordination or the development of national capitalism and control of foreign capital. Their proposals are based upon the concept of national capital operating within nationally integrated economic units, with the state providing a framework of coordination, protection and finance but with capital ownership remaining largely private. This concept borrows heavily from the models established by the Meiji states, the present Singapore state and the principles which underlay the OPS and GPS of Guided Economy.

The creation of such a corporate form of national capitalism requires complex and highly organized forms of state intervention far beyond the capacity of the present state apparatus in Indonesia. Nor is it likely that the Indonesian state apparatus can be transformed in the image of the Singaporean or Meiji states in the foreseeable future. This is largely because the P-B and the larger domestic bourgeoisie find the conditions for accumulation adequately provided by the present structures. Joint ventures with foreign corporations are providing access to capital and technology, while alliances between the specific P-B factions and particular business groups provide channels of access to state credit, contracts, licenses and concessions.

A more fundamental conflict has been that between the smaller indigenous bourgeoisie or petty bourgeoisie and the Chinese. This has been generated primarily by the indigenous bourgeoisie operating in the small-to-medium-scale sector of capitalist production and merging into the petty commodity production sector. Such bourgeoisie and petty bourgeoisie have generally failed to develop their economic power either by expanding their base of capital accumulation or by securing access to the patronage of P-B factions. Consequently they have been politically active in opposing the expansion of the Chinese bourgeoisie, in protesting the alliance of P-B with foreign and Chinese business groups, and in criticizing general state policies which benefit either Chinese or foreign business. This general class-based challenge has spilled beyond immediate economic interests and has come to be associated with a broader Islamic political/cultural challenge to Jakarta and to the Javanese *abangan* character of the military-dominated state.

We must differentiate this section of the indigenous bourgeoisie from those elements which have managed to secure entry to the politico-economic alliances which bind P-B political factions to Chinese and foreign business groups as well as those which constitute the P-B dimension of these alliances. It may be argued that the section of the indigenous bourgeoisie we are considering represents a declining remnant of an earlier merchant capitalist/petty commodity production era. However, such petty bourgeoisie have proven resilient during the drawn-out process of transition to capitalist forms and relations of production. With their political and social links to Islamic parties and the landowning classes of Java, the indigenous petty bourgeoisie of Indonesia have been a persistent problem for the State.

Between 1949 and 1965 several nationally prominent indigenous • traders and manufacturers with an established capital base and lines of political patronage successfully entered the fields of import, distribution and assembly of foreign machinery and automobiles and even into large-scale manufacture, although few of these have managed to survive under the New Order. However, the vast bulk of indigenous accumulators remained at the petty bourgeois or petty commodity production level.

The conflict between the indigenous petty bourgeoisie and the P-B is well illustrated by two situations which developed in the 1950s. The Benteng program, which lasted from 1950–5, was

intended to strengthen indigenous importers by giving them privileged access to import licenses and credit for initial operations.
However, while import licenses may have constituted a primary
source of capital accumulation for Muslim petty bourgeoisie they
were also a potential source of finance for politico-bureaucrats.
Consequently licenses were secured by political parties, individual
P-B, their clients and relatives. In some cases they were channelled to
party-controlled business groups and banks but were predominantly
sold to existing trading groups, mainly Chinese. Indigenous bourgeoisie and petty bourgeoisie secured access to the licenses only
where they enjoyed access to patronage.

A second dimension of the conflict centered around the monetary
policies of the state. Domestic inflation and artificially high exchange
rates for the *rupiah* created a bonanza for the Jakarta importers but
were devastating for outer island producer/exporters and small-scale
manufacturers in Java.

Continuing deterioration in the economic position of the indigenous petty bourgeoisie was reflected in increasing political weakness.
As early as 1955 the state had forced the political activities of this
class into a state-controlled representative body and this official co-
option of business organization has been continued under guided
economy (Bamunas) and the New Order (Kadin). The virulently
anti-Chinese Asaat movement of the late 1950s failed to gain the
support of any party and the interests of the indigenous petty
bourgeoisie received a major setback when the defeat of the regional
revolts and the move to Guided Democracy located power more
firmly in the hands of Jakarta P-B.

Economic nationalization under guided economy did not constitute a move to greater protection, credit or subsidy for the indigenous
petty bourgeoisie. Indeed state capital was seen as the appropriate
vehicle for national accumulation. In addition, the inflation, short-
ages and collapse of infrastructure were particularly severe on the
indigenous petty bourgeoisie who were unable to move their capital
to safer regions until the business climate had improved.

With the introduction of the domestic capital investment law
(PMDN) in 1968, domestic investors were given a variety of tax
and import concessions and were eligible for state credit. The
indigenous bourgeoisie and petty bourgeoisie, hard hit by inflation,
found their liquid assets inadequate, not only for expansion of their
capital base but for collateral requirements for investment under
PMDN. As a consequence only 17% of state investment credit under
PMDN went to indigenous bourgeoisie and it is estimated that only
20% of capital invested under PMDN was indigenous. Of course,

the vast bulk of indigenous petty bourgeoisie operated outside the PMDN scheme and therefore at a considerable disadvantage to PMDN investors with their tax concessions and access to cheaper imports of raw materials and technology.

The protest of the indigenous petty bourgeoisie gathered strength in the early 1970s, parallel with the movements associated with growing student discontent with military rule and the direction of economic strategy. Muslim newspapers *Abadi* and *Nusantara* in particular took an anti-Chinese line and a stance critical of the economic alliances between P-B and Chinese business groups. This was associated specifically with the increasing difficulties of the indigenous textile producers and generally with the ever-present social tension between indigenous Indonesians and Chinese, a contributing factor to the Bandung riots of October 1973, and the Jakarta riots of January 1974.

Following the Jakarta riots the government moved to defuse the tensions by introducing a series of regulations designed to redress the perceived imbalances between indigenous, Chinese and foreign capital. These included:

(1) a requirement that state bank credit be made available only to indigenous companies;
(2) a requirement that within 10 years, companies investing under PMDN (Domestic Investment Law) be 75% owned by indigenous investors, and companies investing under PMA (Foreign Investment Law) be 51% owned by indigenous investors;
(3) an acceleration of credit and advisory programs for indigenous small business.

The first of these requirements directly confronts realities of structures of capital ownership and corporate organization. Indigenous bourgeoisie received such a small share of state bank credit, not only because of lack of political influence but because they did not possess the capital and organizational basis to effectively use such finance. In terms of normal banking criteria, they were generally a poorer credit risk than the established Chinese businesses. In the case of the second resolution, it was revealed that neither the state nor the indigenous bourgeoisie possessed the finance to purchase such equity. In general, the state's ability to move against the Chinese in any decisive way is limited by the fact that the Chinese are indispensible to capitalism as it is now structured in Indonesia and by the more concrete business alliances which tie them to the major politico-bureaucratic powerholders. In any case, if the experience of the past is continued the indigenous beneficiaries of policies to transfer ownership and provide credit will be politico-bureaucrats or those larger indigenous bourgeoisie who have managed to enter the framework of the business and political alliances between foreign and Chinese capital and P-B power.

The central problem for the New Order state is that the protection of the interests of the indigenous bourgeoisie in any substantive way is incompatible with the development of the forces of production in Indonesian capitalism. The most it can do is attempt to buy them off with soft credit: thus the significance of the decision to place greater emphasis upon credit for small-scale indigenous business (KIK – Kredit Industri Kecil) and to establish state instrumentalities for providing credit and advice to indigenous investors. Although clearly inadequate for the purpose of fundamentally altering the situation of the indigenous bourgeoisie and petty bourgeoisie, such credits are politically valuable in that they may counteract day-to-day crises in small business and thereby engage the energies of the indigenous businessman in securing state credits.

A more promising basis for the emergence of an indigenous class of small accumulators is to be found in the countryside where the development of commercial production and the accelerating transformation to capitalist forms and relations of production are accompanying concentration of land ownership and increases in capital investment and wage labor. The landlord classes were the most important allies of the military in the 1965–6 period when the New Order was establishing itself. A powerful rural landlord/kulak class constitutes a significant and strategic base of political support for the New Order state. In the fifteen years since the coup, the New Order state has provided the basis for consolidation and development of a rural landlord/kulak class through provision of rural credit and infrastructure in conjunction with the programs introducing high-yielding rice varieties, insecticides and fertilizers into agricultural production.

The Position of the Politico-Bureaucrats (P-B)

In societies where the dominant economic system is capitalist there is a separation of the political and the economic. Unlike feudal societies, production is not secured by political coercion but in the context of economic relationships between capital owner and free wage labor. Consequently the ruling class is separate from the state although the state may serve its interests. We cannot discover the logic governing the relationship between state and society by simply examining the social origins or ideological attachments of those who occupy the state apparatus. The relationship is primarily structural. The state becomes the political expression of specific processes of class formation and conflict and of the general process of capital accumulation. Its function is to secure the political conditions for the social dominance of the bourgeoisie and to provide infrastructure for the accumulation process.

While the state is relatively autonomous in that it is not the instrument of any single class or class fraction, it is unable to impose fundamental structural changes in the social order unless it is reconstituted on the basis of a new balance of social and political power. The major changes in the Indonesian state in 1949, 1957/8, and 1965 followed major changes *already achieved* in the balance of social, economic and political power within Indonesia.

However, we can only fully understand the New Order state if we recognize the P-B as an *independent* political force with clearly identifiable social and economic interests growing out of their appropriation of the state apparatus. It is this appropriation of the state apparatus and their fusion of political power and bureaucratic authority which makes them quite different from officials of the states of western industrial capitalist societies. The P-B have constructed a powerful and centralized state apparatus autonomous of direct political control by political parties representing the interests of specific social classes. In this sense they are the military-bureaucratic oligarchy of a "bonapartist" state, relatively autonomous of political control by social forces but obliged in the long term to reproduce the social and economic order in which the interests of the dominant class are embedded.

In this situation the specific historical development of the political and economic interests of the P-B become crucial factors in deciding the role of the state during periods of social conflict. During the latter Guided Economy period, the military, as the dominant P-B faction, intervened against the forces of social revolution on behalf of the capitalist economy primarily to secure the institutional basis of its *political* power against the challenge of a mass-based political party. The move to reestablish foreign capital investment was also designed to restore the revenue basis of the state threatened by the economic disintegration of Guided Economy. The most effective means of securing a firm basis of revenue was to rejuvenate export earnings through foreign capital investment, loans and aid and the stimulation of domestic capital accumulation through the infusion of foreign capital. The path of capitalist development also strengthened the social and economic power of the political allies of the

P-B (landlords, domestic bourgeoisie and middle classes) in their conflict with the forces of political revolution.

The decision of the military to intervene on the side of the bourgeoisie was also influenced by the existence of concrete *economic* links between the two. During the decade preceding the coup of 1965 the military had constructed a vast network of business alliances with foreign and Chinese capital by means of their control of strategic state terminals of economic authority, including the major state corporations. Such alliances provided revenues for P-B factions, individual officials, their families and clients, thereby giving the P-B a vested interest in the economic fortunes of their business partners. Since 1965, these business alliances have grown exponentially largely as joint venture partnerships.

There are two factors which threaten to undermine the position of the P-B as appropriators of the state apparatus: the political conflict between the P-B and the middle classes; and the general contradictions between the needs of capital accumulation and the development of the forces of production on the one hand and, on the other, the use of the appropriated economic power of the state by the P-B to sustain the political basis of their position and fuel their personal fortunes.

Any capitalist social formation requires a social force of managers, technicians and intellectuals (generally referred to as a middle class). It is a social class which is relatively influential because of its strategic position in the management, information, administration and educational institutions of society. One of the major weaknesses of the New Order has been its failure to overcome the general hostility between itself and the middle classes.

Despite the criticism of the economic policies of the New Order and the calls for social justice and economic equality by some liberal intellectuals, the middle classes do not fundamentally threaten the structure of capitalism in Indonesia. First, critics amongst the middle class intelligentsia have not developed organized political alliances with other social groups, and consequently they remain articulators of grievances rather than a viable political force. Second, and more important, the upper levels of the urban middle classes have generally done well out of capitalist development in Indonesia. Their interests lie contrary to those of the popular classes. Civil service salaries are consistently rising above inflation levels, there are opportunities for well-paid employment with foreign companies, and more and more upper middle class Indonesians have access to the relative luxury and security of new housing estates. Rising living standards for the middle classes as a whole are providing access to an increased range of consumer goods. They are a privileged social element and it is unlikely that they would support fundamental social restructuring, reallocation of social wealth, expulsion of foreign capital or be willing to undertake the privations or suffer the upheaval which would be associated with a systematic attempt to build an Indonesian capitalist economy upon a basis of domestic capital accumulation and economic control.

Their opposition to the military-dominated P-B stems from widespread resentment of the privileges the military have secured for themselves, the authoritarian nature of military rule, the corruption of the P-B, and the arbitrary application of the law. Consequently they are generally in favor of the termination of the economic and political role of the military, the regularization of the bureaucracy, the liberalization of politics and the institution of rule of law.

While the middle classes have no political base from which to challenge the P-B, they are nevertheless a strategic political group. Their quiescence in the New Order is dependent upon the continuing development of their relative prosperity, which in turn is based upon compounding foreign debt, increasing foreign capital investment, export earnings and commodity imports. If this fragile framework collapses, the middle classes may be expected to seek new political allies.

A second threat to the P-B comes, not from the prospect of a collapse in Indonesian capitalism, but from its entrenchment. As investment in more complex and capital-intensive forms of industrial production is increased, so are the demands for reliable transport and communication systems, effective administration of state functions (e.g. customs, taxation) and a predictable and regularized fiscal policy. In industrial capitalism the state most effectively provides the conditions for accumulation through general fiscal and monetary policies and infrastructure creation which serve the general class interests of the bourgeoisie rather than by specific allocation of concessions to individual companies.

At the moment, the P-B syphon large amounts of state revenue from infrastructure creation into their own political and personal projects. Their interference with allocation of credit, licenses, contracts and concessions means that the criteria for such allocations are determined by the political and personal needs of specific P-B factions rather than by the priorities of long-term economic planning.

Attempts by those elements of the state bureaucracy concerned with economic policy-making and management to regularize the state apparatus have met, for the most part, with failure. Even where the government has felt forced to open enquiries into corruption or to carry out campaigns of eradication of corrupt practices, the major terminals of corruption have been left unaffected. The only significant victory of the technocrats over the P-B appropriators occurred with the replacement of Ibnu Sutowo as President of the state oil company, Pertamina. It is significant that this victory was achieved only when it became clear that the continued appropriation of Pertamina under Sutowo threatened to fundamentally damage the whole fabric of Indonesian capitalism.

In the long term the regulation of the state apparatus and the eclipse of the P-B will depend upon three factors:

1. the degree to which their continued appropriation of state power inhibits the development of capital accumulation;
2. the degree to which the bourgeoisie − foreign, Chinese and indigenous − are prepared to place political pressure on the P-B;
3. the degree to which the inhibitions upon the accumulation process threatens the whole structure of Indonesian capitalism.

At the moment, domestic bourgeoisie are able to expand accumulation within the politico-economic alliances between foreign capital and Indonesian politico-bureaucratic power. Foreign investors may simply direct industrial investment elsewhere without critically damaging an economy bouyed up on export earnings from oil. Export earnings from oil are currently able to sustain the Indonesian economy without a major contribution from industrial production. Indeed, there has been a decline in industrial investment, especially by foreign investors, over the past five years. The state, as it exists, is the logical product of the historical process of capitalist revolution in Indonesia characterized by a weakly developed bourgeoisie, and the partial penetration of capitalist relations of production. The power and the autonomy of the P-B is reinforced by direct access to foreign loans, royalties and export earnings from minerals and oil.

If the development of capitalism remains stalled at this level and export earnings from oil and minerals and the inflow of foreign loans are maintained, the form of the New Order state may well remain intact. However, if the process of domestic accumulation and industrialization intensifies, consolidating the social and political power of domestic bourgeoisie, and if foreign investment in industry becomes necessary to maintain export earnings, the inhibitions imposed upon the accumulation process by the existing form of state power must necessarily be removed.

The form of state typical of highly industrial capitalist economies outside the industrial West and Japan is referred to variously as *techno-fascist*, repressive-developmentalist, modernizing-authoritarian or corporatist. Such states remain free of direct political domination by parties representing the interests of specific classes, although the state apparatus continues to be appropriated by a military-bureaucratic oligarchy. The New Order state already exhibits many of the characteristics ascribed to such states, particularly the ideological and repressive characteristics. However, the victory of the technocratic side of the equation has yet to be achieved. Within the technocratic state, specific political and economic interests of P-B factions have given way to the general needs of the accumulation process as the central determinant of state action. The state has become regularized, the contradictions between capital and the P-B resolved, the appanage-holding generals replaced by generals and political strongmen who are technocrats and administrators (although these continue to appropriate the state apparatus). In the context of capitalist industrialization in the Third World, the technocratic authoritarian state is the highest level of political development.

Part II

Industrialization: Capital and Labor

Introduction

During the last two decades, the Southeast Asian region has seen a rapid increase in the growth of industrialization and in manufacturing output in particular. Whatever economic indices are selected – from the more general such as growth rates to the more specific such as value-added in manufacturing or numbers employed in manufacturing industry – it seems that, at the regional level, there has been a more rapid growth in industrialization than in other regions of the developing world which are conventionally considered to be in the forefront of industrialization, such as Latin America, for example.

These developments have led many theorists to reject previous explanations of industrialization based on perspectives such as growth or dependency, or on models of import-substituting industrialization. Most would now conclude that, after a post-war period in which the major focus was the domestic market, export-oriented strategies have played a crucial role in the recent industrialization of most Southeast Asian economies. National focus has given way to a more internationalist perspective, as it has been recognized that the most developed industrial and manufacturing sectors can only be analyzed adequately if they are placed in the context of their role in the world economy. Many writers claim that this location rests primarily on the attraction of the region for manufacturing sectors in the industrialized economies. Wages are – on average – one tenth of those in the industrialized countries, transport costs have been greatly reduced in recent years, and manufacturing in industries such as electronics has been scaled down to a series of clearly demarcated stages, many of which are elementary and easily movable from one location to another.

Debates currently center on whether or not export-oriented industrial strategies have generated a basis for self-sustaining industrialization in the economies of the region, and whether or not they can lead to significant improvements in the standard of living. Many argue (see Wong, 1979) that in the international environment for development in the coming years, with the probable slackening of world trade and the continued depression of raw material prices, it will be difficult to maintain the high growth rates of previous years, and that, necessarily, the countries of the region will be forced to scale down their growth expectations, and become more domestically oriented, with a focus on a more equitable distribution of the results of growth.

Other authors (Kaplinsky, 1984) focus rather more fundamentally on whether the export-oriented strategy is sustainable in itself, given that one of its major elements – the attraction of cheap wage-labor – may no longer be as important to the interests of international capital in the region. On technological grounds, it is argued that improvements in computer aided design and manufacture, together with changes in the systems of production in such industries as electronics and textiles are influencing transnational corporations to locate less in areas of relatively cheap labor and more in the industrialized countries themselves. This has been the case recently, for example, with the Japanese car industry in the region. Against this it should be said that, while technological change may dictate such a movement, nevertheless, conditions in the world economy – and notably the competition which has emerged strongly in the 1980s between the Japanese, American and European economies over market division and entry – have led many Japanese corporations to maintain, and even expand, their Southeast Asian operations. Commodities produced in Thailand, Singapore and the Philippines are not subject to the same tariff or exchange rate constraints in American markets as are those of Japanese origin. We are thus faced with a rather more complicated development than suggested by the technological thesis – but, either way, the outcome is clearly crucial for the likelihood of the export-oriented strategy being sustained as the basis for industrialization in the coming period.

Faced with the heavy emphasis placed by most development theorists on the nature and patterns of industrialization in the region, it is important to make a number of qualifications. Firstly, on the continuing importance of the agricultural sector. In terms of indices such as structure of production and output, the agricultural sector predominates in the region. Furthermore, in terms of employment, agriculture is dominant over industry in all countries, with the exceptions of Singapore and the state of Brunei. Secondly, it is important to realize that the service sector accounts for the largest percentage of output in all the economies of the region, reflecting the continuing importance of the informal sector, the economic marginalization of many of the population, and the substantial numbers employed in non-productive jobs by the state. Thirdly, indices pointing to regional trends in growth and industrialization should be treated with some caution. As aggregates they conceal marked disparities, since much of the increase in industrialization levels is concentrated in Singapore, and to a lesser extent in Malaysia and Thailand. Other states such as the Philippines and Indonesia are performing at relatively lower levels. Finally, it should be recalled that there are several economies – Vietnam, Laos, Burma and Kampuchea (Cambodia) – whose industrialization, although at much lower levels, remains directed primarily towards agriculture, and whose development strategies place a much greater emphasis on labor-intensive production as a means for creating a viable national economic base.

As several authors have indicated, the state has played a crucial role in the process of developing a domestic base for the indigenous manufacturing industrial classes in several Southeast Asian countries. This has been the case most notably in Thailand, as Kevin Hewison indicates in his article on state policies during the post-war period. He describes how an import-substituting strategy was developed after 1958, and how aspects of this were maintained as export-oriented growth came to the fore in the 1970s. In his analysis he outlines in some detail the economic relations between the state and the various classes in the Thai social formation. He argues that, contrary to the conclusions of dependency theory, the domestic bourgeoisie has been able to use the state to create the conditions required for enlarged accumulation.

During the last two decades Singapore has played an important pivotal role for industrialization in the region, channelling investment, directing trade flows, and manufacturing technology for regional consumption. Hafiz Mirza uses the concept of peripheral intermediation to analyze Singapore's economy. He argues that Singapore's role in the international economy still remains primarily an intermediate one, in which goods and services are produced, utilizing inputs from abroad for the principal purpose of export to other countries. He argues that multi-national corporations remain the most important institutions in this process of intermediation, exemplifying this by reference to manufacturing, servicing and financing. In examining Singapore's role in ASEAN (the Association of Southeast Asian Nations) and the Pacific Rim, Mirza projects future trends in the country's development by focusing on three industries – shipbuilding, electronics and petroleum.

One of the lesser known aspects of industrialization in the region is its impact on those who produce the commodities and services on which it exists. This applies particularly to the industrial workforce. In only a few countries are research findings readily available for such aspects as the organization of the labor process, wages and conditions of work. Consequently, in her article Hing Ai Yun undertakes a detailed empirical study of five factories in Malaysia, in very different industries, both national and foreign owned. She examines conditions of employment, industrial organization, and types of work, in surveys carried out in the early 1980s. She focuses particularly on the impact of technology, examining its influence on the labor processes in industries with differing levels of capital intensity. She concludes by examining the ways in which incentives and bonus schemes are used to socialize workers into the familial ideologies propagated by the companies investigated in her research.

The State and Capitalist Development in Thailand

Kevin Hewison

Marxist discussions of the role of the state in capitalist development in the Third World have indicated that the state and local bourgeois classes can cooperate to enhance domestic capitalism, often in competition with international capital. This research has suggested that dependency theorists have, by their focus on imperialism, tended to obscure the total process of class formation and reproduction and the continuing accumulation of capital in the Third World. . . . Contrary to the tenets of dependency theory, it is clear that some Third World states are not acting in the interests of international capital alone. Domestic bourgeoisies have been able to manipulate the state to provide the conditions they require for expanded accumulation. It is thus important to delineate the strengths of the domestic bourgeoisie if a clear picture of the state's relationship with the bourgeoisie is to be determined. . . . This article will argue that a domestic bourgeoisie, capable of acting as a relatively independent class within the international capitalist system, has emerged in Thailand, and that the state has played a substantial role in securing and expanding this class's accumulative base in finance and industry.

The International Context of Thai Economic Development and the Development of the Thai Bourgeoisie

From the mid-nineteenth century to the 1960s Thailand's role in the world capitalist system was to supply primary commodities for the world market. Throughout the period, rice, teak, rubber and tin accounted for between 50 and 90% of all Thai exports. . . .

Since 1960, however, Thailand's trading position has become less dependent on the export of primary commodities, and this has coincided with a more footloose period for international capital. Transnational corporations have become increasingly interested in taking advantage of such benefits as cheap labor, generous tax concessions, bans on organized labor and growing domestic markets. . . . This restructuring of international capital has also provided new opportunities for the expansion of accumulation by domestic

73

capitalists. . . . In Thailand, the manufacturing sector has seen remarkable growth since 1960 with manufactured exports expanded from just 1% of total exports in that year, to 27% in 1979. While the majority of the Thai people continue to work in the agricultural sector, and while agriculture remains the single most important sector of the economy, Table 1 clearly indicates the increasing importance of the manufacturing sector.

Table 1   *GDP by industrial origin, selected years (%)*

Industrial Origin	1951	1960	1971	1979
Agriculture	50.1	39.8	29.8	25.5
Mining and Quarrying	1.9	1.1	1.5	1.7
Manufacturing	10.3	12.6	17.5	20.8
Construction	2.9	4.6	5.5	5.4
Electricity and Water Supply	0.1	0.7	1.8	1.8
Transport and Communications	3.1	7.5	6.7	7.3
Wholesale and Retail Trade	18.0	15.2	17.1	16.6
Banking, Insurance and Real Estate	0.4	1.9	4.2	5.4
Ownership of Dwellings	3.7	2.8	1.9	1.5
Public Administration and Defence	2.8	4.6	4.3	3.8
Services	6.7	9.6	9.7	10.2

N.B. The 1979 figures are provisional.
Sources: 1951 and 1960 figures are from Ingram, *op. cit.*, p. 234, while the figures for 1971 and 1979 are from Bank of Thailand, *Annual Economic Report*, 1974 and 1979 issues.

The origins of the capitalist class in Thailand can be traced to the middle of the nineteenth century. Its most distinctive feature was its compromised position in relation to the traditional *sakdina* ruling class which held rights to the agricultural and trading surpluses through taxation and trade monopolies. Rather than emerging as an openly antagonistic class, the bourgeoisie found it necessary to accumulate much of its initial wealth by cooperation with the *sakdina* class. This class's functionaries, who were often Chinese merchants involved in monopoly trading, tax-farming and administration, were able to amass large personal fortunes. With the development of commodity production in sugar, rice, pepper, tin, teak and rubber, some of these merchant-functionaries were able to invest their wealth in productive enterprises such as sugar, rice and timber mills, often jointly financed with royal money. Others took advantage of the expansion of European business within Thailand, acting as compradors, and providing the essential link between the foreigners and the local economy. . . .

At the same time the *sakdina* class had begun to invest heavily in land, and within a short time, managed to monopolize much of the best, newly-opened rice lands and most of the valuable urban land, thus augmenting their accumulated fortunes with rent and land sales.

It was from this group of Chinese merchant-functionaries and compradors, and from the upper ranks of the *sakdina* class, brought together in a symbiotic relationship, investing in land, industry, commerce and banking, that the Thai bourgeoisie emerged. . . . Milling, trading, banking and finance remained the principal sources of accumulation for the bourgeoisie until about 1926, when Thailand's trade treaties with Western powers were revised. These revisions allowed the Thai government to increase its import duties from 3% (set in 1855) to a general level of 5%. Coupled with the temporary retreat of European capital during the depression years, higher tariffs stimulated a minor resurgence in the sugar industry, and encouraged a movement into, and expansion of, manufacturing industries.

In 1932 the absolute monarchy was overthrown, and the new, constitutional regime developed a more nationalistic approach to economic development. . . . The new regime sought to move the small industrial sector into "Thai" (ethnic Thai and Sino-Thai) citizens' hands, and to initiate industrial development from this base, in an early attempt at import substitution industrialization. Statistically, the achievements of this policy, prior to 1942, were not impressive. However, they did provide some valuable experience for domestic managers and entrepreneurs, and allowed for some increased accumulation as a number of small, private firms and some larger, government-backed enterprises were established.

The impact of the Second World War upon domestic patterns of accumulation allowed Thai capitalist enterprise to expand quite considerably. . . . The Japanese occupation of 1942–5 meant that all British and Allied business activities were suspended, and local firms had to develop and expand in an attempt to fill the gap, especially in the production of previously imported consumer goods. . . .

Following the war, however, industrial expansion was hampered by war-damaged infrastructure (particularly power generation), and the influx of foreign-made goods. The export of primary commodities remained dominant, partly because the government could not meet the costs of infrastructural reconstruction and expansion, and partly because export was particularly profitable, for both the government and traders, at a time when world demand was exceptionally high. But an important development occurred within this trading sector. Whereas in earlier decades Thailand's foreign trade had been in the hands of Western and Chinese trading companies, with profits either leaving the country or remaining in the sphere of circulation, local banks now took on a new and increasingly important role, and were able to divert some of their profits from financing Thai trade into the productive sphere.

Despite this expansion, significant fractions of Thai capital, including the banking fraction, believed that far more investment capital was required if Thailand was to develop, and if they were to expand their base for accummulation. While the government of Plaek Phibunsongkram (hereafter, Phibun) moved hesitantly in this direction towards the end of its time in office, it was not until after 1958, when General Sarit Thanarat took full power, that new investment promotion and infrastructural development policies were implemented, together with the active encouragement of foreign aid and investment.

Although the Thai economy received tremendous stimulation from foreign aid and investment, and from US military spending, joint-venture arrangements have allowed Thai capitalists to gain access to capital, experience and skills in areas they had previously been unable or unwilling to expand into. In order to expand their enterprises, some Thai capitalists were willing to pay the price of subordinate integration into the international capitalist system. Over the years, however, a number of the capitalists have been able to expand and accumulate in their own right. As a result, the contemporary Thai economy is dominated by domestic capital. In industries promoted by the Board of Investment (BoI), Thai capital accounts for over 75% of total registered capital. In the important financial sector, Thai capital is overwhelmingly predominant, as shown in Table 2. . . .

It seems likely that the power of the Thai bourgeoisie will increase as the secondary and tertiary sectors of the economy continue to grow. Its power is enhanced by the close business and family ties it has both within itself, between the various fractions of capital, and with influential functionaries of the Thai state, particularly the military hierarchy. Additionally, connections between elements within the bourgeoisie and similar groups, both regionally and internationally, are enhancing the domestic power of this class.

With this background in mind, we can examine the role of the

Table 2   *Foreign ownership of the Thai financial sector, 1979*

Financial Activity	No. of foreign companies	Assets (in millions of baht)	% of market controlled
1 Commercial Banks	14	18,106	6.15
2 Life Insurance Cos	3	1,282	32.10
3 Non-Life Insurance Cos	9	447	16.15
4 Investment and Securities Cos (a)	15	13,797	27.58

Note: (a) Includes joint-ventures and foreign-owned companies registered in Thailand.
Source: Krirkkiat Phipatseritham, *Wikhro laksana kan pen chaokhong thurakit khanat yai nai prathet thai,* Bangkok: Thai Khadi Research Institute, 1981, p. 258.

state in the process of capitalist development, emphasizing three aspects of the state's activities, and concentrating on the post-1958 period.

(*a*) *Investment promotion policies and Import Substitution Industrialization*
From the moment he came to power, Sarit made it clear that economic development was to be emphasized in his crusade to modernize Thailand. An IBRD report (1959: 94–106) mapped out the "path of progress" for Thailand. The World Bank reported that it was essential that the "relative importance of manufacturing activity . . . be increased", and that this should be achieved through "private initiative, both domestic and foreign". They urged that the government "restore the confidence of private businessmen and . . . assist them in expanding industry . . ." by granting special promotional privileges, streamlining laws relating to business, improving credit, providing infrastructure, encouraging import substitution industrialization (ISI), and by implementing rational development planning. The initial phase of Thailand's first national development plan followed these recommendations almost to the letter. . . .

While the government was keen to attract foreign investment its promotional privileges were designed as much for domestic investors as for foreigners. While there were some local investors who were opposed to foreign investment, the big, domestic capitalists, and particularly the banks and their industrial allies, were very much in favor of increased foreign investment, and it was this latter group which had most political influence.

At the time, they gave two reasons for "needing" foreign capital: (i) insufficient supplies of local capital, and (ii) lack of local managerial and technical skills. While there is some truth in both of these claims, it could also be said that the promotion of foreign investment, particularly in the form of joint-ventures, provided a sound political basis for the rapid expansion of domestic business. In the first place, many of the promotional privileges provided local capitalists with significant benefits, and in particular, the right to own land, a right which had often been denied to alien Chinese business people in the past. Second, the threat of nationalization of a joint-venture firm, or the harassment of Sino-Thai partners in these ventures, was all the more unlikely if Westerners and Japanese were involved, especially at a time when a staunchly pro-American foreign policy was being followed. Indeed, it was only the big capitalist who could enjoy promotional privileges, as it was necessary for the applicant to prove that a project could be adequately capitalized. Thus, between 1959 and 1965, the average investment of promoted firms was in excess of 23 million *baht*.

The majority of capital invested with promotional privileges went into import substituting industries. While many of the industries established in the 1930s and 1940s had also been import substituting, they had generally been on a small scale, and had not been a part of any overall governmental plan. Despite the fact that many of these industries had only met with limited success, the Second World War had convinced many Thais that ISI was the only sure path to industrial development.

Thus, when the World Bank report suggested that ISI should be encouraged, the Thai government was enthusiastic, as were local manufacturers and potential investors.

Even though the first National Economic Development Plan placed most emphasis on increasing agricultural production, the policy for industry was unequivocally ISI (NEDB, 1964). This policy continued to be followed until 1972 when growing financial problems forced the government to look more towards export promotion as a means of rectifying trade deficits, with the third Plan (1972–6) emphasizing both ISI and export-oriented industrialization. The growth rate of manufacturing industry averaged 11% per annum (at constant 1962 prices) during the 1960s, and its contribution to GDP has grown from 10.3% in 1951 to 20.8% in 1979 (see Table 1).

Those who have most benefited from this growth have been the big banking and industrial capitalists. For example, the Bangkok Bank has grown to become the largest bank in Southeast Asia, with assets of almost 105,000 million *baht* in 1979 (about 40% of total commercial bank assets in Thailand), and has control over more than 40% of all bank borrowing and lending in Thailand. The bank's declared profit in 1978 was 825.5 million *baht*, the largest profit declared by any Thai-registered company in that year. The Bangkok Bank and its principals, the Sophonpanich family, have, since the late 1950s, invested heavily in manufacturing, and together with other large banking and industrial families, have attained monopolistic control over the Thai economy. . . .

The state thus implemented policies in the areas of investment promotion and ISI which advanced the process of accumulation from petty commodity and enclave commodity production to a higher level, ISI. Such policies were of immense benefit to the powerful fractions of the bourgeoisie, in that it consolidated their accumulative base. However, there was a price to be paid – the stagnation of the smaller, less powerful capitalist sector, and the loss of a certain amount of capital as profits to foreign investors. From 1966 to 1978 reported outward remittances (probably underestimated) totalled almost 27,000 million *baht*.

(*b*) *Provision of credit for capitalist development* The World Bank report, echoing the sentiments of local capitalists, made it clear that there would be a need for the development of industrial credit facilities in Thailand, and supported the establishment of an Industrial Finance Corporation. In addition the Bank urged a more active lending role for domestic commercial banks, to be financed by increased deposits; the banks had to be more attractive for despositors. . . . The IFCT had been established in 1959 with two objectives: (i) to assist in the establishment, expansion or modernization of private industrial enterprise; and (ii) to encourage the participation of both domestic and foreign capital in these ventures. These objectives were to be achieved through the provision of medium- and long-term loans to worthwhile private projects. Although intended to be a private company, the IFCT was established by the government with interest-free and low-interest loans. Over the years the government has given considerable support to the IFCT, providing a number of additional loans on soft terms, with the aim of rationalizing industrial financing and allowing the development of modern business enterprises, without the need for the IFCT to make large profits on its lending program. Some 53% of the IFCT's shares are owned by Thais, and Thai bankers hold the majority of directorships. Names like Lamsam

(Thai Farmers Bank), Sophonpanich (Bangkok Bank), Cholvijarn (Union Bank of Bangkok), and Boonsoong (Laemthong Bank) have consistently appeared among the directors of the company. Given that these names are also associated with some of the largest industrial enterprises in the country, it is not surprising to discover that the IFCT has given considerable aid to the large and powerful fractions of the bourgeoisie. The World Bank mission apparently believed that the IFCT would finance small entrepreneurs, but small capitalists have seldom been able to take advantage of IFCT credits.

A strikingly similar pattern of state intervention in favor of big capital can be seen in the commercial banking sector. This sector had received little legislative attention after 1945, but in 1962 the new Commercial Banking Act was promulgated. The basic aim of this Act was to increase public confidence in the banks, so as to attract increased deposits. While some commercial bankers expressed reservations about the new Act, the results over the long term were evidential. Between 1961 and 1965, deposits grew by 240% from 5000 million *baht* to 12,000 million, and by a further 1400% to 170,000 million at the end of 1979.

Soon after the 1962 Act came into force legislation was also created to control the small, "irrational", financial sector. The Pawnshop Act (1962) was an attempt by the government to limit the role of these shops, and to take capital out of their hands and place it in the commercial banking sector. Pawnshops were effectively limited to the poor who did not have investible cash assets.

Certainly, the unorganized capital market still exists, but its role has diminished over the years, while commercial banks have grown ever stronger, becoming more interested in banking proper rather than the financing of trade. The result of this state-initiated reorganization of the capital market has already been noted: the financial bourgeoisie is the dominant fraction of the contemporary Thai bourgeoisie.

(*c*) *State policy towards the urban working class and organized labor* Within the general context of its concern with providing the condition for accumulation, the state has consistently taken the side of capital in its disputes with labor, and has severely curtailed the rights of workers to organize themselves. The result has been that workers' struggles have been most prominent when the state itself has been divided by internal rivalry (e.g. 1956–8 and 1973–6).

Phibun, in his attempts to outmanoeuver his political rivals, Sarit and Police-General Phao Sriyanon, had legalized unions in 1956. No doubt Phibun hoped that he could control the unions to his own advantage, but many of the newly-formed unions organized strikes, demanding better wages and conditions for their members.

When Sarit assumed full control of the government, unions were again banned, and some 200 labor leaders were arrested. Strikes were absolutely forbidden, and although some workers risked imprisonment to demand their rights, the government reported only eighty-two strikes between 1958 and 1968. Both local and international capital were generally satisfied with this situation as it allowed them to keep wages extremely low without too much fear of retaliation from labor. . . .

By 1971 reports of gross exploitation of workers had become commonplace. Some 500,000 factory workers were receiving wages of only 7–10 *baht* per day, which was barely adequate for food alone, and thousands were forced to sleep at their workplace. There was little or no compensation for overtime, holidays, accidents or sickness; there was no guarantee of employment; working conditions were often unsafe and unhealthy; and child labor was not uncommon. While workers paid dearly with their labor, health and lives, capitalists continued to accumulate. Table 3 gives an indication of the surplus-value extracted by industrial capitalists.

Table 3 *Average profits per employee, Bangkok industrial sector, 1972*

Size of firm	No. of firms	Average profit/employee
1–5 employees	9,134	11,300 *baht*
6–9	6,761	7,600
10–49	1,775	9,900
50–99	374	34,100
100–249	184	31,800
250–500	71	61,400
500–1000	24	19,700
more than 1000	17	46,300

Source: Adapted from N. K. Sarkar, *Industrial Structure of Greater Bangkok.* (Bangkok, United Nations Asian Institute for Economic Development and Planning, 1974), p. 31.

Exploitation of the level indicated in Table 3 was compounded in 1971–3 by a domestic slump and inflation, and strikes began to occur with regularity. From 1969 to 1972 there were 108 officially recorded strikes, involving more than 21,000 workers. However, as the demise of the military regime grew more likely, strikes mushroomed, with 501 occurring in 1973. From 1973 to 1976, when workers had far more freedom to organize following the overthrow of the dictatorship, there were a further 716 strikes, involving over 261,000 workers.

Initially capitalists were not too concerned about this increased activity as they were able to resist workers' demands or make but small concessions. However, as the strikes multiplied, the first warnings by capitalists to workers were issued, when Major-General Pramarn Adireksarn, then president of the Association of Thai Industries, and a leading political figure, stated that strikes were still technically illegal, and that there would be serious economic problems if strikes did not cease. Not long after there were declines in both domestic and foreign investment levels, and coupled with the defeat of the US in Indochina, wealthy Thais began to channel their money overseas. Thai capitalists and state officials became increasingly determined to defeat the workers, and the government repeatedly used the state's repressive powers (augmented with privately-hired thugs and assassins) to break strikes. For example, in one instance 100 anti-riot police were used to smash picket-lines established by women textile workers, and in another, about 200 Red Gaur thugs were hired by the management of the Dusit Thani Hotel to break a strike there in 1975.

Nevertheless, in the 1973–6 period unions did manage to double the minimum wage paid in Bangkok. However, the Thai bourgeoisie, foreign investors, and factions within the military had decided that a situation where labor was becoming more militant and where the business and political climate was becoming increasing unstable could not continue. Thus, in October 1976 the military returned to power following a bloody massacre of students at Thammasat University in Bangkok. The new administration quickly sought to rectify the situation for business, allowing previously delayed projects to begin immediately with BoI incentives. Local capitalists felt even more secure when the nominally civilian government of Thanin Kraivichian was replaced by General Kriangsak Chomanan's administration in 1977.

If these state policies of fragmentation and disruption of working class and peasant (see Turton, 1978) movements are compared to the promotional attitudes of state officials towards organization within the bourgeois class (e.g. trade associations, chambers of commerce, Board of Trade), then it is again clear that the state had deliberately represented the interests of capital. Repression of the working class has been one of the state's essential political and economic tasks in providing a climate conducive to the accumulation of capital.

Concluding remarks

Political and economic intervention by the state has allowed the bourgeoisie to expand its accumulative base to the extent that it has moved from a reliance on trade and petty commodity production to financial and industrial activities. While state intervention has also enchanced the position of foreign capital, Thai capitalists were prepared to pay this price.

Clearly, the Thai bourgeoisie is not merely a comprador bourgeoisie, and the state has not acted as a mere intermediary between domestic and international capital. While some Thai capitalists do cooperate with foreign capital, this is a necessary role to be filled in the modern, international, capitalist system, even in the advanced industrial societies. And, the same can be said for the role of the Thai state. It has not just taken a passive, intermediary role, but has actively promoted domestic capital. Indeed, through the BoI and other state institutions, the state has sought to regulate the conditions under which foreign capital operates while, at the same time, being mindful of the fact that the Thai bourgeoisie operates within the expanding international system. No capitalist or capitalist state can afford to ignore this fact.

Peripheral Intermediation: Singapore and the Emerging International Economic Order

Hafiz Mirza

Singapore's pivotal role as a regional and international business center can only be understood in the context of an ongoing global redistribution of manufacturing and service industries. The post-war era has been characterized by a massive global expansion in output and international trade, an unprecedented internationalization of nearly all economies, and the emergence of a "new" international division of labor (NIDL) as part of the redistribution process. The "old" division of labor was created during the colonial era and entailed a specialization in international production and exchange whereby industrialized countries produced and exported manufactured goods, while developing countries produced and exported agricultural goods and raw materials ("commodities"). Though this trade structure still predominates, it has been modified by the rapid expansion of manufacturing and service exports from developing countries. In 1981, for example, 11% of developing country visible exports consisted of manufactured goods, although 85% of this trade was accounted for by just ten countries (including Singapore). The term "new" international division of labor therefore refers to a system of international trade in which there is intra-industry, intra-services specialization between industrialized and developing countries.

The world economic system is dominated by a group of capitalist industrialized countries (North America, Western Europe, Japan and Australasia – the *metropole*) which are surrounded by a large number of "peripheral" (mainly developing) countries whose chief international economic and political interactions are preponderantly with this capitalist "core". Metropole-periphery economic relations have been transformed over the last decade by the advent of a peripheral sub-group of countries which can be referred to as intermediate economies (IE). This small group of countries is involved in a process of peripheral intermediation which can be defined as, the production of goods and services in a given country, *predominantly* utilizing inputs from *abroad* for the *principal* purpose of *export* to other countries. This intermediation activity can be conducted by both indigenous firms and MNCs, but the latter predominate in most intermediate economies. Intermediate activity can be both entrepot (e.g. Singapore acts as a distribution center for commodities and manufactures regionally and globally; it also reroutes excess funds between regions because it is the East Asian center for the inter-bank market) and productive (e.g. Singapore's oil refining; Hong Kong's loan syndication and fund management). Finally, it is important to recognize that while some countries are almost entirely intermediators (Singapore, Hong Kong, the Bahamas), others are only partial-intermediators (Brazil, India, South Korea) and it is necessary in these cases to determine the appropriate activity and the extent of intermediation.

Peripheral intermediation is most marked in manufacturing activity and partly explains the developing countries' share of global trade, and world manufacturing value added which increased from 4.5% in 1938, to 8.1% in 1963, to 11.0% in 1982; and possibly 21.0% by the year 2000). Much of this intermediation has arisen as a result of activity by MNC's attracted by cheap labor, rapidly growing regional markets and other factors.

Intermediate activity generated by MNCs can take the form of exports to the source country or third countries or inputs into export-oriented industries in the host country. All three forms are found in Singapore. Further, the trade engendered by intermediation can be inter-industry (e.g. textiles exported by IEs in return for high technology manufactures), intra-industry (radios and black and white TVs in return for color television) or intra-product (IE subsidiaries of MNCs or indigenous firms are involved in part of a global production process). Again all three types prevail in Singapore.

Although the network of world manufacturing trade is still dominated by industrialized countries, developing countries are increasing their share: in 1970 they accounted for 5% of international manufacturing exports; by 1980 this figure had risen to 10% and is rising. What is particularly interesting is the increase of manufacturing trade between developing countries, from 2 to 4%, which is chiefly intra-IE or IE-developing countries in scope. A large share of metropole imports now come from the periphery, and the share of Asian countries and Singapore is significant. Excluding commodities, the peripheral share of imports is high in chemicals, machinery, transport equipment, clothing and basic manufactures. The high import penetration in basic manufactures and clothing indicates that technology transfer from industrialized countries to intermediate economies continues to be in the intermediate and low technology range.

Manufacturing peripheral intermediation is concentrated in a small number of developing countries: the top five exporters account for 62.9% of the total, while the top ten account for 82.1%. Singapore is the fifth largest exporter. . . .

Financial peripheral intermediation mainly dates from the early to the mid-1970s, and is restricted to a small number of countries. Excluding the European centers, the major centers are Panama, the Bahamas, the Netherland Antilles, Kuwait, Bahrain, the Philippines and especially Hong Kong and Singapore. Singapore is a major intermediary in the interbank market – Asiacurrency loans, Asia-bonds, financial futures, insurance, etc. It is also attempting to expand into loan syndication and fund management in which it is relatively weak. Statistics indicate that peripheral intermediation in the services is very important for Singapore and, in all likelihood, for a number of other developing countries. This is confirmed by a number of recent UNCTAD reports concerning the role of services in developing countries. . . .

Peripheral intermediation is obviously related to the new international division of labor (NIDL), but only partly. The NIDL also encompasses a transfer of technology, industry and services to the periphery for purposes other than intermediation (e.g. the establishment of refineries in OPEC countries). Peripheral intermediation is a vital aspect of the emerging international economic order. Intermediate countries such as Singapore help maintain a world system dominated by industrialized countries: they create a buffer zone between the metropole and the periphery, they permit some flexibility in global industrial restructuring, they offer high growth economies with profitable opportunities for MNCs and indigenous enterprise during a period of world stagnation, and they enable industrialized countries to provide a facade of resource transfer to the periphery when in reality most transfers are concentrated in a few sympathetic regimes.

Singapore as an Intermediate Economy

Intermediation is not a new phenomenon from Singapore's point of view. Since the mid-nineteenth-century the island has been a center for entrepot trade and ancillary services, linking resource-rich Southeast Asia with the industrialized countries; and intermediation remains the island's raison d'etre. What is new, however, is that its intermediary role has been extended extensively into a wide range of manufacturing and service industries. To be sure, some of the output of these industries is sold locally, but most is oriented towards export markets. Furthermore, Singapore is the only peripheral economy which intermediates across the entire range of manufacturing, financial and other service activities and is therefore a vital component of the emerging international economic order.

The rest of this article discusses Singapore's intermediary role both geographically (within ASEAN and the Pacific Community) and industrially (petroleum, shipbuilding and electronics). Initially, however, it is worth posing a question: Why has Singapore become so important in the process of intermediation?

Factors such as state support, investment climate, location, incentives etc. have spurred Singapore's success. GSP, US tariff items 807 and 806.30, and other industrialized country regulations promoting exports by developing countries have helped, but these do not explain why Singapore is relatively more successful in attracting foreign capital and technology. This question can perhaps best be answered by comparing Singapore with Asia's three other newly industrializing countries. All have right wing, authoritarian regimes; few raw materials; are industrially diversified; and possess cheap, skilled, responsive work forces whose power is controlled by tight trade union legislation. Singapore's manifest advantages over the other countries are a high level of inducements, excellent infrastructure and a massive acreage made over to export processing zones. These benefits especially attract MNCs involved in manufacturing peripheral intermediation. Service MNCs are also attracted by Singapore's lack of restrictions, low taxes, and the experience, skills and communication networks developed during its entrepot past. Singapore developed as a distribution center within a worldwide British Empire whose economic pre-eminence was dependent upon free, unhindered international trade and investment: hence the reliance on MNCs and a liberal trade policy.

A recent comparison of Singapore and other ASEAN countries revealed that motivations such as market penetration, raw material procurement and cheap labor were the primary determinants of country choice by multinationals (see Wain, 1979). However, for export-oriented manufactures and services Singapore was the preferred site: factors such as good infrastructure, skilled labor, pacific industrial relations and political stability offset the disadvantageous lack of cheap labor or raw materials.

ASEAN

ASEAN was founded in 1967 as a means of diffusing political conflict among its member states (Indonesia, Malaysia, Thailand, the Philippines, Singapore; and now Brunei). Since then economic objectives have come to the fore and economic cooperation and integration are major issues for discussion on any ASEAN agenda.

Singapore plays a pivotal role in the organization and the island's trade with ASEAN countries accounts for between 20–30% of its total trade. Singapore accounts for 85% of intra-ASEAN trade, 21% of ASEAN's trade with the Pacific Rim countries and 36% of ASEAN's exports world-wide. Thus, though all ASEAN states have considerable trade with other countries, Singapore's share of trade is totally out of proportion to its size; and its intermediary role is clear. The main ASEAN exports to Singapore are petroleum and rubber; and the main imports from Singapore are chemicals, petroleum products, industrial machinery, electrical/electronic machinery and transport equipment. Most petroleum products and rubber products (largely manufactured using ASEAN raw materials) are exported to the USA, Japan and the "rest of the world" (e.g. Hong Kong for petroleum products); and entrepot trade involving ASEAN is also high.

In specific services Singapore is also a pivot (e.g. in the 1970s Singapore-based banks and MNCs supplied 45% of the loans to related companies in Thailand; and these received 51% of Thai financial outflows (see United Nations, 1981). Furthermore, MNCs operating in ASEAN tend to establish their headquarters in Singapore and co-ordinate their Southeast Asian activities from there. Much "Singaporean" investment in ASEAN in fact results from the Southeast Asian operations of multinational subsidiaries based in Singapore. However, though ASEAN is dependent on Singapore, the reverse, also applies. In 1983, for example, Singapore's trade with its ASEAN partners was 26% of its total trade and 50% of its trade with developing countries.

A variety of schemes have been adopted over the last decade aimed at increasing ASEAN cooperation: industrial projects, industrial complementation schemes, joint ventures, preferential trading arrangements, investment promotion and co-operation in banking and services. Through such schemes the intra-ASEAN division of labor maintains Singapore as the advanced nexus of a relatively under-developed region. A recent analysis of ASEAN's trade with the European Community by Schmitt-Rink illustrates this point well. The relevant conclusions are these: (i) Singapore's share of all

ASEAN–EC trade is 23%; (ii) intra-industry trade (essentially in manufactures i.e. along the NIDL) accounts for one sixth of ASEAN–EC trade; (iii) Singapore's share of intra-industry trade is 55%; and (iv) Without Singapore the commodity composition of ASEAN's trade with the EC would be similar to that of other LDCs (sic). In other words: Thailand's, Indonesia's, Malaysia's and the Philippines' trade with the EC still follows the colonial and post-colonial pattern of international specialization namely exchange of raw materials for manufactured products. The benefits of peripheral intermediation in such a context are clear.

The Pacific Community

The countries of the Pacific region range from a multitude of tiny island states (many still colonies) in the Pacific basin to the power-houses of the Pacific rim. The USA, Canada, Mexico, Colombia, Peru, Ecuador and Chile are the largest countries on the Pacific's eastern rim; while the western rim consists of Japan, South Korea, Taiwan, Hong Kong, the ASEAN countries, Australia and New Zealand, as well as four socialist countries, the USSR, China, North Korea and Vietnam. Characterized by cultural diversity, economic disparity and major political rifts, these countries are united solely by their shared geography and economic dynamism. In 1984, the major Pacific countries grew more rapidly than countries in other regions.

International commodity trade is the main integrating force. The majority of exports from each country (or country group) go to another country on the Pacific rim; and total intra-Pacific exports ($459.9 bn in 1983) amount to about 30% of world exports. The USA and Japan are the twin loci of this activity with 24% and 20% of Pacific exports respectively. Their mutual exports alone amount to 14% of Pacific exports; significantly, Japan has a balance of trade surplus ($26.8 bn), while the USA has a deficit (–$53.4 bn). ASEAN is the third largest trading bloc on the Pacific rim with the export of oil and raw materials being most important. Singapore, an exporter of manufactured goods, also has a significant 3.4% share of intra-Pacific exports (thrice its share of world exports), of which two thirds go to non-ASEAN countries. Though the Singapore authorities seek to maintain diversified export markets (like the USA, the city-state's exports are only 55% intra-Pacific), potential trade opportunities arising from increased intra-Pacific collaboration are not likely to be spurned.

Intermediation in Selected Industries

The structure of Singapore's international trade is largely the result of its role as an intermediate economy. Thus, compared to selected NICs, developing countries and industrialised countries raw materials are a very low proportion of its imports. This is chiefly because in the existing division of labor Singapore is used by MNCs to (further) process industrial supplies, fuels and machine parts. Accordingly the bulk of its imports consist of these items and capital equipment. Export-wise, Singapore differs from other NICs by not exporting a great deal of textiles: instead the bulk of its exports are chemicals (including petrochemicals) and machinery (both areas in which MNCs dominate). As an intermediate economy it also differs from Malaysia and India whose exports are dominated by primary products and which broadly still trade on the basis of the old division of labour. In some ways Singapore's export structure resembles that of the UK.

Singapore's intermediation takes a number of forms. In petrochemicals, for example, value added is a mere 12%: crude petroleum is imported from the Middle East, Malaysia and Indonesia, processed and then exported to countries such as Indonesia, Hong Kong, Australia, Japan and Malaysia. Significantly Singapore only uses 13% of the output of its petroleum products industry and most exports are destined for intermediate use elsewhere. In industrial, electrical and electronic machinery the value added is rather higher, but otherwise the process is the same. Parts are imported into Singapore or produced locally (by MNCs); processed/utilized; and the final output is largely exported overseas (most demand in Singapore is, in fact, intermediate). A similar analysis applies to most other industries, showing the importance of entrepot trade, and indicates that MNCs are encouraged to produce locally because of low import duties.

Table 1 indicates that some Singaporean industries and products are significant in world trade; and that most of Singapore's trade is intra-industry, intra-product, i.e. along the lines of the NIDL. As mentioned before, intermediation is most important in petroleum products, machinery and some marine industries. The origin and destination of imports and exports depends on the product in question. Thus, in the case of petroleum products, imports come mainly from the Middle East and South East Asia and exports are directed to East Asia and Australia; with ships and boats, imports derive from industrialized economies and exports go to developing countries; and with televisions, imports orginate in Japan and

Germany (which have a comparative advantage) and locally produced televisions are exported to a great number of countries. Trade
in radios and transistors is interesting. The former are at the end of
their product life-cycle and therefore most imports are from other
NICs and exports are destined for industrialized countries in Europe
and North America. The latter shows a division of labor in East
Asian countries: Singapore imports certain transistors/valves from
nearby countries and exports yet others to these countries – it is not
possible, however, to indicate the basis of this specialization.

Table 1   *Trade in Key Manufacturing Industries and Products, 1982*

	Industry or Product		
	Industrial Machinery	Transistors	Ships and Boats
Imports as a Proportion of World Trade (%)	1.4	8.6	6.5
Main Source Countries of Imports into Singapore	Japan Germany USA UK Netherlands	USA Japan Malaysia Hong Kong Germany Philippines	Japan Norway Germany Sweden UK USA
Exports as a Proportion of World Trade (%)	2.6	7.4	2.3
Main Destination Countries of Singapore Exports	USA Germany France Italy Australia	USA Malaysia Germany Hong Kong UK Italy	Indonesia Saudi Arabia Australia Liberia

Source: United Nations, *Yearbook of International Trade Statistics, 1982*, New York.

The remainder of this article analyzes the process of intermediation
in three key industries in Singapore.

Petroleum Products

This industry accounts for 40% of current FDI in manufacturing,
one-sixth of the sector's value added and over 30% of exports. The
industry is almost entirely controlled by foreign concerns. Shell first
established an oil bunkering and distribution service in Singapore
in 1892 and was the first company to establish a refinery in 1961.

The main reason for establishment was the central position of Singapore in Southeast Asia and the country's strategic location between the Middle East and the growing Japanese economy; soon other oil MNCs followed suit. The proximity of Vietnam during a period of heavy US involvement also played a role in the industry's expansion. Singapore is now the world's third largest refining centre after Houston and Rotterdam with 1.3% of world refining capacity. As demand for some petrol products began to drop in the 1970s, many companies diversified into the production of specialized fuels, oils, lubricants and basic petrochemicals, such as ethylene, butadiene and benzene. With intense over-capacity in the petrochemicals industry world-wide, exports of these products have also begun to falter; and Singapore based companies are presently upgrading their activities to manufacture thermoplastics, synthetic fibres and synthetic rubbers. Further competition is likely to be generated by the Indonesian, Malaysian, Thai and Philippine petrochemical complexes planned for the near future.

Petrochemicals is therefore an intermediate industry with problems, but these are not insoluble. First, diversification can proceed much further and Exxon (for example) has invested in petrochemical chemical additives through its subsidiary Exxon Chemical Singapore (Pte) Ltd. Secondly, the burgeoning offshore oil and gas industry of East and Southeast Asia continues to provide opportunities for Singapore's petroleum related industries. The island can provide: storage and distribution facilities, support services, oil rig construction and integrated petroleum related facilities. Finally, considerable Arab, Chinese and international finance is available for projects.

Petroleum products and related industries are a good example of peripheral intermediation and Singapore's chief benefits derive from the employment generated, employee remuneration and some linkages established with other industries e.g. shipbuilding and repair. There are, however, large costs associated with maintaining this capital intensive, infrastructurally expensive and volatile industry. Furthermore, foreign domination is likely to continue and there has been little technology transfer to indigenous firms.

Electrical and Electronic Products

These two related industries are vital to Singapore and have played a major role in the country's vigorous diversification into more advanced technologies. Their share of the manufacturing sector is large and in 1982 they accounted for 24% of output (of which electronic products constitute 17%), 20% of value added (16%),

27% of employment (22%) and 24% of direct exports (21%). The two industries are foreign dominated in terms of paid-up-capital and the number and size of firms. Both industries were insignificant until the 1970s when US MNCs led a wave of foreign companies intent on establishing manufacturing operations in Singapore. The two earliest firms of note were in fact indigenous and were set up in 1965 (Setron) and 1966 (Roxy) to manufacture monochrome televisions. In 1969 Philips (of the Netherlands) and a number of US companies established labor-intensive, export-oriented plants in Singapore to assemble semiconductor components. Since then the number of establishments, employment and output has leapt enormously. The structure of production has also changed with shifts in Singapore's comparative advantage which itself altered as a consequence of the government's high-wage policy.

The assembly of components is now less important than the production of components, intermediate parts and final consumer goods. In the electronics industry, the number of establishments has increased from 35 in 1970 to 195 in 1982, while output has soared from under $0.1 billion to $2.1 billion over the same period. Consumer electronics (such as televisions, radios, amplifiers, calculators and tape recorders) account for 40% of the 1982 output with electronic components (semiconductor devices, capacitors, cathode tubes etc.) making up a further 55%. The remaining 5% consists of industrial electronic equipment, including computers, peripheral equipment and telephones. There is a constant upgrading of technology with a move into, for example, the production of computers, robots and VLSI, and the introduction of computer aided design and manufacturing (CAD/CA11).

The electrical and electronics industries are also good examples of peripheral intermediation and were established in Singapore essentially for offshore production. As elsewhere, these industries are deployed as part of a strategy of world-wide sourcing by MNCs (in search of cheap labor, low taxes and incentives, as discussed elsewhere) and initially only consisted of low technology products and processes. More recently, however:

> ... computer-based automation is pervading practically all stages of the design, application and maintenance of electronic hardware and complementary software ... [and] ... the internationalization of production and support services in the electronics industry is acquiring new forms and mechanisms. ... The issue for the 1980s is not so much the possibility of relocating industrial activities from [industrialized] countries to the developing countries ... Rather, in consumer electronics and in electronic components, both automation and

industrial redeployment to developing countries are taking place as complementary processes, with automation coming to the fore as the driving force. (UNIDO, 1984).

Curiously then, despite automation, the electronics industry (and, for similar reasons, electrical manufacturing) is likely to expand in Singapore and other developing countries, albeit in an altered form and structure. Ironically this is because of the shortage of skilled labor in industrialized countries, combined with the availability of highly skilled labor and engineers in countries such as South Korea, Hong Kong, Singapore, India and Brazil.

Singapore's present policy of expanding the output of its scientific, engineering and technical manpower is therefore likely to pay handsome dividends. Two subsidiary reasons also contribute to continuing peripheral intermediation in the electrical and electronics industry. First, social legislation is relatively lax in most developing countries, thus making them attractive to MNCs keen on maximizing the usage of costly equipment by running multi-shift operations. Secondly, incentives and low priced infrastructure (especially EPZs and "science parks") are key elements in any MNCs locational decisions. Intermediate economies should be wary, however, because, the developmental benefits of offshore production to be reaped by developing countries in terms of employment generation, skill formation, forward and backward inter-industrial integration and technological spin-offs might become even smaller and less viable than they are today. This is of particular importance to Singapore. Pan Eng Fong and Linda Lim (1977), while acknowledging the patent benefits of Singapore's MNC-dominated electronics industry, suggest further problems: the industry is volatile – in 1982 it shed 10 thousand local workers); there is little technology transfer due to MNC preponderance, the partial transfer of products and processes, and a paucity of local R & D; there are few inter-industry vertical linkages; and there maybe negative effects on local competition. Kwan Kuen-Chor and Lee Soo Ann (1983) agree on the third problem and point out that Japanese electrical firms, such as Matsushita, Sanyo and Hitachi have solved the problem of industrial support by asking other Japanese firms to set up in Singapore. . . .

Shipbuilding and Repair

Singapore's marine industry (i.e. shipbuilding and repairing, oil rig construction, marine engineering and related industries) is one of the country's largest, accounting for about 11% of employment and value added in the manufacturing sector in 1982. About half of the output is exported and this amounts to 5% of the economy's annual merchandise exports. The industry is also significant in two other respects. Firstly, it offers an important supportive and servicing facility to key industries, including shipping and transport, and Singapore is now the world's twelfth largest maritime power; it also has associated petroleum products and related industries, an offshore petroleum extraction industry; and burgeoning aircraft construction/repair and air distribution services. Secondly, unlike the other two industries discussed above, the marine industry is dominated by indigenous firms which wholly or substantially own all but 40 of the 260 relevant establishments. MNCs from the USA, Japan, Switzerland and the UK were the main foreign investors. An orientation towards local industries and the use of sizeable local talent by indigenous firms suggests that the marine industry is generally *not* involved in peripheral intermediation; and the industries being supported are often themselves intermediate in nature.

Though some of the major local shipbuilding and repairing companies trace their origins back to the country's colonial past, many are recent establishments whose development owes much to joint ventures with foreign companies, especially Japanese shipbuilders. Three good examples are: Jurong shipyard founded as a joint venture between the Singapore government and Ishikawajima-Harima Heavy Industries (IHI) in 1963 and now employing over 2000 Workers (IHIs ownership share is only 11%); Mitsubishi Singapore Heavy Industries Ltd, a joint venture between the government and the Japanese concern of the same name founded in 1968 with nearly 1000 workers; and Hitachi Zosen Robin dockyard, a joint venture initiated by the private indigenous Robin Group with over 1000 workers. The transfer of technology, skills and organization was very complex and was chiefly achieved through seconded personnel from the Japanese parent company. In the case of the Jurong Shipyard transfer took a lengthy period of time with a peak of 55 seconded personnel (including scientists, engineers, designers and other specialist staff) in 1965 tapering to the 1983 level of 4 Japanese staff. Despite some tied imports from Japan, these joint ventures have successfully transferred technology to Singapore. However three additional points should be made. First, the government's initiative was vital and a number of other large firms in this industry are state owned enterprises. Secondly, Singapore already possessed many skills and facilities required for marine industries in the 1960s when most joint ventures were inaugurated;

Finally, the success of shipbuilding, repairing and other marine industries would have been impossible without excellent infrastructure and communications and a rapid expansion in related industries: shipping, petroleum, offshore oil, etc.

Conclusion

In this article we have focused on Singapore's role as an intermediate economy by analyzing three key industries. We have shown that the establishment of each of these industries was determined by a varied constellation of factors, including location, incentives, government initiative, and infrastructure. In addition each industry's impact on the Singapore economy was assessed and seen to differ considerably (e.g. the electronics industry created much employment and offered potential access to highly advanced technology; the marine industry was much more successful in transferring technology to Singapore and establishing linkages). . . .

Singapore's role in the NIDL, peripheral intermediation and the emerging international economic order (EIEO) will probably be maintained, but its exact characteristics and dimensions depend not only on future economic trends, but also on political realities.

The world economic crisis, rapid technological change and global industrial restructuring have all contributed to an international power struggle in which industrialized countries have been pitted against each other and against NICs and developing countries demanding a New International Economic Order (NIEO). The EIEO will attempt to resolve this conflict (essentially in the interest of industrialized countries) by reducing inter-industrialized country competition and placing intermediate economies and developing countries in subordinate positions in a new global political and economic hierarchy of alliances and inter-relationships. . . .

The industrialized countries supporting the EIEO are not, however, a monolithic international power structure. In industrialized countries, as in developing countries, elites are divided by their diverse opinions and conflicting political and economic interests. Attitudes vary from the arch-conservative to the liberal and the relatively progressive (the Brandt Commission, the International Progress Organization). Further, many international organizations (UNIDO, UNCTAD, UNESCO) are sympathetic to developing countries; and some of the latter (e.g. OPEC, China, India, even ASEAN) are not entirely powerless themselves. Singapore's economic future will in the last instance be determined by the outcome of the conflicts between these particular groups and states.

Wage Labor in West Malaysia: A Study of Five Factories

Hing Ai Yun

Within Malaysian manufacturing industry, attempts to contain labor are very often already put into gear even before workers join the production line. To ensure that only certain types of worker are taken in, larger corporations such as transnational textile and electronic factories have set criteria for age, sex, working experience and marital status in their choice of applicants.

The large textile company studied, regularly sends recruiting teams to rural centers such as Kulim (in Kedah) and Teluk Anson (in Perak) to recruit the relatively more educated female Malay workers from these poor wage areas. The factory has posted a sign board for female workers between 16–26 years of age. Housed in relatively cheap company hostels – costing only $10 per month with free utilities, TV and transport to work – these first generation workers think twice before leaving, as cheap accommodation and public transport are two rare commodities in Penang. Compared to locals who are well-known for job-hopping, these rural workers with little social contact are more willing to take on shift work and overtime work for small additional allowances (see Table 1 for details of cases studied).

Whereas the larger companies can afford to recruit a specific type of worker, competing smaller companies are forced to take in the "less desirable" workers such as the older married female workers (who tend to be "less stable" due to their triple role as mother, worker and wife) or the young and often recalcitrant unmarried male. Some of the smaller companies solve their labor woes by relocating to rural areas. However, as these young workers grow with the firm their experience does make them bolder and less amenable to strict work routine, but what is even more important is that their salaries soon prove to be more than what the company will bear. They therefore are retrenched at the next recession and new workers taken in at the same time. At this older age too, workers would have got married. Those who are prepared to change their "single" status would be "advised" to leave for their own interest. However, remaining married female workers would soon be termina-

97

ted because they would not be able to cope with the strict rules and regulations of such enterprises.

The tasks of co-ordinating social production and appropriating useful labor are partly achieved through the propagation of countless rules and procedures regulating work behaviour. Penalties for poor performance and rewards for desirable behavior are also carefully spelt out. Rules governing the arrival and departure of workers from their work place are strictly observed, especially in the larger factories. Clocking devices print to the nearest minute the time workers cross the factory gate. Beside getting a stern warning a worker who is five minutes late may have his pay deducted by one hour. To prevent loitering and unnecessary socializing, workers have to obtain a pass to cross sectional boundaries. And, because toilets are situated at the far end of buildings it would be embarrassing to be frequently seen asking for passes to go to the toilet. This prevents workers from using the toilet as a place for relaxation or as an escape from boredom and heat of the factory. Canteens are also closed five minutes before the siren signalling the start of the working day and security guards are posted around the compound to take down names of loitering workers.

Generally the tendency is towards multiplication of rules and increasingly strict rules limiting physical mobility and social interaction in the work place. In the textile company studied, whereas workers in the normal shift (8.30am–4.30pm) were allowed to stop work 10 minutes before time, after April 1981 this was cut to five minutes. This process is clearly illustrated in the development of the biscuit factory studied. One year after it started making a profit, workers succeeded in forcing their employers to recognize the union. This move in turn prompted the management to take steps to rationalize and professionalize production and labor organization. New rules and regulations were formulated and specified in writing and workers were told that these will come with the new collective agreement. Where previously workers had considerable leeway and flexibility in conducting themselves as long as quotas were achieved, the new rules:

1. direct workers to work according to set regulations and procedures;
2. insist on strict observation of cleanliness;
3. request that they work hard (incentives will be provided accordingly);
4. require strict adherence to rest time set out (instead of relaxing whenever they felt like it, as practised before);
5. require workers to clock in and out of the workplace at specified

time (when previously workers entered or left the factory as desired);

6. disallow workers from chatting during work (where before they could talk freely with workmates);

7. prohibit unnecessary movement from section to section (previously if the worker had completed the work allotted he could either leave or visit and chat with friends in other sections. Colored uniforms are now worn by workers from different sections to facilitate identification of loitering workers);

8. prohibit smoking or eating in the factory (this was freely allowed before).

Such rules are complemented and implemented by a hierarchical power structure. Larger enterprises with many more rules also have more complicated hierarchical structures of organization. This invariably results in a narrower span of control averaging about one supervisory staff to five or six production workers and hence a more disciplined workforce. In contrast, smaller companies have wider spans of control with one supervisory staff to between 20–30 workers. Correspondingly these companies carry a smaller number of rules and procedures regulating work behavior. The organizational hierarchies for different companies are shown in Table 1. One clear conclusion is that the very minute division of labor and authority structure in the textile factory narrowly restricts the behavior of workers at all levels. Due to the very specialized nature of the machines even the engineers are confined to their particular section unlike other factories where various sections share a common pool of technicians and engineers. At the production level workers have very specific jobs. For instance, unlike the shoe factory where machine operators also sort, bundle and carry the cut leather uppers to the sewing section, textile workers just leave the product stacked by their side to be carried by specially designated packers to the next section for further processing. Such differences result in varying degrees of physical flexibility and hence social interaction and opportunities for relaxation and "wasting time" favoring more workers in the shoe factory.

While rules in advance can, to a certain extent, bring about desired work behavior, hierarchical authority is still essential for enforcement of these rules. The constraining influence of supervisors is clear from the different conduct workers display in their absence/presence. In the textile factory, when only junior or assistant supervisors are around during the early morning shift (6.30am–2.30pm) workers only start work at 7am. On the other hand, morning shift work ends punctually at 2.30pm. By this time, all

Table 1 *Case Studies*

Paid-up capital ($M)	23,800,000	8,000,000	8,000,000	10,000,000	1,450,000
No. workers	883	1187	1200	400	800
Nationality of owners	90% Japanese	90% Malaysian	Japanese	Singaporean	Malaysian (98%)
Product	Fully integrated factory (spinning, yarn dyeing, weaving & finishing) producing yarn dyed gingham	Wooden kiln-dry furniture (natural resource based)	Silicon Transistors & linear integrated circuits (for use in TV and radio equipment), bi-polar digital ICs (for scientific equipment) & power ICs (for audio equipment), thristors (for current control)	Biscuits & sweets	Canvas shoes
Market	90% export	100% export	100% export	Domestic & Singapore	80% exported
Year	1981	1981	1980	1981	1981
Span of control (ratio of supervisory staff to production operatives)	1:6	1:5	1:5	1:6	1:20

Organization Hierarchy	Dept. Head Asst. Dept. Head Officer-in-charge Asst. Officer-in-charge	Dept. Superintendent (administrative functions too insignificant at this level, therefore combined at factory level)	Production Supervisor	Chief Supervisor	Section Supervisor
	Engineer Asst. Engineer	(specialization only at factory level indicating lower level of technological sophistication)			
	Supervisor Asst. Supervisors Junior Supervisor	Supervisor	Line Leader	Supervisor	Supervisor
	Line Leader Asst. Line Leader	a) Process leadman b) Process leadman	Group leader	Asst. supervisor	
	Production Operators	Workers	Workers	Workers	Workers

managerial and supervisory staff are present (normal shift hours are 8.30am–4.30pm). In addition, normal shift workers are also subjected to the dreaded daily check by department heads who not only demand immediate explanations for defects but who also order workers to carry out specific tasks at once. Afternoon shift workers who have to start work punctually at 2.30pm, in contrast, normally finish work 20 minutes before dismissal time at 10.30pm. Furthermore, they can take their 45 minutes dinner break 15 minutes before time and finish off 15 minutes later. In small factories where supervisors have to control between 20–30 workers spread over maybe two sections, workers are usually more relaxed until time for the regular hourly checks by supervisors. In fact, some of them prefer working the quieter afternoon shift 3.45pm–11.30pm) when they can smoke, chat or sing because by this time most of the management staff would have gone home. Moreover, if they finish work they can nap and not be asked to help out in other sections facing labor shortage.

Even in the presence of supervisors, workers may display different degrees of desirable behavior depending on the supervisor's relationship to the owners. Supervisors who are relatives or friends of the owners (this frequently happens in the smaller Chinese-owned factories) tend to be high-handed, arbitrary, temperamental, unsympathetic and rude, often abusing the workers verbally and in certain cases even physically. In one case a worker was slapped by his supervisor and left the next day, while in another a supervisor hurled a chair at the worker after a heated argument.

On the other hand, supervisors who have risen from the rank and file (due to union pressure internal recruitment is normally practised by the larger enterprises) are commonly more sympathetic to workers. This class of supervisors actually share some of the problems faced by workers such as pressure from superiors. Similarity in experience extends to living in the same neighborhood, traveling by the same bus to work. Moreover, difference in salary is so small that some workers refuse promotion to line leader.

Even if the supervisor has greater freedom to stand and cool himself before the fan, he also gets a shelling if workers cannot fill daily quotas. In fact, some supervisors may cover up when quotas are not achieved for the day and try urging workers to put in more effort the next day to compensate for the deficit.

In view of the shortage of labor especially at the unskilled level over the past few years, workers have the option of leaving if they can no longer tolerate impositions on their behavior. The biscuit factory which has a labor force of around 400 workers, recruited

266 workers mostly between 16–25 years of age between January to March 1982. At the same time 70 workers left their jobs. Those who left were mainly new recruits. Older workers who are already familiar with the work situation and who have worked themselves up the wage scale will lose out if they leave for a new job, as factories taking in new production workers do not differentiate the experienced and inexperienced unless one is technically skilled.

The same phenomenon is observed in the shoe factory which registered a fluctuating labor force of between 475 (in October) and 831 (in January) for 1979. Workers at the biscuit factory gave these reasons for leaving: obtaining a better job elsewhere; bad-tempered supervisor; dislike for the night shift (only for young female workers staying with conservative parents); to continue studying; insecurity of job (daily rated); sacked (e.g. "ponteng" – leave without absence for more than two times); and carelessness.

For the rest of the workers who have accepted their fate as "dumb" and of low status, the power hierarchy does give some hope for mobility. This is much more true in the case of the larger enterprises. For this reason some workers strive hard to exceed quotas or to work beyond what is necessary and acceptable. In this respect rural workers educated in the national language have even less hope of promotion especially if they are working for Chinese-owned companies or large transnationals where the language of management is Chinese and English respectively. Thus we find that 70–80% of the unskilled production workers in non-government-owned factories are Malays, while most of the supervisory and managerial staff are Chinese and foreigners. Add to this cultural differences such as eating habits and the language barrier, hurdles to developing workers consciousness seem almost insurmountable. This does complicate the development of worker consciousness, especially in the Chinese-owned factories where racial consciousness is high and where even ordinary Chinese workers are seen as "powerful" due to the practice of racial favoritism. There is always the pressure against outgroup interaction reflecting the saliency of racial identification nurtured by policies based on race. By contrast, in companies owned by the state and managed mainly by Malays, as exemplified by the shoe factory, anti-management feelings are strong, especially when continued efforts to unionize were unsuccessful as a result of management action (include co-opting the leaders, linking unions to communism and therefore anti-Islamic and anti-government). In such homogeneous factories favoritism may be based on sexual criteria.

Actually, the hierarchical system is not complete proof against insubordination. Supervisors' power of coercion can sometimes be diluted. Supervisors try not to confront the more experienced and older workers who have grown with the company and who have lost all hope of promotion (one worker in the biscuit factory was only promoted after 17 years with the company). They therefore get away with small offences and would "talk back" or ignore the supervisor when ordered to carry out some tasks. In fact, the older workers very often act as "informal" supervisors, guiding the younger recruits and sometimes even informing on them. Maturity of the workforce and accumulated frustrations was the main reason accounting for the spate of worker protests in the second half of the 1970s in the oldest Free Trade Zone of Malaysia in Penang, even though the state had prohibited workers organizations in such zones. Strikes such as those organized by workers of Atlas Electronics in 1974, RUF and Hewlett-Packard in 1980 indicate that electronic factory workers have come a long way since the time when the first company, Clarion, started production in 1971 in Penang.

Rise in labor cost and difficulty of securing a stable and dependable labor force have brought about a corresponding increase in the rate of mechanization especially among the larger companies. For instance, the biscuit company used to cream its wafers manually. But due to the shortage of cheap labor (it is located next to the high-wage sector of Singapore) the company installed a machine to cream the biscuits. Financially weaker companies have resorted to attracting new recruits with higher wage rates than those offered to existing workers, though new workers are not entitled to other benefits given to the existing workforce.

Machines provide an "impersonal" kind of directive to each worker as to what he is to perform. They also establish the pace at which workers have to work. Instead of having at least the opportunity of manipulating the supervisor, the worker is now helpless in the face of a reality fixed in nuts and bolts. If he needs to go to the toilets he cannot plead urgency of his case but is forced to wait until he can get a replacement. Unlike the human supervisor, machines can run non-stop. About the only time that workers can take a rest is when the machine breaks down (this happens more often in small companies using old machines) or when electricity supplies are cut due to power failure. Indeed, the worker cannot make a pact with the machine to compromise the pace of work. Neither can he shout the machine down so he can talk to his colleague. In fact, workers are spaced quite a distance apart. Combine this with the noise of the machine and very little social interaction can take place. Management themselves realize the constraints and loneliness machines impose on the workers. For this reason those who work in the primarily mechanized wafer department (continuous flow production) in the sweet factory are paid 60 cents an hour (for standing the whole day) compared to 55 cents for those in the sweet department where there is free movement and workers are not paced by machines. In addition, a machine operator's annual increment is seven cents an hour compared to six cents for the other workers. The machine tender's job is mainly to feed in the raw materials and to ensure that the product is of a certain consistency or specification. The supervisor is only referred to if the machine needs readjustment to correct the product. When the pace of work is too fast as in the furniture factory, defects are simply ignored in order not to stop the flow of work. The quality of work therefore cannot be ensured by machines. This has actually resulted in loss of business for the company. But because of the high labor turnover in the factory, by the time this is realized the worker responsible for the defect has already left.

However, the pace of machines is determined not only by the maximum speed at which workers can comfortably carry out their work. In the texturizing department of one Hong Kong textile company studied, the older machines and the cheaper quality yarns used dictated that the spindle speed should only be around 350,000 revolutions per minute (rpm). The same process carried out in a modern factory using the latest (Japanese made) machines and good quality yarns could run at a speed of 600,000 rpm without causing frequent breakage to the yarns. With such sophisticated equipment, one cycle of production could last as long as 24 hours without doffing (removing the spun yarns to the next stage of production) and therefore fewer workers would be needed. In contrast, in the less sophisticated factory studied, doffing had to be carried out after every eight hours, thus more workers had to be employed. Comparing the productivity of workers using similar machines, one supervisor estimated that a local worker could only manage two crimping machines, whereas her European counterpart managed seven to eight and the Japanese counterpart, four machines.

As increasing spheres of the production process are subsumed under technological control, the work of an increasing number of workers will assume a uniform character. At this stage of Malaysian industrial development when labor is still cheaper relative to imported machines (one estimate is that Malaysia is five years behind Japan in technology used for production of TV) the use of continuous production flow is still not so pervasive that stoppage of work in one section of the plant can immediately spark off a plant-wide stoppage. The less sophisticated textile company studied had considered introducing a conveyor belt to reduce the movement of workers which was difficult to monitor. But because the cost of the machine ($60,000 exclusive of interest) was way beyond the cost of labor, the management decided to shelve the idea temporarily.

Positive reinforcers such as bonus schemes, monthly attendance bonus, annual picnics and welfare capitalism are also used by employers to maximize workers' motivation. Since the pay is generally low, and during periods of low demand, overtime work has become an incentive much sought after. In the sweet factory, overtime pay represents 20–50% of a worker's total pay. American electronic companies in Malaysia are well-known for their initiative to stimulate the active loyalty of workers to the firm. Married male supervisors are sometimes referred to as bapa (uncle) by female operators to maintain the happy family ideology propagated by such companies.

The circulation of the in-house magazine, the house-union, job rotation and group work in these companies are part and parcel of the happy family image. In fact, some workers in the sweet factory had forgone the one-cent hourly increment for machine operators to join sections where production is based on work teams. Job rotation and work groups provide workers with a modicum of comfort and a little happiness in an otherwise boring and physically unbearable working environment. It was also observed that cooper-ation in work groups transcends even racial barriers as members get to know each other well and do not hesitate to cover for each other. Working in teams may improve productivity, but it also enhances the confidence of workers in themselves – to see themselves as contributors to production and not only as objects to be supervised and talked down to by persons of authority.

Part III

Rural Transformation and Agrarian Differentiation

Introduction

Nearly all Southeast Asian countries are predominantly agrarian, with agriculture contributing a major share of the countries' revenue, and the agricultural population constituting the majority of the population. Singapore is an obvious exception; but even in Malaysia, the most urban and industrially diversified of the other countries, 35% of the working population is engaged in agriculture, and agriculture remains the largest contributor to national revenue. In all countries the rural population continues to grow in absolute, if not relative, terms. And in all countries rice cultivation is of strategic importance, and in most it is the largest branch of agricultural production. The three studies which follow all focus on rice-growing areas.

State policies towards agriculture vary – thus, for example, Malaysia and Indonesia heavily subsidize agriculture, while in Thailand there is net taxation – but all are guided by the dual imperatives of encouraging food production and of political control of the mass of the rural population. The latter is typically by state patronage of dominant rural groups. Over the past fifteen years or so there has been a quite rapid spread of new seed-fertiliser technology and commercialization, leading to greater volume of production and usually productivity. But precisely in those countries where this has been most marked (Malaysia, Indonesia, Philippines, Thailand) there has been an accompanying increase in socio-economic differentiation in terms of wealth and access to and control of human labor and resources.

Proponents of some dependency or structuralist theories have tended to analyze agrarian change – often on the basis of survey data – in terms of what is or is not capitalist or functional for capital. Recent emphasis has been on empirical studies of detailed local processes, mechanisms and contexts – not just indicators – of differentiation. These take into account not only commercialization and technology, but also local and state power structures and their mediations with local, national and transnational economic relations (see Hart, Turton and White, 1988). Many accounts have tended to assume, on the one hand, a baseline of a relatively undifferentiated and egalitarian peasantry, and, on the other, a likely tendency towards polarization of large capitalist landowners and agricultural wage-labor. More recent studies have challenged both assumptions. In particular, while there has been a general increase in landlessness, there has been a marked persistence of small-scale production, due to many and varied mechanisms and a range of adaptations of supposedly "pre-capitalist" labor-tying arrangements which allow landowners greater control over tenants, sharecroppers and hired labor. A pervasive feature in this is the diversification into off-farm and non-agricultural investment and employment by the richest and poorest, respectively for accumulation and survival.

Stoler examines changes in labor organization in rice-harvesting, arguing that these are a sensitive indicator of more general labor relations. The "green revolution", in Java as elsewhere, has reduced production costs relative to returns for the larger landowners and led to less agricultural employment. She analyzes the shift from symmetrical and reciprocal to more assymmetrical and exploitative relations of production and an increase in differentiation among peasant producers. She corrects a distortion in previous accounts which have underestimated the importance of harvesting labor as a household income producing activity, because it was seasonal and female labor. She also explains why landless women receive lower wages for harvesting than small landowners and women from larger landowning households. The importance of examining issues of gender and generation and the diversification of household income strategies is also taken up in articles by Mather and White in Part IV (Production and Gender Relations). Some social and cultural effects of differentiation are documented in Scott's article on Malaysia in Part V (Culture and Ideology).

Anan Ganjanapan shows how Thai state policy instruments (credit, development funds, guaranteed prices) have chiefly benefitted an emergent class of capitalist farmers. The basis of their expanded accumulation and local influence are ownership of land, local political connections, and their ability to take advantage of new technology which permits triple-cropping. They have also diversified into machinery hire, haulage, trade, livestock raising and moneylending. In particular he shows in detail complex ways in which sharecropping contracts have been renegotiated to give landowners greater control of tenant labor, reducing supervisory costs to owners while increasing their control of decision making, and allowing owners to appropriate incremental output. In these conditions the labor of tenants and sharecroppers increasingly resembles wage-labor, and is experienced as such. However, share-cropping continues to provide the tenant with marginally greater security of basic subsistence than wage-labor.

Ngo Vinh Long reviews on a broad scale agrarian changes which have occurred in the southern region of Vietnam, both before and after reunification in 1975, up to 1981. Land reform between 1970–5 corrected some of the gross inequalities in landownership; but American wartime campaigns of forced urbanization, bombing and shelling, dislocated population and destroyed land, forest and cattle. After five years of attempted socialist reforms following 1975, there was still, in the south, a class of rich peasants and rural capitalists (some 4 to 5% of the rural population) and over 20% were still landless or land-poor. The rich peasants and rural capitalists however, accumulated not so much on the basis of ownership of land as through the use of farm machinery and by diversifying into off-farm activities. It is argued that the commercialization of the rural economy and use of capital inputs were among both causes and effects of the slow development of the program of cooperativization. Suggestions are made for the redistribution of all resources, not just land, in a thoroughgoing reform, and for critical state investments and appropriate pricing policies.

Rice Harvesting in Kali Loro: A Study of Class and Labor Relations in Rural Java

Ann L. Stoler

The "Green Revolution" was initially hailed as a cure-all for underproduction in the impoverished countries of Southeast Asia and the Third World in general. Recent critics, however, looking beyond gross national product, have indicated that these programs result in various forms of environmental degradation and increased economic polarization. Technological inputs in the form of high yielding rice varieties, pesticides, and fertilizers have been accompanied by widespread social changes in labor organization, leading to reduced production costs for larger landowners, but also to a large-scale elimination of agricultural employment opportunities.

Although the relationship between increased stratification and larger capital inputs into the agrarian economy in such places as rural Java is well established, the *process* of economic polarization and the internal socio-economic conditions that have fostered these technological changes is yet to be described. The fact that the "Green Revolution" has encouraged new forms of labor recruitment in harvesting, for example, does not explain their acceptance at this particular time, nor does it explain the social consequences for rural society. In fact, the tools that have recently been employed in rural Java (the sickle in particular), and the new organizational features of rice harvesting are hardly new innovations. Explanation of their adoption *now* requires analysis of the relationship between these external factors and the internal structure of rural labor relations. In particular, I shall focus on the shift from symmetrical and reciprocal forms of labor exchange to more asymmetrical and exploitative relations of production. The increase in rural socio-economic inequalities must be understood as a function of historical conditions in the colonial and postcolonial periods. This is not to suggest a lack of stratification in precolonial Java, but rather an increase in *intrapeasant* class distinctions as a result of the colonial encounter.

Javanese rural economy has been characterized by numerous authors who have emphasized apparently contradictory consequences of Dutch colonial rule. Geertz and Wolf have stressed the

111

closed, corporate nature of peasant organization and concomitant leveling mechanisms of wealth redistribution and "shared poverty" (Geertz, 1963). The assertion is that in response to colonial demands on land and labor, leveling mechanisms increased the importance of horizontal ties, and not only spread life risks, but assured access to a limited resource base for village members. Others have argued that communalism, imposed by the Dutch, led to a gradual individualization of landholdings and encouraged economic polarization (Lyon, 1970).

This paper emphasizes that "shared poverty" and the leveling mechanisms inherent in closed, corporate communities represent only a *temporary* adaptation to external pressures. Although colonial rule initially enhanced horizontal ties, I suggest that in the long run vertical structures were strengthened, gained dominance, and thus systematically undermined the basis for "shared poverty," that is, horizontal relations of production and exchange.

Labor arrangements in rice harvesting in particular provide a useful and sensitive indicator of more general labor relations, since they represent one of the rare occasions in village life where these relations emerge in striking and easily observable form. The traditional harvesting system, involving a labor intensive technology and large numbers of women paid with a share (*bawon*) of the harvest, is cited by Javanese as a stronghold of mutual cooperation (*gotong-royong*) and by students of Javanese society as a prime example of "shared poverty". References to the fact that "every woman or child in the village is entitled to harvest" (Wertheim, 1984), or that "all who hear of it may come and join" (Jay, 1969: 29) portray a normative system of equity and sharing that masks the real conditions of socio-economic inequality. A closer examination of the harvest system reveals a delicately balanced set of production and exchange relationships that determines both differential access and returns to harvesting opportunities.

An analysis of that system in the central Javanese village of Kali Loro (where harvesting practices have remained relatively stable) allows me to specify the conditions under which reciprocal labor arrangements are operative and the factors undermining their viability.

Land, labor, and harvesting, and social relations in Kali Loro

The village of Kali Loro is situated in south-central Java, thirty-five kilometres from the city of Yogyakarta. It lies on a narrow plain bounded on the west by an infertile, sparsely cultivated, and lightly populated mountain range, and on the east, by a river that separates Kali Loro from fertile, densely populated, and well-irrigated lowlands. The land area of Kali Loro totals a little under twelve square kilometres and is made up of 32% irrigated rice land (*sawah*), 44% garden and residential land (*pekarangan*), and 18% dry fields (*tegalan*), most of which are eroded and uncultivatable and the remainder are used for secondary crops; this distribution is typical of central Java.

In Kali Loro *sawah* provides a major subsistence resource, and work related to rice agriculture is an important, though secondary, source of employment. However, the distribution of landholdings indicates great variation in levels of participation in rice production and a correspondingly wide range of income differences. Of 478 households surveyed, 6% own more than half of all the *sawah*, 37% are landless, and another 40% work farms too small to produce their basic rice requirements. In other words, at least 75% of the households have to meet their subsistence needs either primarily or completely through sources other than ownership and cultivation of rice land. Among these alternate income-producing activities are agricultural wage labor, various forms of market trade, handicraft production, and mixed garden cultivation for sale and consumption.

As an income-producing activity external to the household, harvesting wages have been underestimated by those studying Javanese society and by Javanese themselves. In part this is because harvesting is a seasonal and female activity. Prior to the completion of a new irrigation channel in 1968, harvesting occurred on a large scale only once during the year. As Boserup (1970: 29) notes, female participation in agriculture is often underestimated since women working only at the peak season are classified as housewives. That Javanese underrate the significance of harvesting is more surprising. This is in part due to its seasonality, but perhaps more importantly, harvesting rights are considered within the context of *gotong-royong* relations, that is, are often obligatory, and fall outside the more impersonal category of farm wage labor (*buruh tani*).

Access to harvesting opportunities is mediated by a number of different kinds of socio-economic relationships that can broadly be classified into three types. Harvesting rights may be considered (1) within the larger complex of reciprocal labor exchange (between households of similar socio-economic status), (2) within the context of a patron-client relationship (an asymmetrical exchange of goods and services), or (3) as a formal and impersonal employer-employee relationship. "Symmetrical" refers to labor exchanges between households of similar socio-economic status with wages paid in kind.

Although "exchange" usually refers to nonwage labor, the term is appropriate here since work opportunities as much as labor are reciprocated and exchanged. "Asymmetrical" labor occurs between wealthier landholdings households and between landless or small landholders. Although all three types are in fact wage labor arrangements, the final one refers specifically to labor performed for households with which the laborer has no long-term social or economic ties. In the first two cases participation and rights to harvesting are part of a larger set of obligations. For the latter of these two, the employer-employee component of that relationship is ideologically obscured. This point will be discussed in more detail below; however, I should note that the somewhat ambiguous and changing relations between harvesters and large landowners (that is, the transition from client-patron to employee-employer) may account for the fact that many women still do not consider their participation in harvesting as wage labor. These categories indicate the varied shares harvesters receive and the different obligations that accompany harvest opportunities.

Rice harvesting methods

Rice is harvested with a small, short-bladed implement (*ani-ani*) that cuts each panicle individually. Such a technology allows "the fullest percentage of the yield to be reaped and leaves the greatest amount of the harvested crop on the field to refertilize" (Geertz, 1963: 35). It also means that harvesting is the most labor intensive of all agricultural activities and demands large supplies of labor at concentrated periods in the agricultural cycle. Thus, even farmers with small holdings are dependent upon outside labor to meet part of their cultivation requirements. Ploughing, harrowing, hoeing, and weeding (all male tasks) require only a limited number of man-days, which can be spread over a relatively long period of time, and these labor needs can usually be met within the household.

Planting and harvesting on the other hand (all female tasks) must be performed quickly and at precise times. In Kali Loro there are two harvests, a main harvest in the wet season (*rendengan*) and a small harvest in the dry season (*gadu*). The new irrigation channel has provided only an extremely unreliable water supply, which makes the second rice crop a risky undertaking and does not allow the staggering of crop cycles and consequent spreading of labor requirements that is found in some of the better irrigated parts of Java. Therefore, whereas the preparation of a small field requires twenty man-days over a period of one month (that is, only one man), planting requires the same amount of woman-days in one morning, and harvesting uses twice as many woman-days for a morning and afternoon. Still, small farmers (who make up 40% of the village) can meet their peak labor demands largely from household members within their *gotong-royong* network.

The large number of women mobilized for harvesting, even on relatively small farms, is not simply a function of the requirements of wet rice production. By allowing members of a neighboring household to participate and by paying them in kind with a relatively large share, a farmer is insured that female members of his or her household will be given reciprocal employment opportunities. Such arrangements are as much a means of spreading the risks of cultivation as they are a means of meeting labor requirements. Larger landowners who own between five and ten different pieces of well-irrigated *sawah* throughout the village have no need to partake in this symmetrical system of reciprocity.

Labor recruitment for planting

Like harvesting, the mode of procurement for planting labor is dependent on the size of the landholding. The smallest landholders (less than 0.1 hectares) usually plant their fields with household labor, while those with slightly larger *sawah* (0.1 to 0.2 hectares) invite close kin and neighbors. During the April planting, when everyone was planting simultaneously, several landholders paid their neighbors in advance to insure that they would be available when needed. However, during the September planting the water supply had been cut short on some fields, and those farmers with irrigated *sawah* complained of an inundation of uninvited laborers.

Although wages in cash rather than kind have been paid for planting for as long as the old people can remember, often the planters request not to be given a cash wage (of Rp.25 = US 6 cents) but opt instead for the right to take part in the harvest for a larger payment in kind. Among smaller landholders this practice is more wide-spread since it benefits both the small farmer who has very little cash to lay out for wages and the planter who gets a much larger money equivalent by waiting for a harvest share (*bawon*). Large landowners, who may employ as many as one hundred women for a morning's work, prefer not to give bigger *bawon* and often force cash wages upon the planters.

Labor recruitment for harvesting

For small as well as large landholders, the bulk of the harvest does not begin until one or two days after the rice is ready. . . . . On the particular harvest day, potential harvesters wait early in the morning beside the field. For small *sawah* the harvest is usually overseen by one of the older women in the household, and even invited harvesters will not begin work until she has arrived. On small fields and in situations where everyone knows one another, the harvest proceeds in a relatively unhurried fashion. Members of the host household usually set the pace as harvesters move in a straight line across the field. Harvesters space themselves evenly; thus plants are less easily neglected or trampled. Young girls are chided for leaving the shorter and hidden plants unreaped. Sometimes women from the same household will back up a young, less experienced harvester by searching out the uncut paddy. Harvesters working for neighbors in general tend to work thoroughly, with the incentive that their own fields will be harvested with the same care.

On larger *sawah*, the harvesting proceeds with more rush and organization. As many as fifty to 150 women are used to reap the *padi* on fields of half a hectare and above. A large proportion are *orang lain* (literally "other people") from within and outside the village who seek out these larger fields where their harvesting chances are greater. Even in these *sawah* some potential harvesters may be excluded. Those excluded may ask permission to glean (*ngasak*) what is left after the harvesters have combed the field. Gleaners have always been present at harvest time; formerly however, they were small children and old women from the poorest families, who were neither agile nor skilled enough to keep up with the quick pace of the harvesting group. With more crowding of the land and more landless families, gleaners now comprise a more diverse group of women.

Several factors have affected the gleaning system. Formerly, when water was unavailable for the dry season, harvested rice stalks were left to decompose in the fields. Thus, gleaners could come at their leisure without asking permission and seek out the few panicles missed by the harvesters the day or two before. Now that a second rice crop is planted, harvesters are followed directly by men who slash, burn, or plough the remaining stalks back into the earth for quicker decomposition. Others carry the stalks home for fodder and garden mulch. Thus the gleaners must be there on the day of the harvest, between the harvesters and clearers.

Unlike harvesters, gleaners come to the fields and leave at their own discretion. With harvesters and gleaners working very close together, it may be difficult for the landowner to distinguish between them. In crowded fields, harvesters may trample deliberately on the uncut rice stalks and leave some low-lying panicles for a daughter or sister gleaning close behind. Although the number of gleaners in Kali Loro is probably less than in other areas of Java, the problems reported are essentially the same. Women overseeing the harvest of fairly large fields use their own relatives to watch over the gleaners. The overseer occasionally calls out, "*sing ngasak, mundur*" "gleaners, move back!", or in the more subtle Javanese fashion, "*ngasak opo derep bu?*" "mother, are you harvesting or gleaning?" – causing a quick retreat of the precocious gleaner.

Bawon: the harvester's share

Bawon payments for harvesting labor have existed in Java for centuries.

> The reapers are uniformly paid, by receiving a portion of the crop which they have reaped; this varies in different parts of the island, from the sixth to the eighth part, depending on the abundance or scarcity of hands; when the harvest is general through a district, one-fifth or one-fourth is demanded by the reaper. In opposition to so exorbitant a claim, the influence of the great is sometimes exerted, and the laborer is obliged to be content with a tenth or a twelfth (Raffles, 1817).

Harvest labor is rarely so scarce now that harvesters can demand a one-fourth or one-fifth share, but it is interesting that even 150 years ago, at particular times when there was an abundance of harvest labor, the shares were virtually the same as they are now. However, the notion that there is one set wage that prevails throughout a region or that applies to all harvesters on all types of land imposes homogeneity on a complex distribution system. Two factors determine the size of the *bawon*: the amount of land the harvester herself controls and her social proximity to the host household.

Bawon normally are decided by the landowner. In the case of sharecropped land, the owner and sharecropper frequently divide the ripe field and harvest their halves individually; thus the *bawon* is decided by each respectively. Close relatives receive from one-fourth to one-half of what they harvest, although a poor relation may be given the entire amount. Close kin tend to demand higher shares and for this reason, some sharecroppers prefer to let the landowner divide the *bawon* at his or her home. Thus, the sharecropper is neither forced to refuse, nor more often, to grant these higher payments. Shares of one-sixth to one-eighth are given to women from neighboring households (*tetangga*), defined not only by their physical proximity to the host household, but by their mutual participation in *gotong-royong* activities. Shares of one-tenth to one-twelfth are given to *orang lain*, that is, distant villagers and non-villagers who fall outside the first two categories. In other villages the *bawon* for this group may be as little as one-twenty-fifth.

The small landowner (who meets labor demands principally by recruiting kin and close neighbors) is forced to give higher *bawon* than the larger landowner (whose labor demands being greater, thus employs a greater proportion of women outside the first two categories). Moreover, neighbors can exert strong pressure on a small landowner to maintain a high *bawon* since both host and harvester exchange labor with one another. On the other hand, larger landowners, in part independent of these reciprocal relations, have a stronger bargaining position vis-à-vis the harvesters. Of the half-dozen largest landholders in six hamlets (478 households), some consistently gave one-eighth while others gave one-tenth and one-twelfth. However, as the election for *lurah* (village head) approached in 1973, candidates from these households gave much larger *bawon* than usual, presumably as a means of gaining political support. After the election, *bawon* payments returned to the usual shares. . . .

Analysis of quantitative data shows that the larger landholders receive the greatest amount of paddy as *bawon* per day of harvesting, that is, they receive the largest returns to their labor. The landless households, on the other hand, use more household members as harvesters than either of the other groups and receive lower returns to their labor.

Why do women in poorer households receive lower wages for the same work? For women in poor households rice harvesting is by far the most productive source of income. Mat weaving, for example, has much lower returns to labor and as a complementary activity does not compete with time allotted to harvesting. Similarly, small-scale trade tends to have lower returns to labor. Women in poorer households trade with very small capital investments, and receive minuscule profits. During the harvest season most stop trading temporarily and continue after the harvest season. More often, though, women in landless and small landholding households combine each of these activities to maximize the opportunities available.

Women from larger landholding households, on the other hand, have a different set of options. Basic rice requirements can be met within the household, and as traders with much larger capital investments, they can insure profits far beyond what they could earn from harvesting. Furthermore, more of their time is taken up with harvest management. They oversee the harvest operation, control the number of harvesters invited or admitted, and decide on the share each harvester receives. Thus they preside over the field operations as well as the threshing, bundling, and distribution of shares that takes place at the home of the landholder.

A second factor determining lower returns to labor for women from landless households is the capacity in which they harvest. Women from larger landholding households harvest only when invited, or not at all. Thus when they do harvest, they receive much higher shares. Small landowners also tend to harvest within a limited social network, for kin and close neighbors from whom they receive higher shares. Landless women, on the other hand, lack the economic flexibility to choose where they harvest. To meet consumption needs they harvest not only for close neighbors, where they are assured a larger share, but are forced to seek harvest opportunities further afield. Thus they receive less rice per harvesting time, in part because their economic situation forces them to harvest more often. *Within* the village, landless households do not have the same access to harvesting opportunities as their somewhat better-off neighbors. Whereas small farmers exchange not only labor but more importantly *opportunities for obtaining rice*, landless households have nothing to offer but their labor. The landless household therefore has to "earn" its "right" to harvest by obligating itself to a patron household for which it will perform numerous other tasks and be paid with somewhat higher shares. . . .

The relative importance of harvesting incomes is very different for poorer and wealthier households. For landless households per capita harvesting incomes provide 20% of the per capita rice requirement per year; for the small-holding category harvesting incomes provide 18%, and for the large-holding group 15% of per capita requirement. The differences in percentages among groups do not seem especially great unless we remember how much less women in large landholding households actually harvest and how much greater are their returns to labor. . . .

"Shared poverty" and hard times

My evidence indicates that the harvesting practices of Kali Loro hardly represent an equitable system of "shared poverty" or for that matter "work spreading". In fact developments during the research period suggest a weakened bargaining position for the poorer members of village society. A comparison of harvesting incomes for each of the land groups for the April and September harvests reveals some interesting contrasts between these groups. For each of the land groups, harvesting incomes for the September harvest were much lower than in April.

Landless households received only 61% of their April harvesting incomes, the small landholders received 70%, and the larger landholders received as much as 80% of what they had earned in April. The "patrons" neither increased the size of the shares to the poor nor was work "shared" by allowing more harvesters on the field. Instead harvesting rights were more limited than in the previous harvest, patrons reserved harvesting rights for a small group of clients, and while clients retained harvesting rights on their patron's land, they were often denied harvesting rights further afield. Thus those poorer women who harvested more frequently outside their kin and *gotong-royong* networks were most severely affected by limited harvest opportunities.

Changes in harvesting practices in other parts of Java

In some of the more "progressive" areas of Java, a breakdown in the patronage system is further advanced. In order to cut harvesting costs and to escape "traditonal obligations," farmers sell their rice crop to middlemen (*penebas*) a few days before the harvest. The *penebas* (who is usually from outside the village) either drastically reduces the number of harvesters (in some cases by issuing invitations that the harvester wears in her hat), or he may bring his own small group of harvesters from outside the village and pay them a lower wage (local police are often employed to insure that the "uninvited" do not enter). Thus the number of harvesters and the total wage paid out are reduced, and harvesting costs are lowered by as much as 42%.

Even more drastic reductions in harvesting opportunities have occurred in many of these villages where the *penebas* employs a small group of *male* harvesters who use a sickle rather than the *ani-ani* and are paid in cash instead of a *bawon*. Quite apart from the reduction in harvesting costs (that is, the total amount made available to harvesters in income), the number of harvesters receiving that reduced income is of course reduced.

The fact that landowners cannot institute these measures on their own but must employ middlemen to do so gives some indication of the pressure that villagers can bring to bear on landowners. However, subsequent research indicates that in the same village after a few seasons of the *tebasan* system, the landowners feel sufficiently free of their obligations to employ the new harvesting methods themselves and no longer resort to the use of middlemen.

Conclusion

. . . Recent changes in sharecropping and harvesting practices reported throughout Java can be understood, in part, as a product of the historical development of a more exploitative patronage system and the emergence of more refined intrapeasant class distinctions, accelerated in recent years by the rapid influx of capital in both the urban and agrarian economy of Indonesia.

To what extent do these processes characterize the development of labor relations in Kali Loro? Some local historical and present conditions that have mitigated against the more drastic changes in agricultural production found elsewhere and that suggest that these changes are not far off are discussed below. Kali Loro was never as directly involved in commercialized agriculture as some of the more densely populated sugar-producing lowlands of Java, and thus pressure on subsistence land was somewhat lower. Also, although population density is about average for Java as a whole, it is much below the density of the more fertile lowlands. Furthermore, until recently rice cultivation was confined to the wet season, and production was not sufficient to involve Kali Loro in rice export. Those "surpluses" that were produced by wealthier households were primarily used to buy more land and to fulfill a host of ritual and economic obligations within the village. Located in a relatively inaccessible, hilly area without an extensive irrigation system, commercialized agriculture could neither be economically nor ecologically "superimposed" on Kali Loro. Thus reciprocal labor exchange and a relatively equitable patronage system remained intact.

Although *bawon* payments have fluctuated over the past seventy years, there does not seem to have been any appreciable long-term change in harvest shares. Before the channel was completed, women traveled further from the village to find harvesting opportunities for smaller *bawon*. During the early 1960s, up until the period following the violent change of government, harvesting shares tended to go down (where they are now one-eighth, they were one-tenth); in response to an unstable money economy, payment was preferred in kind. Although I have suggested a relative stability over time in the proportion of the yield given to sharecroppers and harvesters, this does not mean that the equity of the patron-client relationship has remained unchanged. On the contrary, I would argue that the very stability of harvesting shares in the face of a shrinking resource base and declining incomes may indicate diminishing power for the client in that relationship. . . .

Recent changes in agriculture brought about by the "Green Revolution" (and the completion of the irrigation channel) have given a distinct advantage to the already secure members of village society. Although these farmers have neither employed middlemen for harvesting nor eliminated the *ani-ani*, the fact that they can impose relatively smaller harvest shares indicates that such practices are not far off. It is these relationships between large landowners, and the landless and small landholding households, rather than cooperative patterns of labor exchange, that are dominant and in part determinant in the process of increasing economic polarization in rural Java.

This change in dominance not only provides an economic and social context in which technological change has occurred but has also allowed these techniques to be implemented. By focusing on the mode of production, rather than the agricultural system per se, and hence on labor relations *and* technology, we have seen that significant alteration of the agrarian system does not imply major changes in technology. The technological and social changes I have described do not represent a major transformation in the means of environmental exploitation but do represent a major transformation in the exploitation of labor.

Strategies for Control of Labor in Sharecropping and Tenancy Arrangements

Anan Ganjanapan

The following account is based on a historical study by the author (Anan, 1984) of the development of commercialized agriculture in Northern Thailand from 1900–81 and an intensive anthropological study of Ban (village) San Pong (population 674 in 1980), Ban Kat sub-district, San Pa Tong district, Chiang Mai province, which is situated some 30 km southwest of Chiang Mai city. . . .

An Emergent Class of Capitalist Farmers

In 1980 the ownership of irrigated riceland in the village was considerably skewed towards wealthy villagers, especially an emerging class of capitalist farmers, namely those able to invest heavily in both farm and off-farm enterprises. The seven households of what I here term capitalist farmers hold an average 3.8 hectares compared with an average 2 hectares for "rich peasants". Although representing only 4.4% of agricultural households, they possess 19.5% of irrigated riceland; rich peasants, constituting 20.6% of households, possess 47.9%.

These capitalist farmers are among a selected number of wealthy villagers who, mainly because of their control of a large area of irrigated riceland – but also because of their broadly political local connections and powers – benefited most from the intensive commercial production of the early 1970s and from government policy. After 1975 the state, in addition to outright suppression of peasant radicalism, began to adopt World Bank prescriptions for a rural policy ostensibly to help the "rural poor" (see Feder, 1976: 349–52; World Bank, 1980). However instead of embarking on the implementation of land reform, which might have alleviated problems of tenancy and landlessness, the Thai government concentrated on the transfer of more capital and technology into rural areas. The policy aimed at keeping peasants on their farms as sources of cheap labor for the production of low-cost food and other agricultural commodities, serving further to reinforce existing rural contradictions and increasing the integration of peasants, including those with no surplus to sell, into the labor market.

Three principal policy instruments, all dating from 1975, were Local Development Schemes (*ngoen phan*), subsidized agricultural credit programs, and rice price support schemes. Local development funds were intended primarily to provide wages for off-season employment on local projects. In 1975 and 1976 the Ban San Pong headman and his kinsfolk kept all the wages and compelled villagers to contribute free labor. In 1977 and 1978 wages were paid only to kinsfolk and clients, and in 1979 a rival elite faction removed him from office.

Agricultural credit from government-sponsored cooperatives had been available to a few wealthy villagers in the 1960s and had been used to purchase land from Chiang Mai aristocrats (see Anan, 1984). From 1975 the Bank for Agriculture and Agricultural Co-operatives (BAAC) began to provide subsidized credit at 12% for three-year loans. This was not available to full-tenants or small-owners without collateral. Some small farmer debtors who were unable to repay because of crop failure lost their land; others borrowed at 60% interest per annum from local money lenders, who sometimes loaned at 60% what they had obtained at 12%.

Various rice price support schemes have, over the years, benefited only a very few farmers, especially those who have no rent to pay, have storage facilities, and can therefore benefit from delaying sale after harvest; or those producing on a scale enabling them to benefit from bulk selling prior to harvest and from growing non-subsistence, higher priced, non-glutinous rice.

In response to the agrarian conflicts of 1974–6 (see Anan, 1984; Turton, 1982) several large Ban San Pong landowners transferred ownership of their riceland to their offspring by registering the land in the names of the latter. About 24 hectares of riceland was transferred in this way between 1976 and 1981. In most cases parents continued to receive nominal payments from their children (*kha hua*) which, though sometimes a token amount, can be as much as half the main season crop. These transmissions when both parents are alive are directly contrary to past practice, in which all children can inherit land (usually equally) only after the death of both parents. It is possible that large landowners adopted this strategy to avoid landlord-tenant conflicts and complications arising from the land rent control law, and to avoid renting land to non-filial tenants. The offspring of these large landowners were allowed a free hand to cultivate their parents' riceland with the help of hired laborers. This development also indicates an attempt by parents to alleviate dissension among their children, a phenomenon which has increased considerably as a result of the growing profits from intensive commercial production.

Both agrarian conflicts and intensive cultivation are also major factors influencing the nature of land sales in the period 1973–81. After experiencing a period of intense conflict with tenants at that time, some traders in another village, who owned land in Ban San Pong, felt that income from renting their land was not worth the risk. After 1976 they began to sell all their riceland in Ban San Pong to wealthy villagers. Unlike large landowners in Ban San Pong, the traders could not opt for taking over the cultivation themselves, even with the help of hired laborers or shared-cost leasing arrangements (see below) because they were preoccupied with other more remunerative enterprises. By taking advantage of the high price of riceland, most traders reckoned that they could earn more from interest on bank deposits than from rent.

Land prices have been driven up because of the higher returns from triple cropping and increasing demand by wealthier farmers. Indebted small landowners have benefited in the short run. They can at least hold on a little longer, selling small portions of land to meet debts. However, the landless and other poor villagers are now entirely excluded from the land market. Small landowners have redoubled their efforts to hang on to their holdings; but the reduced incidence of land transfers within domestic groups suggests that kin ties are playing a diminishing role in resisting the process of land concentration. Overall the concentration of riceland into the hands of the wealthy villagers continued its previous increase, if slowly, during the period 1973–81. The process has been assisted by the availability of credit from the BAAC and commercial banks which were set up in the district from 1972.

Unlike the government's financial institutions, the commercial banks encouraged villagers to purchase large tractors and trucks, rather than buy additional land. In this way the banks can benefit not only from the interest on the loans, but also from the profit from sales of tractors, trucks and other commercial transactions in which they have a direct financial interest. The loan policy of commercial banks also began a process of advancing their control over riceland, which is very likely to contribute to the real transfer of riceland ownership from the villagers to the bank, and to have significant repercussions on the agrarian structure and agrarian production in the future.

The capitalist farmers are investing heavily and diversifying into off-farm and on-farm enterprises: trading, machinery hire, haulage, pig raising, and moneylending. Although they are in a better position than others to operate their own riceland using wage labor, they also continue to rent out the largest area of riceland, averaging 2.24 hectares per household, compared with 0.6 hectares for rich peasant households; and a much higher proportion – 52% as compared with 15.4% – to "non-filial" tenants (see below). Capitalist farmers continue to rent out land not only because they are engaged in other enterprises, but also because of an uncertain labor supply as a result of the struggles of farm laborers. These strategies of resistance by labor and response by landlords in devising new and transformed means of control of labor are discussed below. Recently increasing numbers of poor and middle peasants have been forced to rent out their land too, mostly however because of indebtedness as a result of failure in intensive commercial production, or through inability to produce second and third crops for which high capital inputs are required. It is in off-season cultivation that the rental market is most developed. To explain this, some preliminary discussion of the intensive use of irrigated riceland and complex cropping pattern is required.

Triple Cropping

In 1978 Ban San Pong villagers were triple cropping on their irrigated riceland, a practice a few households had begun experimentally ten years earlier. By the 1980–1 season there was triple cropping on nearly 40% (55.04 hectares) of all irrigated land (138.96 hectares) cultivated for main-season rice; a further 5.52 hectares being rented to tenants from other villages. Almost all of the remaining irrigated riceland is double cropped. The main-season rice crop is about 92% glutinous rice, a subsistence crop for the majority of producers. The second crop on most land is soybeans, planted on about 87% (122.36 hectares) of irrigated riceland; of the remainder, about half is planted to a second rice crop, and about half to garlic, onions, and chilli, or left fallow.

The third crop is entirely planted to non-glutinous rice for the market: 90% to the Thai Rice Department's KK7 variety, 10% to KK1. These non-photoperiod sensitive, high-yielding varieties, which can be planted in any season, were first introduced into the area in the early 1970s. They were not adopted on any scale until the late 1970s when more capital was flowing into rural areas and more cultivators could afford the necessary chemical fertilizers, herbicides and pesticides. These contributed to a rapid increase in yield from 3125 kg/per hectare in the early 1970s to 5500 kg/per hectare for main-season rice in 1981.

Improved water supply also facilitates triple cropping. In 1981 thirteen new tubewells, capable of supplying 0.4–1.6 hectares each were added to the existing eight wells. The local irrigation system was also improved with local development funds between 1975–8. Most important has been the introduction of power tillers which increased in number from 12 in 1978 to 26 in 1980. These machines, manufactured in Thailand with imported Japanese engines, cost about 16,000 *baht* or the price of two full-grown buffaloes. They allow cultivators to prepare land in at least two weeks less time than the use of draft animals requires, that can be used after the first rainfall when the ground is still too hard for plowing with buffalo. This is crucial for the triple cropping system because of its extremely tight schedule, with some crop seasons overlapping.

This triple cropping system has led to a complex development of tenurial arrangements which will be discussed in the following section. The development provides opportunities for landless villagers to rent some riceland for particular seasons, but in the long run may jeopardize the well-being of poor villagers because the third rice crop is so highly capital intensive that most poor tenants cannot afford to undertake it. In this case, as we shall see, landowners provide capital and take more control of the management of cultivation in a form of "shared cost leasing" which will gradually force tenants into the role of wage laborers facing an uncertain, subsistence life. Small indebted landowners may benefit however from being able to rent out land for one or two cropping seasons without endangering their main-season subsistence rice crop.

Changing Forms of Tenancy

Prior to the 1970s the principal form of tenancy which had emerged was the renting of land by independent households of children from their parents, which I here term "filial tenancy". The percentage of riceland rented in this way has declined from 70.3% in 1970 to 57.3 in 1980, and has assumed a more commercial character. This has had a more marked effect on poor tenants (renting an average 0.67 hectares) for whom the proportion of land rented from parents has declined from 80% in 1970 to 45.5% in 1980. The proportion rented by middle peasants (average area 1.09 hectares) has remained at about 50%, while rich peasant households (average area 1.62 hectares) *only* rent from parents (see Anan, 1984). Although for the main rice crop filial tenants pay half the crop in rent they have greater security (and some anticipation of inheritance) and are likely to have more assistance with labor and other inputs than "non-filial" sharecroppers. Children of rich peasants and capitalist farmers may pay only a nominal sum (*kha hua*) to their parents, sometimes at their own discretion.

For the second (soybean) crop filial tenants pay no rent, though some are able to rent only for the second crop – in which case they pay a quarter of the cash rent (500 *baht*) paid by non-filial tenants. Only rich peasants are likely to allow their offspring to cultivate the third (rice) crop for no rent (except perhaps for a discretionary *kha hua*). Interestingly, access to land for the cultivation of second and third crops may be extended to offspring still living within the parental household. Thus a household which operates as a single unit in the main rice season separates financially in the cultivation of cash crops. In this way intensive commercial production of cash crops allows children to prepare for separation from the parental household earlier than in the past, and may lead to increasingly commercial relationships between parents and offspring. It also poses problems for approaching households as units of production except in main-season cultivation.

The percentage of riceland rented from other than parents (whether kin related or not) by poor peasants has more than doubled: from 21.5% in 1970 to 54.2% in 1980–1; the proportion rented by middle peasants remained about the same. The most common form of rent (on 74.5% of rented land) was half the crop yield with tenant bearing all input costs. Some landowners who were also capitalist farmers demanded even higher rents: in two cases (5.6% of rented land) two-thirds of the crop; and in two other cases (11.3% of rented land) they demanded an additional advance cash deposit or premium (*wang ngoen*) of about 6250 baht per hectare – on which interest is paid at 60% per annum – returnable on termination of tenancy.

A form of fixed cash rental (*lang na*) has become a viable option for landowners not resident in the villages where their tenants live – and so not having to supervise cultivation – and/or who need large sums of cash quickly. Most land rented in this way is available for triple cropping, though there were several cases of renting *lang na* for a single crop season, especially renting out by small landowners. Rents are lower the longer the term of the tenancy.

I have elsewhere attempted to construct an annual production account for an average farming unit of one *rai* that can support triple cropping, in order to compare the costs and benefits in production as between different cultivating units under various forms of tenure. Here I present only a summary of net incomes. Landowners made approximately the same amount from rent from non-filial tenants as if they had cultivated themselves, except when contracting a cash in advance fixed term tenancy (*lang na*). Filial tenants paying only half of the main-season crop as rent for the whole year have a substantial return. Non-filial tenants renting for a period of years on a *lang na* basis show a very modest return. But non-filial tenants paying half shares for all crops barely break even; and those paying two-thirds for the first crop and half for the other two, and those additionally paying a cash deposit or premium (*wang ngoen*) operate at a considerable loss when their labor is valued in market terms.

Non-filial tenants are able to cultivate because they substitute their own labor for most marketable inputs. These tenants rarely hire labor, and those without draft animals had to contribute household labor to labor exchange networks in order to gain access to power tillers. For off-season rice they cannot avoid hiring power-threshers, because the paddy is reaped when still mostly green and cannot be threshed by hand. For other items like seed, tenants try to produce for themselves rather than buy it on the market, which is more difficult in the case of soybean seed for those who have no upland farms. These non-filial tenants even use their own labor for weeding instead of purchasing the herbicides used in soybean and off-season rice cultivation.

If tenants were to turn to work exclusively as wage laborers, they would face great uncertainty in their subsistence, even though they would sometimes be able to buy rice at lower costs than they would have to spend producing it on their rented plots. Rice prices vary considerably, however, even within the same year. Accordingly, sharecropping provides tenants with some security in the face of seasonally-fluctuating labor and product markets.

From the landlord's point of view, this variety of forms of tenancy and sharecropping represents attempts to capture the largest surplus possible directly from the tenants. With some monopoly control of land, most landlords can present themselves as patrons to their tenants, assuring the latters' subsistence. The landlords in turn are able to use such patronage relationships as a means of securing their tenants' labor supply in an increasingly uncertain labor situation (see below) which makes cultivation on the basis of wage labor highly risky. At the same time, they are ensured a well-disciplined workforce that does not require direct supervision. This is an important advantage, given large landowners' extensive involvement in other activities.

Another reason why sharecropping persists is that a fully developed cash rental market for land does not yet exist. Such a market began to emerge with the development of tenurial arrangements on the basis of fixed cash rents (*lang na*), which through market mechanisms make agricultural production profitable. But this practice requires access to capital and credit, and as long as these markets remain underdeveloped this form of tenancy cannot easily lead to a fully developed rental market. Such tenurial arrangements have been mainly tried by small landowners whose inferior position and need for cash makes them unable to bargain for high rents. Thus a fixed cash rent is not yet a viable alternative either for the large landowners who cannot demand high cash rents or for poor villagers who have limited access to credit.

Although sharecropping arrangements are in many ways functional to both landlords and tenants, they also give rise to tension and antagonism. Generally landlords are careful not to demand more than half of the harvest from main-season paddy as rent, because this rice is so essential for sustaining the life of their tenants. Instead landlords may try to increase rent on other cash crops.

Under these conditions, many tenants in 1980–1 thought that the rice they produced from their rented land was more expensive than rice currently available in the market. Although no tenants yet wanted to leave the land they rented, they voiced their frustration, expressing the opinion that they might be better off working as wage laborers, buying their rice from the market. This effort to squeeze tenants underlies the growing antagonism between landlords and tenants in recent years.

Despite this antagonism, tenants still require secure employment and landlords still need to ensure their labor force. But as agricultural production has come to require more and more new capital in order to increase productivity, landowners have begun to score heavily in their struggle to control labor. Without capital tenants cannot by themselves cultivate intensively. Some landowners who need the labor of these poor peasants turn to what I term here "shared cost leasing" arrangements *yia na pha nai thun*, literally "work the fields sharing with the owner of capital" providing tenants with new inputs that enable them to work the land more efficiently.

The Modification of Sharecropping Arrangements

This arrangement began to develop at Ban San Pong following a wave of evictions during 1976 and 1978. In 1978 a few landowners tried to furnish some of the costs of production as a means of claiming a greater share of the crop from the new incoming tenants. In one case a new tenant received only 36% out of the yield from the main-season crop after paying all input costs. For the second season, however, the landowner supplied fertilizer and soybean seed, but allowed the tenant to cultivate only one-third of the plot without rent while the landowner worked the remainder himself. In another case a new tenant received 30% of 10,000 kg harvest on 2.1 hectares but was entitled to half of any yield above 10,000 kg. This tenant was responsible for all production costs except for chemical fertilizer. In the dry season the landowner supplied onion seed and claimed no rent for that crop.

Thus landowners not only claim more than half the main-season rice crop, but also increase their control over decision-making: the kind of crop to be planted, the extent of land to be cultivated, especially in the dry season when landowners can choose to work for themselves. By imposing all labor costs on tenants, landowners can be relieved of the uncertainty and burden of labor management. This in turn allows them to diversify and assume more entrepreneurial roles (in trading, transport, contract pig farming, machinery hire, etc.). Tenants are increasingly forced into the role of permanent farm workers, and this is clearly how it is perceived by landowners, who insist that they did not rent their land but "hired" (*chang*) their "tenants".

Tenants under these arrangements tended to be paid in fixed amounts of the main-season rice crop, rather than in a percentage of the yield. This allowed the landowners to gain all the benefits from the potential yield increases as a result of the application of new inputs, which they contributed. For tenants this meant a lower return on their labor, as they got less from these fixed amounts than sharecroppers usually get from half shares: in some cases close to a quarter of the yield. Tenants complained that they had to cultivate at a loss. They had to spend roughly the same amount of cash on wage labor or on mid-day meals served to exchange labor, as the price of the paddy they received as their share. This meant that they got close to nothing for their own labor. Most cannot continue to work for more than one season.

In response, large landowners (both rich peasants and capitalist farmers) tried to modify their relationship with contracted workers (now a more appropriate term than "tenant") within the general form I have termed "shared cost leasing". They tended to provide all the capital need for cultivation, which turned them into *nai thun* (capital-owners) in the eyes of the workers. In 1980–1 three landowners supplied all capital inputs for seed, chemical fertilizers, gasoline and power tillers. The contracted cultivators undertake to provide their labor and to engage in exchange networks in place of the owners – becoming more like permanent laborers on the plots – and received only a small fixed proportion of the yield. One of them got only 200 *thang* out of more than 800 *thang* yield from a 10 *rai* plot; he was however allowed to cultivate off-season rice with capital provided by the landowner, including a water pumpset, enabling him to cultivate land that would otherwise have been left fallow. In such cases landowners benefit considerably by deducting all costs of production before dividing the yield equally with the worker. The worker in this case felt morally indebted to the landowner for allowing him to grow the off-season rice which is highly capital intensive and risky.

Thus "shared cost leasing" arrangements amounts to a combination of tenancy and wage employment. Although such arrangements are still minority of cases, their development indicates that more landless villagers are being forced into the ranks of wage earners (*khon hap chang*) who are no longer able to maintain themselves as tenants. . . .

Agrarian Differentiation in the Southern Region of Vietnam

Ngo Vinh Long

The aim of this article is to show that even in an area where land reforms have been carried out, agrarian differentiation can reoccur in a relatively short time given the presence of certain favorable conditions; that a comprehensive effort at rural transformation requires not only the redistribution of land but also of all resources including labor and population; and that if this cannot be carried out because of temporary political considerations, production needs and structural obstacles, then economic measures such as small but strategic and critical investments by the state and appropriate pricing policies could help develop mechanisms for agrarian transformation and development.

Results of a Decade of Land Reforms

Vietnam is traditionally divided into three administrative sections, known as the Northern, Central and Southern Region respectively. The former state of South Vietnam was composed of about half of the Central Region and the Southern Region. Less than 35% of the population of South Vietnam lived in the central area, which was divided into the Central Lowlands with about 30% and the Central Highlands with only about 5% of the population.

The Southern Region, which begins at the southern edge of the high mountains and plateaux, was inhabited by two-thirds of the population of South Vietnam. Some 25 to 30% of the population was in the eastern part of this region, which stretched south to the northern border of Long An province and included Saigon. The rest of the population lived in the western part of the Southern Region, commonly referred to as the Mekong Delta or the Delta. This section was the most populous and it produced 80% of the rice and half of the secondary crops of South Vietnam. For this reason, in this article we will focus primarily on the western part of the Southern Region.

According to statistics provided by the National Liberation Front of South Vietnam, as a result of its land reform program, from 1960 to 1965 it redistributed 1,650,000 hectares of land to the peasants. This amounted to 50% of the total cultivated surface or 72% of all paddyfields. As a result, according to investigations carried out in a number of provinces in the Southern Region and in the Central Lowlands, land distribution by the end of 1965 was as follows:

Social Class	Per cent of Population	Per cent of Land
Middle Peasants	54.3	76.8
Poor Peasants	37.3	14.6
Landless Peasants	2.1	0.1
Rich Peasants	0.55	2.6
Landlords	0.45	4.8
Others	5.3	1.1

In the Mekong Delta, by 1965 peasants became owners of 64 to 70% of the land in areas of average peasant ownership and of 75 to 82% of the land in areas of high peasant ownership.

After the General Offensives of 1968 which the NLF claimed shook the Saigon regime to its foundation in the countryside and drove most of the landlords to the towns and cities, land was again distributed to the peasants. By the end of that year, a total of more than two million hectares, or 80% of the crop land, had been distributed. . . .

A very different picture of land distribution in the Saigon-controlled areas was presented by the American Hamlet Resident Survey of 1967. According to this survey, 50.7% of the peasants in the Mekong Delta were landless. Among them 33.9% were tenant farmers and 16.8% were farm workers. In more tightly controlled areas, such as those near district and provincial towns and along highways, these percentages were higher. . . .

Finally, according to statistics provided by the Saigon regime, by the end of 1969 there were 690,000 registered contracts by tenants working on 1.4 million hectares of various types of land belonging to landlords. Close to 582,000 of these tenants worked on 1.36 million hectares of paddyfields, or about 64% of the total cultivated surface, in the Southern region. In the Central provinces some 109,000 tenants rented only about 36,000 hectares of land.

After three years of studies by a group of specialists from the Stanford Research Institute, much pressure from the United States and $1.2 billion of American money as partial payment for the purchase of land from Vietnamese landlords, on 26 March 1970 the Saigon regime finally passed the so-called "Land to the Tiller" program. According to Saigon statistics, from 1970 to 1972 it distributed over 900,000 hectares of land to about 780,000 peasants. The total number of peasant households engaged in cultivation was officially given as one million. And according to a USAID report, by the beginning of 1975 the Saigon regime had distributed 1.25 million hectares, or 60% of the total cultivated surface in the lowland areas, to the peasants and thereby had reduced the percentage of tenant farmers from 60% in 1967 down to 5%.

In spite of all the claims cited above and in spite of five more years of agrarian reform and socialist transformation, in October 1981 Le Thanh Nghi, member of the Politburo and Secretary of the Central Committee of the Vietnam Commmunist Party, made the following statement on the situation in the Southern region:

"A segment of poor peasants has very little land or no land at all and has to continue to hire out their labor. The peasants of the Southern region, the largest group of whom being middle peasants, hold an important part of food crops and commercial crops. They have economic relations with the government on the one hand, but on the other hand they are still under the control and exploitation of rural and urban capitalists. The capitalist class in the rural and urban areas is continuing to exploit the peasants in many forms and by many means (direct exploitation of labor and exploitation through commercial use of tractors, millers and food-processing machines, through purchase and sale, through usury, etc.) and at the same time taking advantage of its ties with the peasants to compete with the government in buying agricultural produce, to speculate, to hoard and to cause instability to the market."

Origins and Nature of Differentiation

In order to understand the nature of this development it is necessary for us to go back at least to the late 1960s. By the mid-1960s land itself had ceased to be an important source of differentiation. In the NLF-controlled areas land rents had been reduced to only 5% of the crops. Although the American policy of "emptying the countryside" had, by 1967, forced about one-third of the rural population to become refugees at least once and had caused half-a-million hectares of land to be left fallow and thereby produced many landless peasants who had to become tenant farmers and agricultural laborers, an American study claims that for the whole of the Mekong Delta the average land rents in the 1960s had been reduced to 5–10% of the crop as compared to 25–40% during the 1950s and 40–60% before 1945.

By the late 1960s forces such as the commercialization of the rural economy and the use of capital inputs in agriculture (tractors, motor-tillers, oil engines, irrigation pump sets, outboard motors, fertilizers) became deciding factors in rural differentiation. While there is a close relationship between these two forces the commercialization of agriculture came about largely as a result of a drastic movement of the rural population into urban areas and a shift within the rural population from agricultural to non-agricultural activities. The growth in the use of capital inputs in agriculture, meanwhile, was produced by a massive import of farm equipment, fertilizers and oil which was made possible by US aid money, by an enormous infusion of liquid capital into the hands of the landlords through the so-called "Land to the Tiller" program and by substantial loans supplied by the American subsidized Rural Development Bank. . . .

It was clear by the late 1960s that the commercialization of the rural economy even affected the areas under the control of the NLF. The results of the 1969 NLF surveys of the four most typical liberated villages in the Mekong Delta show that while *per capita* landholding of a rich peasant was three times as large as that of a middle peasant, only about 25% of his total income was derived from agriculture. Fifty-six % of this income came from "industrial-commercial activities" (i.e., provision of machine services and crop handling) and the rest from credit.

Meanwhile, the use of capital inputs in agriculture was necessita-ted by a shortage of agricultural labor as a result of the population and occupational shifts already mentioned above and by the fact that tens of thousands of water buffaloes and cattle were being killed by bombing and shelling and by American and Vietnamese soldiers for fun and meat. Another reason was that, with over half-a-million hectares of cultivated land destroyed or abandoned because of the war, the peasants had to rely on the greater use of the water pumps and new rice varieties with a short growing season, among other things, to increase double-cropping in order to maintain or increase production. . . .

All this led, first of all, to a massive import of farm and farm-related equipment from 1968 to 1973. During this period 21,000 tractors and motortillers, 550 harvesters and threshers, 215,000 water pump sets, 3550 insecticide dispensers which aver-aged to about 3 hp each, and tens of thousands of other power equipment were imported. . . .

The growth in the use of capital inputs in agriculture as well as the commercialization of the rural economy inevitably increased differentiation in the South Vietnamese countryside. This situation tended to be much worse in the Saigon-controlled areas partly because of proximity to the provincial and district towns and because of access to the resources provided by the Saigon and US governments through those centers. But there was never any study by either government of this phenomenon. And although Saigon newspapers contained hundreds of articles pointing to agrarian differentiation, they generally cited corruption on the part of the rural elites, land usurpation and usury as the main reasons. . . .

Nature and Extent of Continuing Differentiation

It was not until mid-1978 that a comprehensive study of agrarian differentiation in the Southern Region was conducted by the Committee for Agrarian Reform and Transformation of the Southern Region and the General Office of Statistics in eight provinces of the Mekong Delta. The rural population was divided into five categories and some of the overall results are as follows:

Category I is composed of people engaging in non-agricultural activities. They formed about 2.5% of the rural households and occupied only 0.27% of the cultivated surface.

Category II is composed of poor peasants who did not have any land or did not have enough land and who had to earn their living mainly by hiring out their labor. They comprised, on the average, about 22.5% of the households (31% was the highest in some locations) and occupied about 8% of the land.

Category III is composed of "lower middle peasants" who formed 57% of the households and owned 56.3% of the land, which was just about the right amount of land that their own family labor could work on. They occupied a lower percentage of land, however, in areas where there were more land and more power farm equipment.

Category IV is composed of "upper middle peasants" who comprised 14.5% of the households and occupied 25% of the cultivated surface. They had more than enough land for themselves and had to hire extra labor to work on a portion of their land. They also had a large amount of cash with which they could either extend their operations or invest in other activities.

Category V is composed of rich peasants and "rural capitalists". In areas of little land they formed about 2% of the households and owned 5% of the cultivated surface. In areas with more land and more machines, they occupied about 5% of the households (the highest was 7%) and from 11.5 to 29.7% of the cultivated surface.

On the average, they formed about 3.5% of the households and occupied about 10.3% of the total cultivated surface. Each household in this category owned at least 10 times more land than a poor peasant household. But the main income of the households in this category came from the hiring of labor, machine services and commercial activities. They owned most of the farm equipment and held huge amounts of capital which, as we shall see shortly below, helped perpetuate the differentiation which the use of capital inputs and the commercialization of the rural economy had increased in the first place. . . . Differentiation, however, is indicated not only by land ownership but also by the ownership of the majority of the farm equipment. In eight surveyed hamlets of the above eight provinces there was a total of 7106 hp. About 70 of the 150 households of "rich peasants and rural capitalists" in these surveyed hamlets owned 69 large tractors and four small ones with a total of 4,766 hp, or 67% of the total tractor horsepower. In the three hamlets in the provinces of An Giang, Don Thap and Long An where there was more land and more farm machinery, however, the rich peasants and rural capitalists together formed 5.6 per cent of the households and owned 18% of the cultivated surface and 70% of the tractor horsepower.

The total tractor horsepower in the hands of the rich peasants and rural capitalists far exceeded the work requirement on their land which together totalled 1,070 hectares. This amount of land needed at most only three of the large tractors which were about 68 hp each. Each of these tractors tilled about 400 hectares a year. Hence, the 69 large tractors in the hands of the rich peasants and rural capitalists could work on about 30,000 hectares. For this reason the rich peasants and rural capitalists rented out most of their tractor services to peasants in other categories, the majority of whom were those in Category III.

These services were usually paid in kind and sometimes partly in cash. The net income brought in by one of these tractors was from seven to nine tons of paddy rice a year. In Tien Giang province where payment was in cash, each small 12 hp tractor brought in a net profit of 2000 *dongs* or about 4000 kilograms of paddy rice at the official rate.

But this profit was made not only at the expense of the peasant landowners who had to rent tractor services but also partly at the expense of the workers hired to man those machines. In the surveyed hamlet in An Giang province 10 tractor owners hired 25 operators to provide tractor services to other peasants. On the average each operator brought in a net profit of 2271 *dongs* a year to a tractor owner while he himself received only 678 *dongs* a year in total for salary and food. For this the tractor operator also had to work on the land of the owner since he was a full-time employee. . . .

The relationship between land, labor and machines is thus revealing in terms of rural differentiation.

As far as machines are concerned, the Category V households also owned the majority of other farm equipment (such as harvesters and threshers), irrigation equipment (pump sets and power diggers), processing machines (millers and grinders) and means of transport (power junks and trucks). The provision of these machine services, which was usually paid in kind, enabled these people to exact a huge amount of the peasants' produce to be marketed for extra profit.

But the rich peasants and the rural capitalists themselves did not corner the whole market. The upper middle peasants also had their own share since they had more than enough land, machines and capital for themselves and had the ability to expand their production as well as to hire extra labor. In the eight surveyed areas, although the upper middle peasants comprised only 21% of all the middle peasant households (Category III and IV), they occupied 35% of the land. The average *per capita* landholding of a Category IV household was twice as much as that of a Category III household. As far as pull power is concerned, the Category IV households had 43 tractors with a total of 2079 hp, whereas the Category III households had only seven small tractors with a total of 174 hp. A number of Category IV households provided tractor as well as buffalo services.

Category IV households also hired additional labour to work on their land. Hired work days averaged about 50% of family labor. Most of the labor supply came from the Category II households which provided 50% of their hired labor to the Category IV households, over 25% to the Category V households and the remainder to the Category III households. . . .

The commercialization of the rural economy and the use of capital inputs in agriculture continue to be enduring forces affecting differentiation in the territory of the former South Vietnam. The Vietnamese government reported in early 1981 that while the rich peasants and rural capitalists formed only about 4–5% of the rural households in this region, they still controlled an important amount of cultivated surface, most of the large farm equipment, a large number of the draft animals, and the majority of commercial and food crops.

A comprehensive survey of about 80 rural areas of the Southern

Region – 57 of which were in the Mekong Delta – conducted by several governmental agencies and numerous scholars in 1981 shows that:

1. About 5% of the rural households were now engaging in non-agricultural activities (Category I). This is about twice the percentage given in the 1978 survey. Many of these people had had to sell their land, much of which had been distributed to them by the government after 1975, because of lack of means of production and know-how.

2. There were still 5.7% of the peasant households who did not have any land and 18.8% who did not have enough land (Category II). Together they formed about 24.5% of the households, which is about the same as the 1978 survey (22.5%), and controlled about the same amount of land.

3. Lower middle peasants formed 56.2% of the households and occupied 59.5% of the land. But more than half of them – about 70% in most provinces – did not have enough draft animals and farm equipment and so they had to be dependent on the rich peasants and rural capitalists for these means of production.

4. Upper middle peasants formed 12% of the households and are said to have more than enough land for themselves (about 27%) so they either had to rent out their surplus land or use hired labour to cultivate it. They also had more than enough farm equipment and machinery for their own use and they either provided machine services or rented the machines out. Compared to the 1978 figures of 14.5% of the households occupying about 25% of the cultivated surface it seems that some differentiation had taken place at this level because the percentage of landholding of this category for all of Southern Region should be much lower than that for the Delta alone.

5. Rich peasants and rural capitalists formed only 2.5% of the rural households but owned over 7% of the cultivated surface, 58.5% of the larger tractors of 25 hp and above alone, 50.5% of the millers and threshers, 52% of all the sugar processing machines, most of the means of transportation on land and on water (trucks, junks, etc.) and a huge but undetermined amount of cash which was used for usury and commercial activities. Because the figures given for this category here include all the rural areas of the Southern Region and not just of the Delta where there was a higher concentration of rich peasant and rural capitalist households, they seem lower by comparison to the 1978 figures at first glance. But the 1981 survey indicates that, first of all, the *per capita* income of a rich peasant was now 10 times that of a middle peasant. This income

was made possible through the provision of machine services, purchase and sale of government-issued materials, land rent and sharecropping, usury and forced purchase of peasants' produce at low prices through debt and other means. Second, the survey states that rural differentiation continued.

And third, it says there were basically three types of rich peasants and rural capitalists in the Southern Region: those who invested principally in land, those who invested both in land and in commercial and industrial activities and those who engaged only in commercial and industrial activities. It is obvious that these rural capitalists who now engaged exclusively in commercial and industrial activities formed a new distinct group not mentioned in the 1978 survey. In the past these people usually lived in the district and provincial towns and hence were classified as "urban capitalists". But due to the official policy of restricting movement into the towns and cities many of the rural capitalists who had moved out of farming altogether partly because investment in commercial and industrial activities had become more profitable than investment in agricultural activities simply had to remain in the countryside and be counted as "rural capitalists". The figures given on the percentage of land and farm equipment held by the rural capitalists, therefore, do not reflect their real economic power since they obviously derived much of their incomes from non-agricultural sources.

Socio-Economic Impacts and Policy Implication

It is clear from the above discussion that there was still differentiation in the rural areas of the Southern Region and that, as a result, exploitation under various forms continued to exist. Furthermore, the convergence of all these factors has had definite impact on production. The result of a 1981 survey in An Bien district, An Giang province, shows, for example, that the average yield of paddy rice per hectare per year was 1642 kilogams for the Category I households, 1624 kilograms for Category II households, 1955 kilograms for Category III households, 2086 kilograms for category IV households and 1765 kilograms for Category V households. The reason for the low yields at both ends of the spectrum was the fact that poor peasant households could not afford capital inputs, while the rich peasant and rural capitalist households did not want to make the necessary labor and capital inputs since investment in land yielded lower returns than other types of investment.

Obviously concerned about the exploitative situation and its impact, on 9 November 1981 *Nhan Dan* editorialized: "The sluggish development of the agricultural co-operativisation program is a reason making the exploitative situation in the rural areas slow to be put under control and production yet to take off strongly." This point was made to underscore the information given in the October 1981 speech by Politburo member Le Thanh Nghi which was printed in the same issue of the paper: "The development of collective economic organizations in agriculture is still very limited. Until now they cover only 9% of the peasant households and 7% of the cultivated surface. The pilot program to establish agricultural co-operatives has yet to create a model. Land readjustment is still unaccomplished."

While it is true that exploitation continues to exist because of the sluggish development of the cooperativization program, it is also true, as we have seen, that it exists because of continuing differentiation whose major causes have been the commercialization of the rural economy and the use of capital inputs. Of the capital inputs, tractor horsepower seems to be the most pertinent factor. But although there was a substantial increase in the use of tractor horsepower during the late 1960s and early 1970s, the rate of increase and the number of tractor horsepower units per thousand agricultural workers were still among the lowest in South and Southeast Asia during those years.

The fact that such a relatively small amount of horsepower could have done so much to create and perpetuate agrarian differentiation and to alter the organizational structures in the Mekong Delta in such a short time has been due to an abundance of land available, lopsided distribution of population and labor and lack of productive means in the hands of the majority of the rural population. We have also seen the dramatic residential and occupational shifts during the war years that have resulted in an extremely uneven distribution of population and labor. . . . Most important of all, we have seen that the lack of the means of production by the majority of the peasants has allowed them to be exploited by the rich peasants and rural capitalists and even by the upper middle peasants. We have seen that more than half of the middle peasants do not have, or do not own enough draft animals and farm equipment and have to depend on the rich peasants and rural capitalists for these means of production. Worse still, more than 20% of the peasant households who do not have any land or enough land have to hire out their labor to the rich peasants and upper middle peasants. Moreover, most often these poor peasants who do not have enough land, enough pull power and enough capital, get to own lands which are deep in the interior and distant from irrigation and water sources. Many times they own lands in other localities which are quite a long distance from the villages they reside in. For all these reasons, even though they themselves have excess labor they do not have the necessary means and conditions for intensive agriculture. And because they do not have the means of production, many of them have either refused to accept land granted to them by the government or have received it only in order to resell it immediately afterwards.

It is clear from all this that redistribution of land without redistribution of other resources, including population and labor, would not do much to bring about agrarian and social transformation. Redistribution of resources, however, is a long and slow process for reasons of structural obstacles, post-war production needs, and political considerations – not to mention inappropriate administrative measures and ineffective political persuasion – as the experience of the last eight years shows. Peasants have resisted the cooperative program, for example, precisely because of the existing lopsided distribution of resources in the Mekong Delta. But the policy implication of the differentiation situation is that since such a low capital input can have such great impact on the organizational structure of the land system, the Socialist Republic of Vietnam could with small, strategic, critical investment develop a mechanism for getting the southern peasants into a cooperative framework.

First of all, the SRV could invest in tractor stations for key areas of the Southern Region to provide the necessary machine services at low and competitive rates to producing peasant households. Better still, in order to minimize bureaucratic hassles and even petty corruption, as succinctly expressed by the peasant saying "Trau den an co, trau do an ga" (Black buffalo eats grass, red buffalo (i.e., tractor) eats chicken), the government could sell tractors to groups of peasant households or production teams on an easy-term instalment basis. This would not only lower the investment and maintenance costs on the part of the government but it could also encourage the rich peasants and rural capitalists to sell some of their surplus tractor horsepower on competitive terms since their investment in tractors obviously would not bring them that much profit anymore.

Second, the government could establish credit institutions to provide the producing peasant houeholds with the necessary capital to pay for production costs so that they do not have to go to the rural and urban capitalists for usurious loans. In this connection, the government could also sell directly to the producing peasants items such as fuel, fertilizers and insecticides on an instalment basis either in cash or in kind or both. This would not only help free the peasants from middle men and from labor bound by debts but it would also help the government to compete effectively with the rural capitalists for the peasant's surplus.

Third, the government could offer to buy surplus land (any land that cannot be worked on by family labor with available machinery) from the rich peasant and rural capitalist households on an instalment basis or guarantee the sale of such land to poor peasant households at a reasonable rate, say 25% of the crop for three years or 15% for five years. It is understandable that since more than two-thirds of the rich peasants and rural capitalists have come from middle-peasant, poor-peasant and even landless-peasant backgrounds (i.e., most of them had been beneficiaries of the various land reform programs and supporters of the revolution) that the government does not want to antagonize them in one way or another, especially in a post-war situation when their productive capability is much needed. But there is no reason why they should not want to sell their surplus land at fair prices, especially when investment in land does not yield returns comparable to other economic activities.

Fourth, the government should turn any surplus land – land bought from rich peasant households or virgin land – into state farms or joint ventures with certain villages or co-ops and should not try to force it on landless peasants who do not have the necessary capital or know-how to work that land themselves. Instead, they should be employed as workers in these state farms or joint ventures or in some other work projects.

Finally, the government could invest in crop handling and crop processing facilities in certain key areas in the Delta to enable the producing peasants to turn over their surplus quickly as well as obtain the necessary items for reproduction more easily and timely. In this connection, even before it could make the necessary investment, the government could encourage the peasants to bring their produce quickly to the market as well as to increase production by providing them with a stable but competitive pricing system that would allow them a certain margin of profit after production and transportation costs. All these would weaken the hold of the rural and urban capitalists on the peasants and allow the government to extend its influence deeper into the rural areas. . . .

Part IV

Production And Gender Relations

Introduction

Analyses of gender and gender subordination in the Southeast Asian region have developed in a number of directions during recent years. Writers have focused primarily on areas such as the impact of technological change, migration, household production, conditions of work, and the disadvantaged position of female-headed households in the development process.

In these, the focus has been largely on detailed empirical studies, and has revealed a considerable variance between societies. Much of the work has adopted a "before/after" approach, in which the impact of externally-induced changes on a particular sector of society has been the major concern. Analyses of production and cultivation have been the primary reference points, rather than politics or culture. Women have always played a crucial role in production, not only through their labor in both household and rice cultivation, but also in off-farm, non-rice tasks, such as handicraft industry, trading, and foodprocessing. These have been vital to the reproduction of local agriculture, in which women have always worked longer hours than men. In addition to these roles, however, women are now playing an increasingly important part as wage labor in both industry and agriculture in world-market factories, local labor-intensive industry, and in cash-crop agriculture. In Malaysia, for example, women comprise 57% of the work-force in the rubber plantation sector. Similarly, young women now form the majority of those who migrate from the rural to the urban areas to take up jobs in the industrial sector.

One of the results of these changes has been to produce rather different forms of subordination than existed previously. New aspects have been introduced and traditional forms have been reinforced for different purposes. For example, work in export-processing zones is characterized by the strengthening of traditional sex-roles and patriarchal authority; in industry, despite a general improvement in living standards, women workers receive lower wages than men; the possibilities for upward mobility are more limited than those for men. While working, women are still expected to be responsible for child rearing, and there has been no change in the sexual division of labor in the family. Similarly, in the rural sector, technological change and the development of cash-crop cultivation have often led to an increase in the labor-intensity of women's work, both inside and outside the household, as men are drawn into more capital-intensive sectors. Similarly, planning has given the central roles to men, rather than women, thereby eroding their position further.

The articles in Part IV address these varying types of subordination. Celia Mather shows how the provision of a cheap and compliant labor force for industry is both socially and culturally determined. In her study of three villages in the Tangerang region, west of Jakarta, she analyzes the ways in which traditional generational and gender values, reinforced by aspects of Islamic ideology, are used in the socialization of a young, predominantly female work force for industry. Rosalinda Pineda-Ofreneo's work is based upon interviews conducted with workers in free-trade zones in the Philippines at the high-point of the export-oriented development strategy adopted during the Marcos government, in 1980. She describes the conditions of work, employment, and living standards of the workers in the sorts of zones which have proliferated in the Philippines, Malaysia, Singapore, Thailand and Indonesia since the early 1970s. Christine White's contribution analyzes the ways in which the transformation of the agricultural sector and gender relations have been intimately connected in Vietnamese collectivization. She shows how the family economy has been extended since the mid-1970s, and how a return to household organization of production has occurred in many areas of the labor process. She concludes that this has led to the more labor-intensive tasks being undertaken increasingly by women, and to a strengthening of patriarchal authority.

Subordination of Women and Lack of Industrial Strife in West Java

Celia Mather

The availability of a compliant, cheap labor force has been a major element of the Indonesian government's attempts both to attract foreign investors and to strengthen weak domestic capital for its industrialization program. . . .

Here I discuss how the dominant ideology of what women and young people are and should be, do and should do, is actively promoted by an alliance of village "leaders" and industrial capitalists, to help create a subdued industrial labor force. I focus on three neighboring villages in the Tangerang Regency of West Java, on the western edge of the periurban zone around the capital city Jakarta.

The Creation of an Industrial Labor Force

In 1972, the Indonesian government announced that Jakarta was "full" and began encouraging industries to move out into the city's hinterland. During the 1970s, the Regency of Tangerang saw a remarkable explosion in industrial investment. . . . As this industrialization pushed outwards along the main road running westwards from Jakarta through Tangerang town, many previously rural villages became saturated with manufacturing and speculative capital. The three neighboring villages of my survey, here together named Kelompok, house a total of about 18,000 people in 14 hamlets (*kampung*). Lying some 35 km west of Jakarta and 6 km west of Tangerang town, these villages sit on the very edge of the industrial area. Though they still appeared largely rural at the end of the 1970s, industrial development had already become the dominant force, unfluencing all aspects of social, economic, and political life there. . . .

From the early 1970s to early 1979, some 56 factories were built in Kelompok, mostly producing consumer goods for the domestic market, including tyres, plastic goods, pharmaceuticals, air-conditioning units, electrical cables, steel rods, motorbike parts, confectionary and biscuits, and textiles and garments. Most were owned by some combination of national and foreign capital: national capital was usually from domestic Chinese sources in collaboration with individuals from the national or local bureaucracy, and foreign capital ranged from American, Japanese and Thai sources, but was mostly from overseas Chinese interests in Singapore, Hong Kong and Taiwan.

In 1979 of the 41 factories in production, 17 were large firms employing 100 or more workers; 19 were medium-sized with 20–99 workers; and five were small, with 5–19 workers. The labor force of all these factories together numbered some 6000 people, of whom just under half were women.

The majority of the enterprises had a short-term strategy. They used low-technology equipment with low productivity and specialized in simple manufactured products selling at low prices. To achieve profits under these conditions, they kept unit costs per worker as low as possible, paying very low wages, and usually not allowing even the barest minimum of "extras" such as paid holidays or sick leave. Also, because many of these enterprises were highly susceptible to financial fluctuations, they insisted on the right to lay off workers during a crisis, and this they frequently did. Many workers were employed on a casual daily (*harian lepas*), seasonal (*musiman*), or short-contract (*kontrak*) basis, or as "probationers" (*percobaan*) even for many years, so that they could be laid off at a moment's notice. Therefore factory jobs in Kelompok were very badly paid and insecure. The people recruited to do them were those who were most likely to accept work under these conditions, usually the very young, from 13–20 years old, and ill-educated – typically those with only a few years at elementary school. A common pattern inside many factories revealed large numbers of barely-educated girls or, in other factories, boys, supervised by young men with high or middle-school education.

Industrial wages in Kelompok were extremely low. The lowest wage recorded (Rp.150, about 12.5p) was only enough to buy, say, a litre of rice and two bananas. This meant that most wages were not sufficient to support dependants, children, or ageing parents. Indeed, most adults with dependants to support regarded such wages as impossibly low, and insecure too. They preferred to continue taking their chances on petty trade, *becak* (pedal cab) driving, seasonal agricultural employment, and so on. However marginal and insecure, these were nevertheless familiar ways of earning a living. Instead, they sent their young daughters and sons, or sisters and brothers, into the factories. The wages of these young workers were then regarded by both parents and employers as "supplementary" rather than the central source of income, even though they were the only *regular* cash income coming into many households.

A young woman's wages were more likely to be contributed into the household than were those of young men, who had more of a discretionary right to spend their wages as they wished.

Low wages meant that workers could not support dependants, but also caused these young workers themselves to be dependant upon others, their parents or older brothers and sisters, for a good proportion of their subsistence needs. When asked why they let their daughter work for money which could not feed her, parents replied that "she would in any case eat from our rice". In other words, whatever work she was doing, they would be responsible for feeding her. There was, then, a tacit agreement between parents and factory managers that these young workers, especially daughters, were dependent, and this allowed the investors in the area to pay wages which did not cover the daily subsistence cost of their workforce.

Not only were industrial wages in Kelompok absolutely low, but they were also low relative to those in other industrial areas. Wages here were, for example, up to 50% below those generally paid in Jakarta. This was not because prices in this part of Tangerang were lower; in some cases (including rice) they were slightly higher. Yet in spite of this difference, the workers of Tangerang seemed much less willing than their counterparts in Jakarta or Bogor to the south to engage in industrial action to improve their wages and other conditions of work. Strikes and other forms of direct action did occur from time to time in the factories of western Tangerang but they appeared to be much less frequent than in other areas. This suggested that the workforce here was more subdued than elsewhere. Since many of the conditions found in other industrial areas – state repression, high levels of unemployment, recruitment of only certain categories of people into factory work, and so on – applied here too, it seemed necessary to seek out further explanations for the especially high degree of domination exercized over the Kelompok workforce.

The Domestication of Women

Some have observed that women in Java have a remarkable degree of independence from their menfolk. Whatever the situation in other areas, it is not possible to be so optimistic about the autonomy of women in the villages of western Tangerang, particularly if the discussion includes not only property rights, but also questions of the "domestication" of women through marriage and within families. For though Kelompok women enjoy comparative freedom in some areas of property ownership, when it comes to their sexuality and child bearing capacity, the dominant ideology of what is permissible to women ensures considerable control over their lives, as we shall see.

Like women in other areas of Java, the women of Kelompok have traditionally sought incomes at one time or another outside the household. Apart from handicrafts (bamboo woven hats, now nearly defunct) and rice planting, weeding, and harvesting within the orbit of the hamlet, they also engage in their own trade (usually foodstuffs, *batik* cloth, and household goods) which can take them touring other hamlets, and young girls have undertaken domestic service in the towns. Their income is usually their own to spend. Women in wealthy households, though more secluded than poor women, can and do own capital and inherit land and goods in their own right. The property they take with them into marriage remains their own upon divorce, and they are entitled to half the property gained during marriage.

Women's property rights and their contribution to production are in practice recognized as secondary. Many women complain that they do not usually receive their full divorce entitlement. In inheritance men are generally said to have "more of a burden to bear than women" and are entitled to (though do not always claim) double the share of their sisters. Moreover, the work women do is generally gender-specific, that is "women's work" not done by men. The domestic tasks which are always carried out by women are considered women's primary work. Indeed, women's work other than domestic tasks, for example, handicrafts and petty trade, is often termed *pekerjaan nanggur*, literally "the work of the unemployed", suggesting that it is thought secondary both to their own domestic work and to men's work. . . .

Women in this and probably most other parts of Java are dependent upon men in that all women must marry. In both my and the Serpong (Zuidberg and Hasyir, 1978) surveys, there were no households headed by women who had never married, and this has above all to do with the control of their sexuality and reproductive powers, the supervision by men of women's sexuality and their capacity to bear children. Any woman who does not conform to this pattern, who makes her own decisions about her sexual life and bearing children outside marriage, is called "immoral", a prostitute, and is ostracized. Marriage is almost universal for men too, but it does not bind them to women to the same extent that it does women to men. Men can make their own independent decisions about their sexuality and procreation of children, are able to form liaisons with divorced and widowed women (*janda*) without stigma to themselves, and able, if they wish, to engage in polygamy. . . . Marriages are not necesssarily long-term; divorce is frequent (22% of marriages reported for Serpong women ended in divorce). Divorce rights, however, are not equal. As the Serpong Project says, "a husband can easily divorce his wife for adultery, disobedience or barrenness," simply informing her verbally or by letter, whereas a woman can only appeal for divorce to the local religious (male) official responsible for questions of marriage (*penghulu*), and must prove her case against a miscreant husband.

Rather than being stigmatized, divorced or widowed women are very soon remarried. They are considered desirable by men for their sexual and other marital experience, and for their child bearing capacity. About a third of all Serpong women marry twice or more, one husband following another in fairly quick succession. Women heading their own households, then, do exist (12% of both Serpong and Kelompok households), but they are considered "unfortunate", and where the woman is still young she is said to be in a transitory state: "between husbands". . . .

A woman is not considered an adult (*dewasa*) until she marries, a stage reached by boys at a much earlier age after their circumcision (usually between 7–10 years, but can be as early as five or as late as 12 years). But it is upon bearing children that a woman gains her full social identify. Bearing and rearing children are considered women's most important tasks, their God-ordained role; and children, "gifts from God", are the most prominent aspect of the lives of most women.

According to Islamic teaching, a man may demand sexual intercourse from his wife whenever he wants (apart from the prohibited periods surrounding birth). It is a sin for her to refuse, for "the wife is the field to be sown". In practice, a wife may refuse from time to time without serious retribution, but since divorce and polygamy are permitted and frequently occur when a husband is not satisfied, wives feel themselves constantly under this threat. A marriage is not considered successful unless there are many children, and as we have seen, childlessness is justification for a man to divorce his wife. . . .

Children, then, are the focal point of women's lives and by them they are identified. But this is not to say that women have a greater claim than men over their children. In contrast to the data from

Central and East Java, divorced mothers do not necessarily retain their children. While the mother continues to care for babies and toddlers, children over the age of five are encouraged to follow their divorced father into his new or other marriage(s). In practice this may not necessarily happen, and we find a greater range of patterns, with children attached to grandparents, elder brothers and sisters, uncles and aunts, etc. Even so, the father is recognized to have priority, first right of option over his children.

The Islamic Patriarchy

Men's rights over women and children do not rest upon individual power relationships but are embedded within the prevailing ideology and promoted through an organized Islamic patriarchy. As both "Islamic" and "patriarchy" are concepts under considerable debate, the use of this term needs some explaining. . . .

Kelompok straddles a frontier area, on the edges of the urban area radiating out of Jakarta to the east, and at the same entering into the rural area of Banten to the west. Banten is particularly noted in the Indonesian context for its comparatively orthodox and scholarly (*santri*) Islamic principles, with a conservative (*kolot*) stream of thought currently influential. Here, male Islamic leaders head a long-established and well-organized hierarchy, promoted through complex networks of mosques (*mesjid*), shrines, religious schools (*pesantren, madrosah*), associations (*tarekat*), and traveling preachers (*kiyai*). It is to Banten that the people of Kelompok have long looked and traveled for their spiritual and ideological inspiration.

In describing social relationships surrounding gender and age in Kelompok as Islamic, I am here using the categories of the people of Kelompok themselves. . . . Kelompok people have a category "social custom" (*adatistiadat*) separate from Islamic practice (*menurut agama*) and past feudal relationships in this area will have had a major significance in shaping social relations as they are now. However, for an outsider to distinguish between this as "feudal custom" and that as "religious practice", independently from the categories of Kelompok people themselves, is a dubious undertaking. Islam is recognized by Kelompok residents as far more than a set of abstract beliefs, and few elements of life are distinguished as "social customs" divorced from their religion, certainly not those as deeply part of the moral code as are questions of the relationship between men and women, the legitimation of children, and the control of women's sexuality.

Nor are many of the values relating to gender and age relationships described here exclusive to the Muslim religion. Elsewhere in the world one might find a similar ideology promoted through, for example, Christian values and organizations. This might give grounds for arguing, as many have, that they are not "Muslim" or "Christian" as such, but rather part of a virtually universal patriarchal ideology which is somehow "misusing" religion. However, I see all religious ideology and organizations as political constructs, and do not discriminate between them. In the present case study, patriarchal values subordinating women and youngsters are promoted, not exclusively, but most importantly, through mosques, prayer houses, schools, and other institutions, by teachers, preachers, judges, officials, and others, all with reference to Islamic scriptures and practices.

In the Kelompok context the term patriarchy appears to have some usefulness to convey the presence of a hierarchy, which is organized and with concrete form, led by particular adult men (*tokoh*, village leaders), who also have a systematic body of ideas on which to draw. It seems to me that if used in this sense, then the word "patriarchy" need not be completely abandoned.

In Kelompok there exists a category of local male dignitaries, *tokoh*. Exactly which men are *tokoh* is not fixed, and would be disputed between individuals, but there is a general consensus. They come from the wealthy landowners and traders and the functionaries of the various mosques. They include several men honored by the title *kiyai* (preacher) and many of the respected *haji* who have made pilgrimage to Mecca, especially if they own their own prayer houses (*langgar*), or are otherwise active in the religious community (*ummat*). Some of these are also hamlet heads (*jaro*), and just a few hold other positions in the village-level (*desa*) administration, though because of the suspicion in which officials of the local state are often held, most of them, especially those appointed from the outside, would be excluded from the *tokoh*. So, the *tokoh* include men identified by economic, political, and religious interests. Many of them share class interests (but not all do, and the role of the state would be particularly contentious between them). In any case, to define their class interests separate from, or more important than, their interests in gender relations would be to miss how integral their shared ideology of what women and young people are and do is to the totality of their interests.

Above all, the *tokoh* promote their interests using Islamic and feudal ideals of justice and a social order based on hierarchy and paternalism. In particular they encourage notions of themselves as guardians and "father-figures" of the community. Young men in Kelompok also find themselves subordinate to those higher in the patriarchy. However, my focus is on young women workers, who are trebly subordinate, as client-employees, and as young people (as are young men workers), but additionally as women.

I have mentioned how the religious authorities stand guard over marriage, controlling, for example, women's access to divorce; they also arrange marriages in order that no child is born without a recognized father (providing one when the genitor of a baby is unknown). They are responsible for overseeing and will intervene in any circumstances which threaten the prevailing moral code. The new generation learns of this not only through socialization within the home but also through Islamic education. Though the balance is probably now shifting, it is arguable that Islamic school (*madrosah*) education in Kelompok remains as important as secular state education, both for boys and girls. Many children attend the *madrosah* in the afternoons, after secular schooling in the mornings. Even at secular school, religious education is given a priority, and local Islamic leaders are engaged as teachers.

There is some seclusion among women of more wealthy and orthodox *santri* households, and also in one hamlet noted for its adherence to orthodox principles. Even the most secluded women do not wear a veil, but they do cover their heads with a light cotton or chiffon head-scarf when in public. This is considered appropriate (*cocok*) for all women, but most young women now ignore this except when engaged in religious duties. However, the separation of women runs deeper than the seclusion of some, and partial wearing of head-scarves.

The public attitude deemed most appropriate for women, and to a lesser degree for young men, especially of poor families, is *malu*. This refers to both mental and physical attitudes, encouraging them to appear shy, embarrassed, and retiring, deferring to superiors and remaining at a distance from them, averting their eyes, and so on. They are also encouraged to feel afraid (*takut*) of new experiences and new people. The opposite, *berani*, applies to behavior which is assertive and forceful, and this is considered most inappropriate, even dangerous, for the women of Kelompok, though as with much that is dangerous it holds its own fascination. Any strongly independent spirit in a woman or among women is strictly limited, by calling it *berani*. The attitudes of *malu* and *takut* encourage women to identify themselves publicly with their husbands (*ikut suami*) or fathers (*ikut bapak*) and not to cooperate together outside the limited spheres of the home or harvesting, or outside the supervision of the Islamic authorities. The only organizations which exist specifically for women are the Islamic women's council (*Majlis Tak'lim*) and communal *Qur'an* reading sessions (*ngalih*). The secular women's organizations which had begun to penetrate the rural areas before 1965 have been completely dismantled. Even in women's trade, there is no evidence of the capital-sharing groups (*arisan*) now common among urban bourgeois women. In sum, however they behave in the confines of their domestic life, in public Kelompok women do not gather together to organize their own lives, but are separated and identified with reference to the men who dominate and to whom they defer.

An Alliance of Powerful Men

By recruiting young people, especially young girls, from the hamlets of Kelompok into the factories, the industrial capitalists are able to make use of the traditional forms of subordination of women to men, and youth to age, to create a labor force which is cheap and relatively easy to dominate. I have noted previously that wage levels are partly determined by categorization of these young workers as dependants. Once inside the factories the young girls consistently (and young men occasionally) say that they feel too *malu* and *takut*, so deferential to their bosses (usually older men) that direct confrontation, individually or in groups, is almost unthinkable. They say that they are too *malu* to be straightforward about any grievances, too *takut* to complain about low pay or unfair treatment, and would rather leave the factory than "make trouble" (*daripada bikin ribut, lebih baik pulang saja*). They show an unwillingness, based on their inexperience, to organize together and it is easy for the management to atomize them and isolate one from another, to dismiss those who "create scenes" or engage in other types of inappropriate (*berani*) behavior.

Moreover, as well as benefiting from previous socialization of the young, factory managers attempt to ensure that their workforce is pre-selected. They do this by entering into a direct alliance with the local male dignitaries. Contact is made by inviting the *tokoh* of the nearby hamlets to a meal to celebrate the building of a particular factory, where willing *tokoh* can be identified and enlisted. Interviews with such dignitaries in Kelompok revealed that a substantial proportion of them were retained by local factories. For example, every *jaro* head of the Kelompok hamlets was hired by one or more factories in his locality, as were a number of men with important positions within various mosques.

These men (none of these hired agents are women) have two functions. The first is to recruit laborers for the factories, for most factory jobs are not obtainable on a free labor market; they are usually obtained through having a "contact" (*kontak*) already inside a factory. . . .

The second way in which the *tokoh* work on behalf of the factories is as security agents (*jago keamanan*), responsible to the factories for ensuring peace in their hamlets. For this they normally receive a monthly salary (typically Rp.30,000, about £25). As security agents, the *tokoh* are also in an unrivalled position to detect and attempt to eliminate potential trouble from within the villages aimed at the factories. In these ways, the *tokoh* leaders become mediators in the relationship not only between capitalists and their labor force in the factories, but also between the factories and the surrounding communities.

This arrangement does not eliminate the airing of grievances by the industrial workers of Kelompok, but it may be one reason for the comparative lack of industrial unrest in the region. In other industrial areas where strikes and workers' organizations have been developing, it may be that the incoming investors recruit on an open market, and do not benefit from a workforce subdued by such deeply patriarchal relations in the surrounding villages as exist in the Kelompok area. When workers in Kelompok do get upset about the conditions of their work, this more usually takes the form of mass hysteria. Occasionally production is held up by mass weeping, or rumors that dangerous spirits infect the machinery or the factory site (especially after a series of accidents). Such sporadic and spontaneous outbursts are often resolved by bringing Islamic leaders into the factories to calm the workers down again.

That state-appointed officials (in all three villages the administration was not popularly elected) should ally themselves with industrialization is to be expected, but it is perhaps at first sight surprising that other village leaders who so strongly enunciate Muslim principles should do so. In Indonesian Islamic and nationalist circles there is a considerable body of opposition to the government's "development" programme with its emphasis on outside, "Western"-led growth. It is quite conceivable that the leaders of the established Islamic hierarchy in this part of West Java would feel themselves threatened, and react negatively. For example, they might well feel their position undermined by the employment of large numbers of village girls in the factories, which takes the girls away from the domestic hearth and allows them to gather together, meet "outsiders" and learn to exchange new aspirations.

It should be noted that the girls who go into the factories are from landless or land-short families who have always sought an income outside the home. Factory work is thought as legitimate a way as any for them to do this. The daughters of relatively orthodox, usually more wealthy, families, who were traditionally secluded, do not go into the factories.

Within the factories the girls are in a highly controlled environment, supervized by older men. Outside the factories they return to their homes, where as wives, mothers, sisters, and daughters they are still subordinated. Since the factories are built on the edge of, or even within, their own hamlets, there is not even a long journey home which the girls might make their own. Moreover, industrial production lines are not composed of a random selection of males and females but are clearly defined by gender, and so do not rupture Islamic ideals of the separation of the sexes.

Therefore, the employment of certain categories of young person from Kelompok in factories does not particularly interfere with their domestication, and does not necessarily threaten the prevailing ideology. Indeed, there is a convergence of opinion between the incoming capitalists and the village patriarchs, who both see women and young people as submissive, dominated objects. Individual Islamic leaders can therefore justify encouraging this form of recruitment for their own gain without serious challenge to their own views concerning women or young people. . . .

Philippine Domestic Outwork: Subcontracting for Export-oriented Industries

Rosalinda Pineda-Ofreneo

In 1980 three export processing zones were in operation in the Philippines, two more at the development stage and ten more due to be launched within a few years. There has been a phenomenal increase in manufactured exports, with garments, electrical and electronics equipment, and handicrafts taking the lead. These are part of the export-oriented industrialization now being pursued upon the recommendation of the World Bank and other international lending agencies; they fall into an "outward-looking" pattern of development which has serious repercussions on the situation of women workers in both factory and cottage industry.

What is happening in the Philippines is not an isolated or unique case. Many other developing countries are undergoing the same process under the new international division of labor. In this system of internationalization of production devised by the transnational corporations based in the United States, Japan and Western Europe, the role of the developing economies is to be (1) the geographical site of labor-intensive manufacturing for worldwide markets, (2) the supplier of low-priced consumer products, and (3) the source of cheap labor. Three main factors have made this possible: (1) the virtually inexhaustible worldwide reservoir of potential labor found mostly in Asia, Africa and Latin America, where workers earn wages roughly 10–20% of those of their counterparts in the advanced industrial states; (2) the development of modern transport and communication technology which makes possible the relocation and control of operations over wide geographical distances; and (3) "job fragmentation" or the breaking down of complex operations into simple units so that even unskilled workers can perform them.

Under the new international division of labor, transnational corporations set up branches or subsidiaries in the so-called "low-wage countries." They also go into joint ventures with local capitalists, a convenient arrangement wherein the foreign partners have the upper hand by virtue of their control of technology, access to the world market and large capital. Lately, however, the trend is for transnational corporations to develop supplier or subcontracting firms in the developing states. These firms, which may be branches and subsidiaries of TNC, joint ventures, or "independent" local producers, are dependent on the contractor corporations and perform the ancillary role of processing materials supplied by the latter and/or manufacturing or assembly of components. International subcontracting reduces the visibility of the TNCs in terms of direct equity investments, marks a shift from equity control to market and technological control, and avoids the problem of nationalization in cases when the suppliers or subcontractors are industries wholly owned and operated by the "natives themselves". . . .

Subcontracting is the wave of the future, as evidenced by developments in the Philippine setting. It is being practised in one form or another in the following industry lines: car manufacturing, electronics, leather, garments, toys, handicraft, food processing, textile, musical instruments, paper/packaging products, plastic and rubber products, and metal fabrication. In agriculture, contract growing exists in the following sectors: banana, rubber, poultry, piggery, beef cattle, feed grains, rice and shrimps.

The pattern, however, is clearest in the garments sector, which started as a basically subcontracting re-exporting industry where raw materials are shipped from abroad for processing (cutting, embroidery, sewing, etc.) and then re-exported. Part of the production process goes into the factory but the bulk is subcontracted to cottage-type producers in the rural areas.

In the decade to 1978 the US textile and clothing industries combined had suffered an estimated loss of 300,000 jobs; in Western Europe, the job loss totalled one million in 12 years. The jobs went to countries like the Philippines, where the industry itself has grown into some 900 to 1000 establishments and some 2000 manufacturers employing directly or indirectly about 450,000 to 500,000 homesewers on contractual basis and 214,000 factory and home workers. This expansion is matched by the phenomenal increase in exports: From 1971 to 1977, the value of garments sold abroad jumped 560% from $35,730,000 to $249,700,000. Philippine dollar earnings from garment exports were $405.4 million in 1979, indicating a tenfold growth in just a decade. In 1980, it was estimated that the foreign demand for Philippine garments is approximately 64% of the total demand". . . .

The distinctly smaller part (about 214,000) of the dual labor supply are the full-time factory workers employed as designers, cutters, sewers, inspectors, packers, engineers, sales representatives, accountants and clerks in sites located within Metro Manila, a few other cities and towns, and the Bataan Export Processing Zone.

The greater part of the labor force are cottage industry workers who get paid on the basis of piece rate. These cottage industry workers are again subdivided into the directly employed workers who constitute only 25–35% of the total, and the more numerous indirect workers who labor in their own homes for the cottage enterprises or for agents connected to factories.

One source reported that "subcontractual arrangements with garment firms in Batangas, Bulacan, Laguna and Negros Occidental account for around 40% of total production." Further down the line, "groups of families with 15 to 20 sewing machines are sub-contracted for piecework, thereby engendering the growth of cottage-type sub-industries". The cottage industry workers are provided with materials for sewing, knitting, and/or embroidery and are paid when the goods are delivered to the factory for finishing, pressing and packing. In 1975 they received from P35 to P240 ($4.98 to $34.50) a week, today the figure may be from P50–P300 ($6.00–$36.50) a week, depending on the availability of orders, the ownership of the machines and the nature of production relations, e.g. whether they are employed or self-employed.

It is estimated that more than 90% of workers in the garments industry are women, who are generally the ones relegated to monotonous, tiresome work requiring finger dexterity. Their labor costs much less than that of men. For example, for the second quarter of 1978, female production and related workers in urban areas earned P917 ($127.36) on the average compared to P1345 ($186.80) of their male counterparts. The docility of female labor is also considered desirable by employers. Youth, single status and inexperience are likewise preferred in factory-type employment because with such a background, workers would tend to accept lower pay and are not likely to assert their rights, particularly those related to maternity benefits. In the rural areas, the average wage differential between male and female production and related workers is even wider: For the second quarter of 1978, the former got P901 ($125.14) while the latter received a meagre P381 ($52.92).

More than 50% of garment firms in the Philippines are foreign-controlled, 28% by American interests. Twenty-three per cent are controlled by other foreigners (Japanese, Taiwanese, Korean, Hong Kong, British and German) who have recently moved in as "quota refugees" since the quotas for their respective countries have already been filled up. In addition, there is the advantage of being able to make use of cheap Filipino labor. In 1973, Filipino garments and textiles workers earned $38.40 a month on the average, while Korean workers received $45.10 and Japanese workers $257.60. . . .

If one were to devise a ladder to show who really benefits from the labor of countless women workers in the Philippine export garments industry, at the very top would be the "foreign principals", mainly transnational corporations with branches, subsidiaries, joint ventures or subcontractors in the country. Whether foreign or Filipino, however, the large garment firms find the dual labor supply very useful. First, cottage industry workers are generally not covered by minimum wage legislation and other protective labor laws. Second, they can be used as a weapon against the urban wage workers when the latter make demands. When in mid-1977, there were secret attempts to form a union among the 1800 workers of Greenfield and Santiago, the management fired the union leaders and suspended the union members. The reduction in the regular work force and the consequent lag in production was overcome by giving more jobs to domestic outworkers paid on the basis of piece rate. Third, the latter's volume of work can be adjusted according to demand. When the demand is high, they can be made to produce more and when low, they can be made to produce less or not at all, without cost to the company.

Layers of Exploitation

Rural piece workers who are at the very bottom of the subcontracting ladder are a much exploited lot. Since all they see are the agents from their areas who distributed the jobs to them, they are hardly conscious of the fact that their labor redounds to the immense profits being raked in by the foreign principals abroad and by the large Manila-based manufacturers-exporters.

In 1973, according to the National Demographic Survey, 17.53% of employed rural women were dressmakers, sewers and embroiderers (not in a factory). The same survey showed that 59.3% were farm workers, compared to 18.44% who were farmers and farm managers. This indicates a marked trend in the countryside: the phenomenal increase in the ranks of the landless rural poor who generally find seasonal employment working for farmers with land to till and who manage to survive off-season by taking odd jobs. this trend has been aggravated in the rice and corn areas by the Green Revolution technology purportedly designed to increase agricultural productivity and which has created a huge market for the fertilizers, pesticides, tractors, and other machinery being peddled by the transnational corporations based in the United States, Japan and Western Europe. The high cost of these farm inputs has led to the pauperization and ruin of many small farmers who have sold their land or their tenurial rights and have joined the ranks of the landless. There is thus an increasing labor surplus in the rice and corn areas, which is compounded by the use of labor-displacing tractors and threshers. Within this context, more and more rural women find it necessary to engage in income-generating activities other than farming or farm work, not only off-season but the whole year round. They are thankful for any work that comes to them, no matter what the terms. They say it is better than nothing.

Separate interviews conducted with rural women in the province of Bulacan confirm some of the above observations, and at the moment are the only sources of relevant data in the absence of organized research on the matter. The sewers and embroiderers know that their conditions are worsening. For example, two sisters who have been sewing baby dresses for almost 20 years observed that the payment per piece in real terms declined. Today, the predominant figure is 50 centavos (roughly six cents) when in 1962, it was 30 centavos (roughly eight cents at the exchange rate then), which is much bigger considering the steady erosion in the value of the peso. The most that a sewer can finish is a dozen baby dresses a day, for which she gets paid between P6.00 to P9.00 ($0.73 to $1.10) at 50 to 75 centavos per piece. However, work is available only about two-and-a-half to three weeks a month so total monthly earnings only amount to P102.00 to P109.00 ($12.43 to $13.04). From these earnings are subtracted the cost of the thread and the transport going to and from the agent. Income derived from sewing is thus only supplementary in nature because the main source will still have to be farming. In fact, when it is planting or harvesting season, the sisters prefer to work in the fields because they can earn more – at the rate of about P15 to P18 a day ($1.83 to $2.00). It is significant to note that as regards the subcontracting ladder, the sisters are aware only of the fact that they are sewing baby dresses for export and that the agent in the next barrio, with whom they have been dealing for almost 20 years, supplies an Indian exporter. They say that this agent is not really better off and likewise provides labor because she does the cutting.

A separate interview with a group of embroiderers together with their respective agents revealed many problems and contradictions. These women have given up farm work altogether to concentrate on embroidery. They claim that conditions have deteriorated in the last few years. For example, in 1975, an embroiderer could earn as much as P150 ($21.34) for two to three days' work; today, she would be lucky to get P70 to P80 ($8.54 to $9.76) a week. In 1975, she was paid about P27 ($3.89) for working on one Maria Clara (an elaborate national costume); today, her labor would be worth only P13 ($1.59) and the design is even more intricate!

As the conversation rolled on, it was apparent that the embroiderers felt some antagonism towards the agents whom they perceived as exploiters. According to them, some agents get as much as 50% of the amount paid by the factory contractors for the labor of the workers and earn much more than the latter even when "just sleeping". There are also those who make the embroiderers (particularly the unmarried ones) stay in one place (usually the agent's home), make them work 15 hours a day, and subtract from the latter's pay the cost of food, water, electricity and the monthly instalment for the machines. In some cases, too, there are too many agents situated at different levels from Manila down to the barrio, all directly or indirectly profiting from the labor of those at the bottom, who get very little as a consequence. As many as six agents form the ladder to the top.

The agents present countered that they too suffer, especially when they are caught between the factory contractors and the embroiderers. In the first place, many of them also provide labor in the sense that they launder, dye, iron and cut the cloth. They also have to produce cash to buy thread or to give to the embroiderers when payments are delayed, or when factory contractors short change them by paying less than what was agreed upon on the pretext that deliveries did not arrive on time and therefore were late for shipment. The gravest problem, however, is the intense competition between the subcontractors or agents in getting job orders from the factory-based manufacturers/exporters. Some offer a very low price per piece to the management, on condition that all the job orders would be monopolized by them. In this sense, not only the other agents or subcontractors suffer but also the embroiderers who would be paid much less for their labor.

As a result of this exchange, the women saw the need for uniting the forces of both the embroiderers and the agents so that they could fight against the big fish more effectively. They were already talking about possibilities of organizing garments piece-workers in the province of Bulacan.

There must, however, be a broader unity. Cottage industry and domestic outworkers are not aware that they are being used against their sisters in the organized manufacturing sector. Just how is shown in an interview with militant union members in Uniwear, a large Manila-based garments factory, whose products are sold solely to foreign buyer/distributors based principally in the United States.

The union was formed early in 1981 and practically forced its recognition by going on strike in April. As a result of their action, the workers were able to get what was due them under the law, which means on the average, about P29.60 ($3.60) a day. To counter this, the Filipino-Chinese management is increasingly resorting to subcontracting. Now, it has 200 outworkers in Tanauan, Batangas alone and has more in Bulacan. The president of the company told the union leaders that he could close the main factory in Makati, which has 362 regular workers, anytime because he has enough, as well as cheaper, labor supply in the provinces. . . .

Conclusion

It is obvious from the above discussions that more and more Filipinos are being drawn into production as domestic outworkers under the new international division of labor. They get a mere pittance in exchange for their labor which is being harnessed by foreign global interests and big local manufacturers/exporters to amass super profits. They work under harsh conditions, are deprived of their rights as workers, and are hardly aware of the roots of their oppression. Without their knowledge, they are being used as weapons against their sisters in the organized manufacturing sector when the latter seek to acquire what is due them.

Within the context of international labor policy, the very existence of industrial home work is anomalous and should ultimately be abolished. Where this is not yet possible, efforts should be made to extend to industrial homeworkers the same rights and benefits that the factory workers have. . . .

In the Philippines, the policy is to encourage industrial home work through subcontracting, with the prodding of the World Bank. Under these circumstances, it is up to domestic outworkers and their organizations to protect and advance their interests, together with their sisters in the factories.

Socialist Transformation of Agriculture and Gender Relations: The Vietnamese Case

Christine Pelzer White

Although a great deal has been written both on the socialist transformation of agriculture and on women in socialist societies, there has been little overlap in the concerns of these two fields of inquiry. This is surprising given the crucial economic and social importance of gender relations and the sexual division of labor in the predominantly peasant agriculture of most pre-revolutionary societies, the continued importance of the "family" sector in systems of collectivized agriculture, and the fact that women form the majority of the agricultural labor force in many socialist countries.

How do we account for the lack of integration of these two areas of analysis? In the Marxist-Leninist tradition there is some attempt to link the two, but "relations of agricultural production" are considered to be primarily a class question. Although Lenin referred to women's subordination within the Russian peasant household and there is some analysis of a pre-revolutionary "patriarchal mode of production", the question of relations of production within the patriarchal rural household has been far outweighted by the emphasis on the class status of the household as a unit relative to other households (see Stanis, 1976).

Furthermore, whereas classes are defined in terms of exploitation and subordination within relations of production, women have been often thought of as a category marginal or extraneous to production and therefore production relations, engaged primarily in "non-productive" domestic labor within the household (Molyneux, 1981). This derives partly from the fact that Marx focused on capitalist societies in which production had in large part been removed from the family workshop or farm and reconstituted in class terms in factories or as proletarianized agricultural labor for large landowners.

However, the division of workplace and the home, the spheres of production and reproduction, is not typical of pre-industrial, agrarian societies, and within recent years a growing literature has established the key role that kinship relations play in structuring production relations in peasant societies. Moreover, cultural phenomena often seen as "superstructural", such as marriage customs and inheritance patterns, are important mechanisms by which access to and control of the means of production (primarily land and labor) are regulated and by which women are subordinated to men in peasant societies. Since most socialist revolutions have taken place in agrarian societies characterized by a high percentage of family organization of labor (whether on peasant smallholdings or tenant farms), the question of socialist reform in agriculture and transforming gender relations are therefore intricately connected.

> For example, a land-owning peasant patriarch may well have different interests and attitudes with regard to collectivisation of his land from those of unpaid and landless 'family labour' (wife or wives and children), but this point is not made in the standard analytical literature on collectivisation.

As conventionally defined, socialist transformation of agriculture entails moving from small-scale subsistence and petty commodity production by peasant households to large-scale cooperatives, collectives and state farms involving a formally organized labor force. Small-scale production in family farms or workshops has been seen as "backward": historically (pre-capitalist), economically (low productivity) and socially (low degree of division of labor and social cooperation), as well as politically suspect (a seedbed of capitalism).

There are striking parallels between this and the socialist program for the emancipation of women. Just as small scale household production is associated with economic backwardness, isolated domestic labor within the confines of the household is held responsible for women's inferior social position. The proposed solution has been to involve women in social production outside the home and to socialize women's domestic work through the provision of crêches, canteens, etc. In this light, agricultural collectivization has been seen as a major contribution to rural women's emancipation, providing both formal organization and recognition of women's work in agricultural production and such social facilities as crêches and maternity clinics.

However, along with this fit between the standard socialist solution to the peasant problem on the one hand and the women's question on the other, there are contradictory aspects which appear most clearly in conceptions of the relationship between production and reproduction and policies toward "the family". The "socialist family" has been promoted as the appropriate social context for biological reproduction and the "basic cell of society" because of what is generally seen as its "natural", psychologically and economically irreplaceable role in the rearing of children and the care of old people. Moreover, it remains a widespread social assumption that the care of these people not yet or no longer engaged in productive labor is primarily women's work if social provisions outside the family are not available. In consequence, the family has occupied a highly ambiguous position: as a *social* unit, it is associated with women, notably the "sacred task" of maternity; as an *economic* unit it has tended to be associated with "individualism", the "petty producer mentality" or capitalism.

In the concrete context of collectivized agriculture, it is the household or "private" plot within the collective farm or co-operative which has been the primary embodiment of this ambiguous relationship between the spheres of production and reproduction. The continued resilience of this household or "private" sector has long been considered problematic for socialist agriculture. It is equally problematic for the enhancement of women's socio-political role. Since women do the majority of work on the "family plot" in addition to their "non-productive" family tasks and "social production" in the collective (socialist) sector, the concrete form that collective agriculture has taken has often contributed to women's work burdens. Not only do women have less time than men to devote to social, economic and political activities in the wider community, but their social and economic activities on behalf of the family are devoted to a sphere defined as ideologically inferior to the socialist sector.

In a number of socialist countries the strength of the household economic sector, and problems with productivity on state farms and collectives has led to a partial rethinking of the traditional socialist identification of large-scale agriculture with high productivity. In both China and Vietnam recent reforms have encouraged collective farms to subcontract agricultural production to peasant households. This innovation called "subcontracting of agricultural production" in Vietnam and the "responsibility system" in China, sits uneasily with traditional thinking about socialist relations of production in agriculture and cannot adequately be analyzed without reference to gender relations.

From Family to Collective Agriculture

My aim in this section is to summarize briefly the impact of the major structural changes from the pre-colonial system to the present on two basic and long-standing institutions, the village/cooperative and the farm family/household.

In pre-colonial Vietnam, villages were organized as collectives of male household heads governed by councils of notables and endowed with legal, administrative, cultural and economic personalities, rights and responsibilities. The village's economic base was communal landholdings which included some fields earmarked to provide income for administrative, cultural, defence and social welfare costs, with the rest distributed on a regular basis among adult male villagers for usufruct for a period of a few years as "subsistence shares" (see Ngo Vinh Long, 1973).

While some land ownership was communal, farming was not organized on a communal basis but by household, with some traditional forms of labor exchange. Although the distribution of communal land, as well as the inheritance of private land within the village, went to male villagers, agricultural production was not an exclusively male activity. A man could not farm without female labor. The very word for the verb "to farm" in Vietnamese, *cây cây*, contains the words for "plough" *(cây)* "transplant (rice seedlings)" *(cây)*. These two verbs express a symmetry between the two essential steps in rice production which in traditional Vietnamese culture were the most strictly sex-typed: men plough, women transplant. This involved division of labor within a family unit, as well as neighborhood groups of same-sex workers.

Despite their crucial role in agricultural production, which extended to marketing activities outside the village, women were subordinated in both village and family. They were excluded from membership in the council of notables and from participation in village meetings, while within the household, few women had independent access to land. A widow's husband's land was generally inherited by a son or male relative, and any communal land allotment usually was taken back by the village.

French colonial rule brought new forms of community relations, but hierarchial pre-colonial social structures, including patriarchal relations, survived and were in some ways intensified. The dramatic rise in landlordism and decline in smallholder agriculture was not accompanied by a radical change in the organization of agricultural production (except on the relatively small plantation sector). The peasant smallholder, the tenant and the holder of a plot of communal land all generally farmed with household labor supplemented only at peak periods with mutual aid or some hired labor.

Following the expulsion of the French, the Vietnamese Communist Party completed a land reform which created relatively egalitarian distribution of land and other means of agricultural production. The land reform campaign (1953-6) eliminated ownership of land by non-tillers, abolished the vestiges of traditional communal land ownership and universalized a pattern of small peasant-owned holdings farmed by household labor. However, ownership was not explicitly patriarchal, and for the first time women did receive land in their own name. Many women emerged as radical activists during the mass mobilisation against "landlord exploitation" because of their additional suffering and resentment over patriarchal forms of exploitation. In a marked break from the traditional all-male pattern of village government, many women were elected to leadership posts during the land reform period.

Following the land reform, marriage and kinship remained the major form of labor recruitment in the now universalized "family mode of production" (see Friedmann, 1980). It is probably not coincidental that new marriage legislation which outlawed polygamy, child marriage and parental control of their children's choice of marriage partner was introduced at about the same time that cooperativization began the transformation from family to a larger. non-kin group as the main unit of agricultural production. Traditional forms of marriage which were disguised forms of labor recruitment had continued after land reform, such as the practice of finding a strong young woman to work as unpaid family labor by marrying her to a son below working age. Not surprisingly, young women caught in such marriages often became activists in the campaign to form cooperatives, as membership in a newly-formed cooperative gave them independent access to employment. Moreover husbands tended to be more reluctant to join cooperatives than their wives, because of the threat to their "independent" status as household head managing a family farm. In one village the difference was so marked that original household land was divided in two, with the women joining the cooperative and their husbands initially staying out (see Pham Cuong and Nguyen Ba, 1976: 35).

As Vietnamese cooperatives developed, land ownership was collectivized and agricultural production on 95% of each village's cultivated land was formally organized on the basis of work teams. All adult working members of households joined cooperatives, with men and women becoming cooperative members on an equal footing. The sexual division of labor within this larger unit of production generally continued the traditional pattern (e.g. male work teams for ploughing, female work teams transplanting), although during the wartime absence of many men, women carried out traditionally male tasks.

With the formation of cooperatives, women's agricultural work previously thought of as "supplementary" or "secondary", was measured, like that of men, in work points. According to Tran thi Hoan, a Woman's Union cadre who had been involved in the campaign to form cooperatives, "some husbands were very surprised when they saw how many work points their wives earned. Before they had thought that it was they who fed their wives, not their wives who fed them". Another advantage of cooperativization was the possibility of giving pregnant women lighter work because the unit of production was larger.

While men had previously been the "directors" of the family farm, the formation of cooperatives made it possible for women to be elected to management positions. During the war, when a large percentage of the men of working age were away at the front, there was an active policy of training and recruiting women for cooperative management posts.

The dependence of children and old people on the family was modified by new collective institutions. Crêches were set up in co-operatives, and a uniquely Vietnamese institution, the old people's orchard, with a shaded rest place or house, provided a social meeting place and profitable economic activities for cooperative members who no longer had the strength to work in the rice fields. In a cooperative visited by the author in 1979, the old people's team even played a role in making marriage a cooperative rather than just a family affair; their garden provided flowers for weddings and furniture for new households was made by their carpentry workshop.

However, the system of collective (in Vietnam usually termed cooperative) agriculture did not entirely supplant the role of the household in the organization of production, let alone in the sphere of "reproduction". Although agricultural land was collectivized, each household retained its house and garden and also had usufruct of a small portion of the cooperative's land for use as a "family plot". As the household remained the residential unit, the conditions for a home-based "family economy" remained within the cooperative.

The coexistence of family and collective organisation of agricultural production in Vietnam could be characterized as a symbiosis, as the family economy has not been neatly contained within the confines of the house and yard and the family plot. To a remarkable extent formally collectively organized steps in the production process on cooperative land were dependent on inputs from the household/family sector unless modern inputs were available from the state. For example, household pig manure provided the major source of fertilizer for the collective fields on an obligatory delivery basis, and seed storage and the care of cooperative draft animals were commonly subcontracted to cooperative households. Some cooperatives found it more economic to rent draft animals from private owners than pay the cost of machines from the district tractor station. The cooperative and family economic sectors were frequently in competition: for work time, for pig manure, and even for the harvest on cooperative fields, (e.g. mothers harvesting for the cooperative reportedly would drop grains for their children to glean for the household or for their private ducks to eat).

One of the most paradoxical aspects of Vietnamese socialist rural development is the extent to which the development of the cooperative economy has been accompanied by an expansion in the infrastructure of the family economy. Whereas capitalist development erodes subsistence production and family based petty commodity production, Vietnam's form of socialist development has had an opposite effect. The cooperative system ensures that the house and access to a small plot of land, the basis of small scale peasant production, cannot be lost through bankruptcy. A peasant house is not just a place of residence but a place of production including pigs and chickens in the courtyard, home handicraft manufacture in the slack season, etc. Much of this work is considered "women's work" due to the compatibility with women's other household chores. Before land reform and cooperativization, only a handful of landlord and rich peasant families in each village had tiled-roofed brick houses, brick courtyards to dry their rice and solid piggeries. Now a large percentage, in many areas the overwhelming majority, of cooperative members enjoy such quarters built in the 1960s and 1970s with bricks, tiles and lime produced by cooperative workshops. In other words, the cooperative system has helped to build up the infrastructure of the family economy.

Another development of the 1960s and 1970s was that collective agriculture became and remained a socio-economic sector with a primarily female labor force (at least 60% and often much higher, depending on the region and the intensity of wartime mobilization). Because of what are seen as women's "family responsibilities" for the care of the young and old, far more men than women have been recruited from the villages for state sector jobs and duties, whether in the army, in urban industry, transportation or administration. The combination of cooperative agriculture with the family social system facilitated military mobilization since soldiers could rest assured that the cooperative would guarantee their family's economic needs and that their wives would take care of both their children and their husbands' aged parents, an aspect of traditional patriarchal culture strongly encouraged by the socialist government.

In sum, a number of economic and social aspects of "the family" were strengthened in symbiosis with the collective agricultural system. New aspects of sexual division of labor began to emerge, with more men in the state sector and more women in the cooperative sector.

Subcontracting: a New Sexual Division of Labor?

In the orthodox Marxist-Leninist conception the "peasant question", which in Vietnam in particular largely overlaps with the "woman question", is to be resolved by the eventual establishment of large agro-industrial complexes and the merging of the peasantry into the wage-earning working class. Towards the end of the war there was a strong policy push in this direction in order to move beyond the wartime situation of relatively limited commoditization, semi-autarkic cooperatives, and a strong family economy sector. . . .

In a post-war context exacerbated by the conflict with China this policy did not succeed and food supply problems reached crisis proportions. In 1979, at the Sixth Plenum meeting of the Party leadership, a dramatic new policy direction affirmed the key importance of small-scale production at Vietnam's present stage of economic development and opened the door for the "family economy" to make use of economic resources, including land, not being utilized by the cooperative. This was followed in late 1980 and early 1981 by government advocacy of subcontracting cooperative land to cooperative members for the final stage of the production process, a *de facto* encouragement of household organization of agriculture going far beyond the previous symbiosis of cooperative agriculture and the family economy.

Because of the increasing sociological differentiation within northern Vietnamese villages which has begun to be documented in household surveys within the last few years, (see for example, Houtart and Lemercier, 1981) along with diversity between villages and regions, the range of social relations involved in the new subcontracting system is quite wide. Furthermore, ambiguities in policy and practice over whether the subcontracting is to individuals or to households makes it particularly difficult to clarify the sociological implications.

In part, the analytical confusion stems from the fact that a rural agricultural producers' cooperative in Vietnam is an economic unit of production based on place of residence (a hamlet or village made up of household units) in a country where social relations are becoming increasingly complex (through increased mobility and occupational differentiation) but where kinship ties are still very strong indeed, with economic as well as social aspects. Therefore, each "individual" cooperative member is simultaneously part of several wider social entities, including the cooperative, a kin network ("family" consisting of relatives whether resident in the village or not) and a unit of residence ("household", usually a subset of the wider family group).

To simplify the picture it is possible to hypothesize that two major and very different patterns would emerge depending on the pre-existing mix of state and family sector inputs. In the first type, a high level of state-supplied inputs would enable the cooperative to continue to organize a number of steps of the production process effectively. This is the pattern which the government would prefer to see generalized since it maximizes control by the socialist sector. It is probably no coincidence that the model for the subcontracting system is the Haiphong area (near the major port) which has an exceptionally high level of mechanization and other state-supplied inputs. However, in the more typical situation of low state inputs and heavy cooperative dependence on family sector contributions, it is likely that the new system entails a return to household organization of production for all steps of the labor process. The implications for gender relations in the two patterns are quite different.

The first type received most publicity as it was the officially encouraged model. The government policy directive on subcontracting makes no mention of households, only to "giving groups of workers and individual workers contracts for product quotas". The directive stresses that the new method must not allow "any individual cooperative member to take charge of the whole process of production – from ploughing to harvesting". Instead, the co-operative and production teams must be "directly responsible for carefully organizing labor in specialized teams and groups to perform important operations requiring technical expertise and the use of collective technical and material facilities". On the other hand, "operations requiring manual labor that can be satisfactorily perfor-med by individual workers" are not to be directly managed by the cooperative but contracted out to "groups of workers or individual workers".

In both Vietnam's traditional and present existing sexual division of labor, those tasks defined as "important" and "technical" which are to be directly organized by the cooperative sector include all the steps done exclusively or primarily by men (ploughing, irrigation work, uprooting seedlings . . .) while the implicitly less "important" tasks suitable for an individual labor process and to be subcontracted are done primarily by women (transplanting, weeding, harvesting). . . .

While there are obvious negative implications for women in a system which associates collective work and technical expertise with men's work, the subcontracting system does highlight women's manual labor input as crucial to the success of the harvest and may strengthen women's collective bargaining position.

On the other hand, in the second type of contracting where the entire labor process is subcontracted to a household head to mobilize and deploy household and family labor, the result could be a strengthening of traditional patriarchal authority. However, in rural Vietnam there are many female household heads, both widows and women with husbands virtually permanently absent in the army, administration or industry. Even where a man is present, women sometimes control the disposition as well as the generation of the family economy; traditionally women are the family accountants. Where women do control the family economy in all senses, the present relaxation of administrative controls on women's income-generating activities, including marketing (as women are traditionally the rural market sellers in Vietnam) could have a partially beneficial effect for women. One aspect of the new system is to allow greater freedom for agricultural producers (the overwhelming majority of whom are women) from interference from administrators (the overwhelming majority of whom are men).

Whereas the intent of most previous structural reorganizations in agriculture had been to increase the formal organization of the work force, to specify universal norms for production and distribution and to transform the social structure, the new policy is an attempt to mobilize existing informal social ties in order to increase productivity. It is left up to the existing social relations between individuals within households and families which have received land on subcontract to determine what the distribution of work and product will be. Government policy is only concerned with the contractual relationship between the cooperative and the contractee (obligation to deliver a certain quota of production). Discussions of the new system make it clear that individual sub-contractees are expected to mobilize labor within the household (e.g., children and old people) as well as family members not resident within the household (e.g., husbands or other relatives working in urban jobs in industry or the civil service who could ask for leave to participate in family agricultural production).

Unlike the cooperative workpoint system, which quantified the labor inputs of household members on cooperative fields separately, the new system could once again create undifferentiated "family labor" without any external norm as to how the workload or income should be distributed within the household or family. As we have seen, one of the advantages for women of cooperativization was that the workload could be shared more widely; unlike in the family farm system, pregnant women did not have to do heavy labor such as transplanting. The new system appears to be increasing productivity by intensifying women's workload with negative results for women's health, as well as making it more difficult to compare the relative economic and labor contributions made by men and women.

Productivity is up because women are given the financial incentives to work harder, but meanwhile women's burdens in the sphere of reproduction have also increased. The new system has reportedly had a negative impact initially on the collective child care system, as crêche workers found it more lucrative to take up a contract for agricultural labor and crêches have difficulty getting staff. The population implications of a family farming system (especially in wet rice agriculture) where there are economic advantages in having many children have been well documented. If population growth is not checked, it will quickly negate any improvements in productivity.

In sum, the new system seems to accentuate already existing tendencies toward a new form of women's subordination, with men concentrated in the state and cooperative (socialist) sectors and women's labor power mobilized as "subcontracted" manual labor on an individual or household basis. Women's "privatized" work within the family, the sphere of reproduction, has spilled over into the de-socializing of their work in agricultural production.

Conclusion

The present policy to harness the economic potential of small-scale production is a major reversal of orthodox socialist thinking about "economies of scale" in agriculture, and as such seems a very positive development. At the present time, the subcontracting system is still under debate, with the orthodox seeing it as a temporary tactical retreat in the forward march toward "large-scale socialist agriculture". However, debates over scale are largely beside the point unless there is creative thinking by socialists in Vietnam and elsewhere about a new sexual division of labor and new means of coordinating the spheres of production and reproduction so that men and women can function effectively as workers and parents and as individual and social beings.

Part V
Culture and Ideology

Introduction

Culture has been called "the missing concept" in studies and critiques of "development" (Worsley, 1984). It is often ignored in approaches which tend to reduce society to political-economy or social structure. It is argued that attention to cultural dimensions of social realities may reveal some of the historical specificities of constraining and enabling features in the development of particular societies. These concrete and local cultural factors are scarcely treated in general and abstract theories of dependency, mode of production, world system and the like, which limits their heuristic value. Another way of saying this is that normative values and sanctions must be considered in their connection with remunerative (materially rewarding) and coercive or physical, even violent, sanctions.

This notion of culture refers not to elite conceptions of culture as the superior values in society, or to holistic or pluralistic views of culture as, respectively, a whole shared way of life, or a more or less balanced co-existence of distinct value systems and codes of social behavior. Rather it is the concept of a hegemonic culture in which values and behaviors are imposed on the majority by dominant classes and groups; or, better, where there is a sustained, persuasive effort to assert their political and moral legitimacy and acceptability. The concept of hegemonic culture builds on and develops some of the senses of ideology, which can be retained to refer to those aspects of culture – from "Great Traditions" to common sense – and its formation and dissemination which concern the interests of dominant classes and groups, and the tendency for existing social forms to be represented as natural, uniquely legitimate and rational, unchallengeable and unchangeable. In other words, it refers to the power dimension of cultural production, and the ways in which alternative or oppositional cultures are co-opted, downgraded or silenced in dominant discourse. In this view, ideology is not necessarily only the ideas of the ruling class, not inherently or totally "false", nor necessarily a coherent and systematized set of ideas and values, nor only those propagated in the more obviously "ideological apparatuses" or institutions of the state.

The idea of a contested, changing hegemonic culture directs attention to areas of social and cultural creativity – and its denial – to processes in the formation of social consciousness. These processes and their outcome may or may not be congruent with classes conceived in terms of production relations. It suggests the value of attending to ways in which both class and "non-class" (gender, national, regional, ethnic, religious, personal, etc.) identities and loyalties are asserted and contested in struggles to establish new forms of social subjectivity. These are struggles in the course of which various social groupings, strata or classes may come to define themselves and create new forms of association and alliance. The approach directs our attention, too, to the more fragmented, less articulate, everyday elements of popular culture, including those which have been inherited and transformed over generations, and those in the process of emergence.

Kahn argues against concepts of ideology as mere reflections of social structure, or as mechanically determined, or as "false consciousness". He argues for an analysis which goes beyond conscious models or "folk models", in order to be able to explain disjunctions between ideological categories and other economic and political realities. The three models he examines are those of ethnicity, patron-client relationship, and *aliran*, an Indonesian word for a kind of "vertical" alliance. Though these notions do indeed have a phenomenological reality, do indeed refer to observable behavior and social interaction, they are but the "raw material of ideology". They are inadequate for use as explanations of social structure, though many social scientists writing on Java have raised them to this generalized status. Thus the patron-client relationship is based on a perception of a social gap which it "bridges", but this is, Kahn argues, a physical, spatial gap (e.g. between town and village) and not a social-structural gap. For example, villagers in different relations of patron-clientage, *aliran* or ethnic alliance, are involved in the same relations with national and international markets.

Ileto considers perceptions of nationalism and revolution by peasant and popular classes from the anti-colonial revolution in the Philippines of 1898, through the period of American colonization, and up to a dramatic incident in 1967. His work has important resonances for understanding the explosion of what has been termed "people power" against President Marcos in 1986. He challenges received academic judgment that popular political ideas had no meaningful existence apart from their articulation with elite ideology; and he challenges notions of Filipino masses as fanatic and irrational, or contradictorily, as passive acceptors of change. He urges the need to "decode the language and gestures of peasant rebels". This he does not through historical documents compiled by elite sources, but through popular songs, plays, processions and experiences surrounding Holy Week and other ritual occasions celebrating the life and death of Jesus. This is summed up in vernacular epics of the *pasyon*. These contain images of hope, redemption and social deliverance that nurture a popular undercurrent of millennial beliefs. They contain themes of critical rejection of social hierarchy and inequality, and affirmation of the potential power of the "poor and ignorant", religious meanings which overflow into the socio-political life of the participants.

Scott gives us valuable insights into some of the cultural dimensions of agrarian differentiation, here resulting from the introduction of new technology and production relations following the "green revolution" in Kedah, West Malaysia. He suggests that ritual gift exchanges between rich and poor are sensitive indicators of shifts in class relations and incipient awareness of them. He shows, with detailed instances, a decline in the practice of giving Islamic tithes and village feasts, both obligatory and voluntary, which were designed to promote social harmony between rich and poor – and validate status in the previous social order. There is not only an overall decline, but also a new selective use for the "deserving poor". Thus marginalization in the ritual life of the community accompanies economic marginalization. Humiliation and bitterness result, but also forms of criticism of the newly rich and attempts to sanction their behavior in religious idioms, where economic and coercive sanctions are not available.

Finally, Turton proposes ways of thinking of dominant ideology not as a separate, "superstructural" realm of ideas, nor as merely part of state ideological institutions, or even of any "institutions" as such, but as an integral part of new processes of capitalist production, exchange, advertising and consumption. He shows how new ideas, norms and values of work, time and consumerism, even of health and religious practice, are inculcated in daily social and economic life.

Ideology and Social Structure in Indonesia

Joel S. Kahn

In this article I want to discuss a number of issues that have arisen out of my research into the structures of underdevelopment in Indonesia. First, some concepts that have been used in the analysis of Indonesian social structure will be examined. I shall show that these concepts, used in many cases as analytical tools are, in fact, aspects of peasant ideology. As such they should be objects *of* analysis rather than tools *for* analysis. The three concepts discussed in the first section of this paper are: the *aliran*, or vertical alliances described by Geertz and other members of the Modjokuto research team; ethnicity; and patron-clientage. . . .

In order to understand any system of thought, whether we choose to label it ideological or not, we must recognize that every view of "reality" is the product of a cultural code. It follows from this that what is perceived, the "facts" of any thought system are, by and large, constituted by the system itself. Systems of social classification employed by Indonesian peasants, such as the aliran framework, are based on certain principles of constitution which must be uncovered by the social scientist.

Similarly, it is fruitless to distinguish views of reality according to their relative correctness simply on the basis of assumed closeness to reality. For if it is admitted that all systems of thought, both scientific and ideological, constitute their own "facts", then all systems of thought define their own separate reality with which they are, by definition, in close harmony. While, therefore, we may disagree with a Modjokuto peasant who argues that the main principles of social classification derive from differing degrees of religious piety, we cannot disagree that this view has what Geertz has called a certain "phenomenological reality". This is to deny that ideology, religious or otherwise, can be distinguished as a mode of thought which is non-empirical. Neither is the term "false consciousness", frequently appearing in highly materialist interpretations of Marx, an adequate description of the complexity of any accepted or shared thought system.

Indeed it often seems that "closeness to empirical reality", at times used to distinguish science from ideology, can cut both ways.

In most cases it is ideology rather than science which is more directly concerned with and based on reality as it is directly perceived. I shall argue that the ideologies of aliran, ethnicity, and patron-clientage in Indonesia rest on certain directly perceivable aspects of personal appearance and social interaction, taking what *appears* as crucial to a definition of the structures which generate appearance.

This leads directly to a consideration of the relation between social structure and ideology. The concepts of reflection and mechanical determination of superstructure by infrastructure must be abandoned because economic and political structures are not directly perceivable and because ideological systems are themselves semi-autonomous – the product of their own internal properties as much as of economic and political constraints.

This is not to argue that ideology must be analyzed entirely without regard to relations of production and authority within a social formation. It seems most useful to conceive of the relation between different levels of social reality in terms of what Friedman (1974) among others, has called a hierarchy of constraints. Ideological systems thus become subject to the constraints of functional compatibility between different structures which go to make up the total formation. How would a hierarchy of constraints operate on the formation of ideology? I would susggest, on the basis of the preceding discussion, that it is through "empirical reality" that economic and political structures operate on thought systems. If thought systems are directly related to observable interactions, and if these interactions are generated by social structure, then it is in the generation of the raw material of ideology – social appearances – that social structure affects the perception of social reality. The relationship between social structure and ideology, when perceived in this way, becomes a negative one, in the sense that the systemic requirements are that ideology does not contradict appearance. At the same time there need be no reflective process at all, since interactions and other àppearances are not themselves direct reflections of underlying social structure. . . .

Aspects of Indonesian Peasant Ideology

Aliran

This Indonesian word meaning stream has, through the work of Clifford Geertz on Java, entered into common anthropological usage. While Geertz's definitions of the aliran are not entirely consistent, he suggests that they represent a form of social organization which arose to fulfill certain social needs in the years after Indonesian independence. The aliran were formed around the "four major all-Indonesia political parties" and consist of both local party organizations "plus a whole set of organizational appendages" such as women's clubs, youth and student groups, labor and peasant unions, religious and charitable associations and the like. To quote Geertz:

> Each party with its aggregation of specialized associations provides, therefore, a general framework within which a wide range of social activities can be organized, as well as an over-all ideological rationale to give these activities point and direction. The resultant complex . . . is usually referred to as an *aliran*. (1963: 15)

Writing of the period in which he did fieldwork, Geertz (1963: 15) further tells us that "it is the *alirans* which today form . . . the core of Modjokuto social structure, replacing the status groups of the pre-war period."

In spite of the relative clarity of this formulation, there is some confusion in Geertz's earlier work over the exact naming of these aliran. In *Peddlers and Princes*, as the above passage indicates, the different aliran are said to correspond to political parties – the Nationalists (Partai Nasional Indonesia), the Communists (Partai Kommunis Indonesia) and the two Muslim parties – Masjumi and the more conservative Nahdatul Ulama. Elsewhere the aliran are distinguished more on a religious than a political basis (Geertz, 1960). The major groups are now the Muslims (*santri*), the Hindu-Buddhist elite (*priyayi*) and the peasant syncretists (*abangan*). The santri are Muslim purists, hostile to the religious syncretism of both priyayi and abangan. Abangan religion is a mixture of Islam and aspects of Java's pre-Islamic religious heritage. Priyayi are those who adhere broadly to the traditional ideology of the Javanese court, with its emphasis on the maintenance of highly institutionalized status differentials, ascetic mysticism, and a uniquely Javanese Hinduism. These in turn are roughly associated with political allegiance: priyayi with the Nationalists, santri with the Muslim parties, and abangan with the Communists.

Finally the aliran are sometimes described in terms of the occupations of the main adherents of each stream. The santri are traders and entrepreneurs; priyayi are both the feudal landlords and the civil servants; and abangan are the peasants.

Geertz is not the only one to have used this model of Indonesian society. In one form or another it is one of the most widely used characterizations of postwar Indonesian social structure. . . .

That the aliran are really an aspect of Javanese peasant ideology, and not social structure as the earlier work of Geertz sometimes implies, is made clear in a more recent book by Geertz on Modjokuto. Here he tells us that he is concerned to develop a model of social structure employed by the Javanese themselves. The model, which he calls a "cultural paradigm," "is essentially a symbolic structure, that is, a system of public ideas and attitudes" (Geertz, 1965: 8). Elsewhere in the same book he writes: "The categorizations were phenomenologically real; that is, they were objects of direct experience for the Modjokuto population taken as a unit" (1965: 124).

It is clear from this that aliran are first and foremost principles of ideological classification and not "the core of Modjokuto social structure". The social aspects of the aliran might better be termed behavioral, because the models influence, or at least have influenced, the behavior of those who adhere to them. Unless it is assumed that there is an isomorphic relation between social structure and ideology we cannot use the aliran as a basis for our own models of Indonesian social structure.

While based on an acceptance of the validity of the aliran concept, this criticism of its use perhaps goes deeper than criticisms which rest on empirical refutation of the concept alone. Utrecht (1972: 24ff), for example, takes issue with Geertz by arguing that the santri-abangan distinction is unimportant to many Indonesian peasants. He cites examples of political alliances which cross-cut aliran ties in East Java and throughout Bali. Wertheim (1969) in an excellent article shows how the vertical santri and abangan alliances, which Jay suggests demonstrate the unimportance of classes in the Javanese context, gave way to class struggle and the breakup of aliran along class lines during the period leading up to the terrible massacre of communists in 1965.

Given, however, that aliran refers to an aspect of peasant ideology in particular periods of time in specific areas of Indonesia, it is not surprising that conflicting ideologies can and have been described for different places at different times. The criticisms leveled by Wertheim and Utrecht merely raise the question of why it should be that the ideology has been transformed, and how it is that these transformations have taken place – questions which can only be answered within the context of a general theory of the formation and transformation of thought systems.

Ethnicity

This has become very much a part of Indonesian thinking, used by some to explain the obstacles to true nationalism, economic development and the like, and by others to describe the particular strengths, or weaknesses, of some groups as opposed to others. Swift, for example, uses what seems to be the spirit of the Minangkabau ethnic group to explain economic structures in West Sumatra, manifested in the great success of small-scale entrepreneurial activity:

> I suggest that the intense competitiveness of the Minangkabau is such that success as a part of a group is not satisfying for the personality and culture drives involved. I see the genius of the Minangkabau as most suited to a quick perception and grasping of short term opportunity, best exemplified in the world of petty trading (1971: 265).

Ethnicity has also been used to analyze political behavior. Liddle, for example, has "explained" voting patterns in the 1955 elections in part on the basis of ethnic identification. He concludes his study of political organization in East Sumatra by saying that ethnicity "has provided a focal point . . . for the individual's . . . conception of his relationship to the Indonesian polity" (1972: 174). As a result particular ethnic groups – the North and South Tapanuli Bataks and the Javanese – have allied themselves with particular political parties.

Similarly Bruner's analyses give primary importance to ethnic identification. He compares the "structures" of two Indonesian cities, Medan and Bandung, concluding that "The major line of social differentiation and cleavage in Medan society is undoubtedly ethnic. . . ." (1974: 261) For Bruner, ethnic groups in Indonesia are determined according to linguistic and geographical criteria, as well as by stereotypes formed by other Indonesians. Some, he argues, are known as good businessmen, others as puritans, and others because they fight with knives.

Urban Minangkabau and non-Minangkabau in Jakarta with whom I talked gave me similar criteria of ethnic identification. The Minangkabau, they said, were good businessmen (on a small scale), puritanical Muslims, firm adherents to matrilineal *adat* (custom), bad employees because they were generally unwilling to relinquish their independence and, if they turned to crime, pickpockets.

Ethnic identity, of course, takes different forms in different periods of time. In the period of my own fieldwork in West Sumatra (1970–

2) there was a strong feeling of Minangkabau ethnic solidarity. This was continually expressed in the stress placed on adat (custom law), the independence and strength of Minangkabau culture, and so on. It is also interesting to note that non-Minangkabau, or Minangkabau who identified with the national elite, often cited the strength of adat as the main obstacle to economic development.

Similarly in the period of the regional rebellions in the late 1950s the solidarity of the Minangkabau was a constant theme of discourse. Again solidarity was directed against the cultural domination of the Javanese, as well as Javanese economic and political hegemony. In contrast to this it was the splits within Minangkabau, rather than ethnic solidarity, which received greater emphasis in the period leading up to the abortive communist uprisings of the mid-1920s.

Ethnicity, then, is clearly a part of the Indonesian ideological formation. As a shared system of thought it also motivates behavior based on ethnic solidarities and divisions. Ethnicity alone, however, is of limited explanatory value. To ask ethnicity to "explain" voting patterns, or social interaction as do Liddle and Bruner, is to become trapped in the tautological circles of ideology and behavior. Why certain ethnic characteristics should be significant in some periods, and insignificant in others no amount of allusion to the relativity of ethnic identification can explain.

Patron-clientage

Along with ethnicity, the patron-client model has been used widely by sociologists and anthropologists, particularly with reference to precapitalist or transitional societies. Perhaps most frequently patron-clientage has been used to describe a dyadic tie between individuals with differential access to wealth and/or power.

As a model of social structure patron-clientage is something quite different. For Barth (1959), for example, the nature of patron-client contracts appears to determine political structure. This has been criticized recently as a political formalism (Asad, 1972). Perhaps more important, however, recent studies of patronage (Li Causi, 1975, Gilsenan, 1977) show that in particular cases patron-clientage is an aspect of the folk model, built up on the perception of structural relations of economic exploitation and political domination.

Patron-clientage then becomes a conscious model for behavior in particular kinds of social formation. It is also a model of social structure built up on the observance of all interactions between inferiors and superiors whose differential access to wealth and power are defined by their place in the class structure. The existence of this model in Java, as Wertheim clearly shows, corresponds with the aliran system which serves as an overall framework for linking patrons and clients within the same social group.

Aliran, ethnicity and patron-clientage all have this in common – they are all aspects of peasant ideology in Indonesia, or, more accurately, they have all been a part of Indonesian ideology in particular periods of time. As, to use Geertz's terms, models of the appearance of social reality (interaction), they are clearly at the same time conscious models *for* behavior. To equate ideology with idealization is to take an extremely narrow view of ideology.

Ideology and Reality

I have argued that in many cases the formation of ideology rather than taking place in a vacuum is directly based on empirical reality. The relation between aliran, ethnicity and patron-clientage as thought systems and reality as it is perceived by Indonesian peasants – and anthropological fieldworkers – is a very close one.

Folk models based on ethnicity, patron-clientage and aliran all rest, in one way or another, on an equation of social grouping on the one hand and physical space or distance on the other. In Geertz's (1965) discussion of aliran, for example, it will be noted that the different layers are distinguished according to spatial distance from the urban centers. The distance from the rural mass of the bottom end to the intelligentsia at the top is a spatial distance, the product of the application of a geographically defined rural-urban continuum to groups of people. In other words one of the principles of social classification employed by people of the Modjokuto area in the period of Geertz's research was not social at all, but geographical.

While perhaps not so crucial for ethnic identity, geography also serves partly to define ethnicity. People are grouped together not according to social criteria but according to place of origin or in terms of residential proximity. At the conceptual level, then, spatial affinity is equated with social similarity in the ideology of ethnicity.

Spatial concepts also enter into the patron-client concept, although in a slightly more complex way. Patron-client is based on the perception of a social gap, which is bridged by the patron or the "broker". In fact, it will be noted that this gap is a physical one, in many cases corresponding to the rural-urban gap itself. The gap separates town and country and, more precisely, village from the outside world. This gap is experienced by villagers if only because to bridge it themselves they have to leave the village periodically –

to go to market, to visit government offices and the like. While this is not a gap in social structure – villager and town dweller already form part of a social unity, their roles not defined by place of residence so much as by social factors – for the villager it is real because it is experienced. When an outsider bridges this "gap" the act is taken to be a basic social relationship linking town and country. The ideological model of social structure, based on this vertical linkage, again fuses physical with social space.

Finally for the aliran, as described by Jay (1963) the whole basis of the santri-abangan split is geographical. Jay describes the associations of "social" units – residential groups, neighborhoods, villages – with the one or the other of the secular-orthodox positions. In fact, what is taken for social affinity is geographical proximity. The fact that people live together does not mean, of necessity, that they occupy similar places in the social structure. But in the folk model the two ideas are fused. The ideology aliran implies on the one hand a concept of the social solidarity of geographical units, and on the other their association with or opposition to other spatially defined units. This assumed homology between social and geographical space is, then, an important feature of the three ideological systems.

A second important feature of these systems is the emphasis given to observable behavior and social interaction. These are taken, in the ideology, to be reflections of social structure, and hence in themselves used to define the structural relations of society. For example local, geographically defined units acquire a semblance of structural solidarity because people in these units interact with each other. Patron-clientage seems to be a basic structure of social organization because this is one of the few interactional ties between these different categories of people. Where patron-clientage has become part of local ideology then it is based on an assumed coincidence between interaction and all the important social (economic and political) relations.

A third characteristic of these systems, and of aliran and ethnicity in particular, is their similarity to the taxonomies produced by Lévi-Strauss's *bricoleur*, who builds with a repertoire given to him. He "has to use this repertoire . . . whatever the task in hand because [he] has nothing else at [his] disposal" (1966: 17). The repertoire here is that array of observed odds and ends thrown up by ethnic differentiation: language, dress, eating habits, styles of interpersonal behavior and the like. The "ethnic bricoleur" draws on this source of readily identifiable characteristics to build his models of society, and then to act on them. What his informants tell him is often taken at face value. When I was in Jakarta talking to Minangkabau and non-Minangkabau alike, I was constantly reminded of the reputation of the Minangkabau as fanatical Muslim purists. This contradicted my own experience in Minangkabau villages of a rather tolerant people whose observance even of required ritual tended to be rather lax. What counted, of course, was not ritual observance or textual expertise, but the universal proclamation by the Minangkabau themselves of their attachment to Islam. In many cases one would suspect that the difference between santri-abangan has little to do with secularism or orthodoxy, but rather with external proclamations of faith, and the cultural trappings of Islam – dress, the use of a few Arabic utterances at appropriate times, obtrusive disappearances at prayer times, and breaking of the fast only behind closed doors. Ethnicity and aliran are in this way most directly concerned with things as they appear.

In a very real sense, then, ideology in Indonesia is directly related to, if not obsessed with, reality, if reality is defined at the empirical level. In spite of the apparent superficiality of its underpinnings, Indonesian ideology is a strong force for motivating behavior, and its strength must not be underestimated. Nonetheless, while it seems to be compatible with existing social structure it must not be confused with social structure. In spite of the phenomenological reality of these principles of ideology, other approaches to the analysis of Indonesian social structure yield different models altogether. A structural analysis of political and economic organization would reveal a disjuncture between the categories of ideology and the principles of social structure. It is precisely because these underlying structures do not receive physically perceivable verification – and it is the perceptual level which provides the raw material for the ideological *bricoleur* – that a disjuncture develops between ideology and social structure. . . .

An analysis of economic and political structures of the Indonesian social formation does not coincide with the folk models nor with appearances. Economic and political structures, for example, are in no way determined by physical space. Villages which are associated with one aliran or another are distinct neither in economic nor in political terms, although they may be separated in their ideology. Two villages may both produce cash crops for national and international markets. The subsistence sector in both villages helps equally to reproduce commodity production within the villages and outside them. Neither are the two villages politically autonomous – they occupy the same niche in the state administrative structure. In economic and political terms there is no way of distinguishing the two. Nonetheless they may be opposed in the local folk model, one being a santri, and the other an abangan village.

Similarly the Indonesian village economy is an integral part of a total economy which is rural, urban and international. Village producers stand in a class relationship to others, not on the basis of whether they live in rural or urban areas, but according to their productive or distributive role. Petty commodity producers are not restricted to any particular residential niche. And yet in ideological terms the rural is distinct from the urban. There is an ideological – not a social – gap between town and country. Indeed the relationship between town and country appears to be restricted to dyadic relations across this "gap". Political patrons recruit followings in villages. The patron appears to come from nowhere, although in fact he is only a representative of a pre-existing political hierarchy. . . .

What I have tried to show is that a model of Indonesian social structure which distinguishes different systemic levels illustrates a disjunction between economic, political and ideological systems. There is no neat isomorphism between levels. An analysis which goes beyond the conscious models of peasant villagers allows us to understand the discontinuities in the system.

Toward a History from Below

Reynaldo C. Ileto

One Sunday morning in May 1967, residents of Manila awoke to find a strange uprising in their midst. A little past midnight, street fighting had erupted along a section of Taft Avenue between the constabulary and hundreds of followers of a religiopolitical society calling itself *Lapiang Malaya*, the Freedom Party. Armed only with sacred bolos, *anting-anting* (amulets) and bullet-defying uniforms, the *kapatid* (brothers) enthusiastically met the challenge of automatic weapons fire from government troopers, yielding only when scores of their comrades lay dead on the street. When the smoke from the encounter had cleared, only a few, if any, of the country's politicians and avid newspaper readers really understood what had happened. Who or what would shoulder the blame: depressed rural conditions, trigger-happy police, religious fanaticism, or, as intelligence reports claimed, Communists? After some weeks of public uproar, the incident quickly faded in people's memories. Except for those who had joined or sympathized with the uprising, the whole event was a momentary disruption of the familiar and explicable pattern of the nation's history.

The leader, or *supremo*, of the Lapiang Malaya was a charismatic Bicolano named Valentin de los Santos. Eighty-six years old at the time of the uprising, he had been involved with the militant sect since the late 1940s, building it up to a membership of around forty thousand drawn from the southern Luzon peasantry. De los Santos's goals were very basic: true justice, true equality, and true freedom for the country. But it was his style of portraying and attaining these goals that made him appear a hero to some and a madman to others. He was, for example, a medium regularly communicating with Bathala (supreme god) and past Filipino patriots, above all Rizal. He linked the attainment of freedom with the Second Coming prophesied in the New Testament. And he subscribed to ancient beliefs in the magical potency of sacred weapons, inscribed objects (anting-anting) and formulaic prayers. Thus, when he declared himself a presidential candidate in the 1957 and subsequent elections, his challenge was regarded with amusement by regular politicians. His demand, in early May 1967, for the resignation of President

191

Marcos was his final act of defiance against the political establishment which he believed at least since 1966 to be currying too much
favor with alien powers. The supremo's demand was summarily
dismissed, contributing to the mounting tension that exploded in
the infamous "Black Sunday" massacre.

The Lapiang Malaya affair is not an isolated event in Philippine
history. It is not an aberration in an otherwise comprehensible past.
We should be able to find meaning in it, not resorting to convenient
explanations like "fanaticism," "nativism," and "millenarianism,"
which only alienate us further from the kapatid who lived through
it. But what we modern Filipinos need first of all is a set of conceptual
tools, a grammar, that would help us to understand the world of
the kapatid, which is part of our world.

The "Revolt of the Masses"

Anyone familiar with Philippine history will recognize the Lapiang
Malaya's continuity with the Katipunan secret society of 1896. The
triangular symbols, the colorful uniforms, the title "supremo" and
even the very idea of a radical brotherhood stemmed from the
Katipunan experience. In fact, our difficulty in understanding the
Lapiang Malaya can be stretched backward in time: do we really
understand what the Katipunan uprising was all about? . . .

The Katipunan uprising in 1896 triggered the revolution. But by
1897 the original secret society was superseded by a revolutionary
government with republican aspirations. The Philippine republic of
1898 was the culmination of nineteenth-century developments. It was
short-lived, however, not only because the Americans successfully
invaded the country but also because the republic's Western
influenced (*ilustrado*) leadership was weak.

Teodoro Agoncillo's *The Revolt of the Masses* attempts to rectify the
tendency of historians before him to regard the revolution as the
handiwork of upper-class, Hispanized natives. He stresses instead
that the Katipunan movement was initiated by petty clerks, laborers,
and artisans in Manila, and that it was only later that educated and
propertied Filipinos were, with some reluctance, drawn into the
struggle.

The physical involvement of the masses in the revolution is pretty
clear, but how did they actually perceive, in terms of their own
experience, the ideas of nationalism and revolution brought from
the West by the ilustrados? Agoncillo assumes that to all those who
engaged in revolution, the meaning of independence was the same:

separation from Spain and the building of a sovereign Filipino nation. We can rest assured that this was the revolutionary élite's meaning.

But the meaning of the revolution to the masses – the largely rural and uneducated Filipinos who constituted the revolution's mass base – remains problematic for us. We cannot assume that their views and aspirations were formless, inchoate, and meaningless apart from their articulation in ilustrado thought. . . .

Eventually, the problem we face is how to categorize the activities of post-1902 katipunans, religiopolitical societies and other peasant-based groups that waved the banner of independence and plagued the new colonial order up to the 1930s. The bulk of the principales (a prosperous class of mestizos and native elites) who supported and led the revolution had accepted a revised program for the attainment of independence. Ilustrado politicians now proclaimed themselves at the helm of the revolution, pragmatically setting the groundwork for independence as promised by the Americans. How then are the "troublemakers" to be viewed? Were they romantic idealists who failed to adjust to the "realities" of post-1902 colonial politics? Were the various religious leaders – messiahs, popes, supremos, and kings – who with their peasant followers formed their own communities, harassed landowners and confronted the armed might of the constabulary, simply "religious fanatics" or "frustrated peasants" blindly and irrationally reacting to oppressive conditions? Were nationalist Filipino leaders justified in helping the colonialists suppress these "disturbances"? Even well-meaning historians tend to answer these questions affirmatively. Others regard these movements as curious, interesting but nevertheless minor sidelights compared to the politics of the metropolis. Still others sympathize to a great extent with their anticolonial and antielite aspects but fail to understand them in their own light. "Blind reaction" theories prevail; intentions and hopes are left unexamined. This leads to the foregone conclusion that early popular movements were largely failures, and continued to be so until they turned more "rational" and "secular". . . .

Sturtevant, for example, in his *Popular Uprisings in the Philippines* concludes that the peasant-based, religious-oriented challenges to the republic were antinationalist, irrational, and doomed to fail. Because of his inability to decode the language and gestures of peasant rebels, Sturtevant could at best interpret them in the light of psychological stress-strain theories. He says, for example, that they were "blind" responses to social breakdown. In contrast, he ascribes "rational" and "realistic" goals to elite-led movements. In his effort to classify each peasant movement according to its proportionate ingredients of the religious or secular, rational or irrational, progressive or retrogressive, nationalist or anarchist, he explains away whatever creative impulse lies in them rather than properly bringing these to light. . . .

Understanding Philippine Society

All around us we hear of the need to define the Filipino personality, style of politics, and social system. Yet aside from their presence in idealized portraits of rural life or quaint non-Christian tribes, the masses are hardly encouraged to participate in defining this tradition. It is the elite, particularly the middle class, that puts its imprint on everything – from culture to national development. The common interpretation of the revolution in terms of the ideas and goals of the ilustrado class is symptomatic of the widespread acceptance among scholars of the educated elite as articulators of Filipino values and aspirations. . . .

If we accept most current definitions of the Filipino, we come up with something like the image of the smiling, peace-loving, religious, deferential, hard-working, family-bound and hospitable native. The masses, in particular, are regarded as passive acceptors of change on which the modern mass media can effectively train its guns. "Politics" for them is but a game they can allegedly do without or at least simply pay lip service to in lieu of direct participation. There is a lot of validity in this image. Social mechanisms do tend to preserve the existing socio-economic structure.

However, we should guard against reducing Philippine society to this image. We should take into account the innumerable instances in the past when popular movements threatened to upset or overrun the prevailing social structure. Social scientists unable to view society in other than equilibrium terms are bound to conclude that these movements are aberrations or the handiwork of crazed minds, alienated individuals, or external agitators. On the other hand, many scholars sympathetic to these movements tend to fit them into a tight, evolutionary framework that leads to a disparagement altogether of cultural values and traditions as just a lot of baggage from our feudal and colonial past.

To write history "from below" requires the proper use of documents and other sources "from below." Anyone who plows through the range of materials available, say, in Tagalog, soon realizes why a history from the viewpoint of the masses has been long in coming.

Although most of the sources used in this work – poems, songs, scattered autobiographies, confessions, prayers and folk sayings – have been published or were known to previous scholars, they were utilized only insofar as they lent themselves to the culling of facts or the reconstruction of events. For these purposes, Tagalog sources have proven to be of limited value. That is why, in studies of popular movements, Spanish and English-language sources constitute the bulk of the documentation. But since a language carries with it the history of its speakers and expresses a unique way of relating to the world, the exclusive use of, say, ilustrado Spanish documents in writing about the revolution, is bound to result in an ilustrado bias on issues and events which offer multiple perspectives. If we are to arrive at the Tagalog masses' perceptions of events, we have to utilize their documents in ways that extend beyond the search for "cold facts". . . .

The *Pasyon* and the Masses

One of the principal ideas developed here is that the masses' experience of Holy Week fundamentally shaped the style of peasant brotherhoods and uprisings during the Spanish and early American colonial periods. Like other regions of Southeast Asia which "domesticated" Hindu, Buddhist, Confucian, and Islamic influences, the Philippines, despite the fact that Catholicism was more often than not imposed on it by Spanish missionaries, creatively evolved its own brand of folk Christianity from which was drawn much of the language of anticolonialism in the late nineteenth century. The various rituals of Holy Week had in fact two quite contradictory functions in society. First, they were used by the Spanish colonizers to inculcate among the Indios loyalty to Spain and Church; moreover, they encouraged resignation to things as they were and instilled preoccupation with morality and the afterlife rather than with conditions in this world. The second function, which probably was not intended by the friars, was to provide lowland Philippine society with a language for articulating its own values, ideals, and even hopes of liberation. After the destruction or decline of native epic traditions in the sixteenth and seventeenth centuries, Filipinos nevertheless continued to maintain a coherent image of the world and their place in it through their familiarity with the *pasyon*, an epic that appears to be alien in content, but upon closer examination in a historical context, reveals the vitality of the Filipino mind. . . .

If we, for the moment, limit our attention to one version of the epic, the *Pasyon Pilapil*, its bearing on popular movements and social unrest can already be seen. For one thing, the inclusion of episodes relating to the Creation of the World, the Fall of Man, and the Last Judgment makes the *Pasyon Pilapil* an image of universal history, the beginning and end of time, rather than a simple gospel story. In its narration of Christ's suffering, death, and resurrection, and of the Day of Judgment it provides powerful images of transition from one state or era to another, e.g., darkness to light, despair to hope, misery to salvation, death to life, ignorance to knowledge, dishonor to purity, and so forth. During the Spanish and American colonial eras, these images nurtured an undercurrent of millenial beliefs which, in times of economic and political crisis, enabled the peasantry to take action under the leadership of individuals or groups promising deliverance from oppression.

The pasyon text also contains specific themes which, far from encouraging docility and acceptance of the status quo, actually probe the limits of prevailing social values and relationships. Take the extensive treatment of Jesus Christ's preparation to depart from home. This is a classic exposition – found in common soap operas and novels – of the role of *utang na loób* in defining an adult's response to his mother's care in the past. For all the comfort and love (*layaw*) that she gave her son, Mary asks, why must she lose him? Jesus, despite his attachment to his mother, can only reply that he has a higher mission to fulfill – to suffer and die in order to save mankind.

There comes a time in a man's life when he has to heed a call "from above." In the pasyon it is God's wish that is carried out; but what was to prevent the Indio from actualizing this "myth" by joining a rebel leader who was often a religious figure himself? To pave the way for this experience, the pasyon posits the possibility of separation from one's family under certain conditions. In a society that regards the family as its basic unit even in the economic and political spheres, this certainly goes "against the grain".

An even more significant idea found in the pasyon is that social status based on wealth and education has no real value. Traditional Tagalog society has, of course, been stratified according to wealth and education. The principalia class needed wealth to attract and maintain followers, using debt relationships to this end; education perpetuated this class and enabled a select few from below to enter it. The pasyon, again, contradicts this model by stressing the damage caused by "over-education" and wealth on the individual *loób* (inner self), which is where the true worth of a person lies.

From the Spanish perspective, what could be a more effective tool than the pasyon to discourage Indios from enriching and educating themselves to the point where they might constitute a threat to colonial rule. But from the perspective of the mass audience, the identification of the wealthy, educated pharisees, maginoó and *pinunong bayan* (local leaders) with Christ's tormentors would not fail to have radical implications in actual life. . . .

The most provocative aspect of the pasyon text is the way it speaks about the appearance of a "subversive" figure, Jesus Christ, who attracts mainly the lowly, common people (*taong bayan*), draws them away from their families and their relations of subservience to the maginoó, and forms a brotherhood (*catipunan*) that will proclaim a new era of mankind. The friars must have been bothered occasionally by the political implications of the lowly Christ-figure, but the story could not be altered. . . .

The way that Christ's following multiplies presents quite a contrast to the traditional patterns of Philippine politics. This leader does not offer weapons, money, and security in exchange for loyalty. In fact, his followers must leave all these behind as the apostle Matthew did to his tax office and cash collections. The kind of commitment to the cause that this leader evokes transcends personal consider-ations to the extent that his followers are willing to sacrifice their lives. The much-beloved story of Longinus, the soldier who pierced the side of Jesus, illustrates this. Having witnessed (and been transformed by) the blinding light of the resurrected Christ, Longinus informs the local authorities who, fearing the consequences, entice the other witnesses not to spread the news around.

As might be expected, particularly in a Philippine setting, the soldiers succumb to the bribes. Longinus, however, continues to announce the resurrection of Christ all over town until he is captured. Before he is stabbed to death, he confesses that in the past he was blind, but recent events enlightened (*lumiuanag*) him, showed him the right path (*daang catuiran*), so that he is willing to die as his way of participating in Christ's passion. . . . Jesus Christ in the pasyon text appears as a rather harmless leader of humble origins but he manages to attract a huge following mainly from the "poor and ignorant" class. His twelve lieutenants are said to be neither principales nor ilustrados, nor the leader's relatives. They are simply

'poor and lowly people without worth on earth, ignorant people without any education.'

Yet, the pasyon account continues, these lowly men were charged by Christ with a mission and given special powers to carry it out.

The pasyon abounds with passages suggesting the potential power of the *pobres y ignorantes*, the "poor and ignorant," to use the common ilustrado term for the masses. Whether the pasyon encouraged subservience or defiance, resignation or hope, will always be open to argument. The fact is that its meanings were not fixed, but rather depended on social context. Thus a historical approach is necessary.

A problem in dealing with early peasant movements in the Philippines is figuring out the extent to which they were religious, social, or political. Reflecting upon the pasyon text alone, I cannot see how the above categories can be strictly separated. It is true that many parts of the text exhort the audience to cleanse their souls in anticipation of a heavenly reward; it is equally true that the pasyon as a whole is about salvation. But the most dramatic and memorable parts of the pasyon are those whose meanings overflow into the socio-political situation of the audience. . . . I am not suggesting that the masses drew a one-to-one correspondence between pasyon images and their oppressed condition, although this may in some instances have been the case. What can be safely concluded is that because of their familiarity with such images, the peasant masses were culturally prepared to enact analogous scenarios in real life in response to economic pressure and the appearance of charismatic leaders.

Before the abolition of friar censorship by the republican and American colonial governments, the pasyon was one of the few literary works available to the rural population, and therefore could not fail to shape the folk mind. Its impact derived from the fact that, in the course of time, it co-opted most of the functions of traditional social epics. . . .

The widespread use of the pasyon not only during Holy Week but also on other important times of the year insured that even the illiterate tao was familiar with the general contours of the text. . . . There were other public rituals that taught or reminded the people of the basic themes of the pasyon, the *huling hapunan* (Mass of the Last Supper), the *salubong* (meeting) of Christ and the Virgin Mary, the sermons of the parish priest, and the many processions.

The point of all the rituals was not merely to entertain or dazzle the masses. Undoubtedly there were lively moments, particularly in the *sinakulo*, or staged performance, with its many episodes sprinkled with folk humor. But even these can be interpreted in the general context of narrowing the gap between "biblical time" and human or "everyday time." In traditional Tagalog society, at least, Holy Week was that time of the year when the spiritual and material planes of existence coincided; when, to put it in another way, the people themselves participated in Christ's passion. . . .

The pasyon, then, was not simply sung, heard, or celebrated by the masses in the nineteenth century. It was lived, both individually and socially, during Holy Week and oftentimes beyond it. Furthermore, its meaning went beyond the doctrine of Christ's redemption of man by his passion, death, and resurrection. For traditional Tagalog society, Holy Week was an annual occasion for its own renewal, a time for ridding the loób of impurities (shed like the blood and sweat of flagellants), for dying to the old self and being reborn anew, and, through its many social events, for renewing or restoring ties between members of the community. . . .

Rituals of Compassion and Social Control

James C. Scott

In Sungai Bujur, as in any peasant society, there is a large variety of ritual ties which lie beyond immediate relations of production, and which serve both to create and to signify the existence of a community – one that is more than just an aggregation of producers. Those particular ritual ties which involve gifts and exchanges between rich and poor are sensitive barometers of the vicissitudes of class relations. While they are not, by any means, connected to production relations in some crude mechanical fashion, they are nonetheless sensitive to changes in the realm of production. Using these gifts and exchanges as a valuable window on the transformation of class relations, it will become apparent that as the poor have become increasingly marginal to the growing of paddy, so have they become increasingly marginal to the ritual life of the village.

There have traditionally been three major forms of ritual gift-giving joining the rich and poor of Sungai Bujur. They include what villagers call the *zakat peribadi* or "private" Islamic tithe, *sedekah* or *derma* gifts, and *kenduri* or ritual feasts to which other villagers are invited. All are either required or at least sanctioned by Islamic law as it is understood in the village. After a brief explanation of each form, we will examine how each has changed and how those changes have been experienced by classes in the village.

The *zakat peribadi* is to be distinguished from what most peasants call the "*zakat raja*" – the sultan's or government's *zakat*. The latter is the "official" *zakat*, owed by all but the very smallest cultivators, collected in paddy by an appointed local official (the *amil*) and paid to Kedah's Department of Religious Affairs. Although the proceeds are devoted to specified works of Islamic charity the tithe is generally resented – and widely evaded – by cultivators for its perceived inequities. *Zakat peribadi*, on the other hand, is viewed in a more favourable light because it is not compulsory and because the beneficiaries are local, if not within Sungai Bujur itself. A part of this *zakat peribadi* is collected by the *amil* at the same time as the *zakat raja* and is designated by the giver, according to his or her wishes, as a contribution to the mosque (*zakat mesjid*) in nearby Sungai Limau Dalam, to the village hall (*zakat madrasah*) – which functions as prayer house, religious school room, and meeting place – and/or to the *imam* of the mosque. Private donations are also given personally to the mosque caretaker and to the popular religious teacher whose religious classes include many local children. Collectively, this portion of *zakak peribadi* might be termed gifts for religious services, and it comprises roughly two-thirds of all *zakat peribadi*. The remainder is given to other individuals including especially poorer relatives, neighbors, and friends and wage-workers who have helped with the planting or harvesting. It is this last category alone that might be called redistributive. We are by no means, however, dealing with vast quantities of paddy; the total *zakat peribadi* given out by villagers amounts to less than 2.5% of an average village harvest. Of that amount, the potentially redistributive share is less than 1% of the harvest.

The *zakat* is, of course, one of the five pillars of Islam – a sacred obligation. The religious and social reasoning behind it is best illustrated by the pamphlet distributed by the State Religious Council of Kedah. After noting that Islam does not discourage the faithful from becoming rich, it asserts that the rich have an obligation to share a portion of their wealth with those who are poor and without property, and quotes an injunction from the Koran: "And those who store up gold and silver and do not follow the path of Allah, let them know the sharpest torment". The purpose of the *zakat*, it continues, is not only to discourage stinginess (*sifat-sifat bakhil*) but to promote *social harmony* among the rich and the poor. The *zakat* is accepted by villagers in much the same spirit. They typically say that they give *zakat peribadi* in order to "cleanse [from sin] (*cuci*) their property".

The degree to which property is cleansed by voluntary *zakat* gifts varies enormously in the village. A few substantial property owners are quite generous with *zakat peribadi*, while others give almost nothing. A small number of quite modest peasants give prodigiously, considering their means. Some others give nothing. It should be noted that *zakat* is essentially a transfer of grain among *men*. Thus, with rare exceptions, widows or divorced women who are poor wage-workers receive no *zakat*. The amount of grain which poor villagers receive as *zakat* depends on their reputation, how good the paddy crop has been, and how much they have worked in a particular season. What is notable here is that when the poor receive *zakat*, it is almost entirely from their employers and its payment is rather carefully calculated according to the respectability of the recipient. It functions not only to "cleanse property" but also as a method of labor control and social conformity.

Sedekah and *derma* as forms of alms or contributions are almost interchangeable. Unlike *zakat*, *sedekah* is not tied to the harvest; it is not always paid in paddy; it is as often requested by the needy as given unasked; and it is almost exclusively given to the poor. *Derma* differs only in the sense that it is more often a collection made house-to-house for a charitable purpose – commonly to help a poor family pay funeral expenses. Both *sedekah* and *derma* are seen as "good works" in the context of Islam for which the benefactor, if of pure heart, will be rewarded. In the village context, at least, such gifts are small – for example enough milled rice (*beras*) for a few meals.

The third major form of what might be considered "charity" are the *kenduri* or feasts which constitute the basis of much of the village's ritual life. Unlike *zakat* or *sedekah* they are collective rituals marked by both prayer and a communal meal which the sponsoring family provides to invited guests. *Kenduri* may be held for a host of reasons but the most common, roughly in order of frequency and importance are: marriage feasts, feasts to pray for the dead, circumcision feasts, pregnancy feasts, cradle feasts, infant hair-cutting feasts, house moving feasts, new house feasts and feasts for a fulfilled wish, often for a child of the sex desired. Both rich and poor sponsor *kenduri*, but the rich are naturally expected to sponsor them more often, more lavishly, and for a larger number of guests. Expenses, especially for sponsors of modern means, are partly met by donations in kind or cash by guests, although poorer guests may avoid this by helping with the food preparation. For the village poor, *kenduri* are virtually the only occasions when meat is eaten. Ritual feasts of this kind are the traditional means by which the well-to-do validate their status by conspicuous consumption in which their friends, neighbors, relatives, and often the entire village is invited to share.

When any form of charity is discussed by villagers, there is virtual unanimity for the view that, as a species of social relations, it is threatened with extinction. Even the well-to-do farmers are in accord on this point, although many of them hasten to exclude themselves individually from the charge, while pointing their finger at those who are even better-off. The village headman, Haji Hassan, says the decline in charity began with double-cropping. Kodit, a fairly well-off tenant, gives voice to the general consensus when he claims, "The rich are arrogant (*sombong*); they don't take [the plight of] the poor seriously; [they're] cheap with *sedakah* and [they're] reluctant to give it." The village poor often put the facts bluntly: "The rich don't give anything to the poor".

There is also a consensus about the decline of *kenduri*, albeit with one important historical exception. For initially, the new profits of double-cropping in 1972 unleashed a memorable burst of feast-giving which was unprecedented in Sungai Bujur. Nearly everyone, including small tenants and landless laborers, took advantage of their new-found prosperity to celebrate rituals they could not have afforded earlier. The *kenduri* of the poorer villagers were necessarily more modest, but even they were able, for a time at least, to emulate the ritual decencies previously denied all but the middle and rich peasantry. The poor became, if only briefly, full participants in the ritual life which helps to define citizenship in this small community. After this short period of euphoria, both the frequency and scale of feasts have, by all accounts, been sharply reduced. The reason for the curtailing of ritual feasts by poor peasants is obvious; since 1976 at the latest, their income has become more precarious. For richer peasants, the decline in the quality and number of *kenduri* is more a question of attitude than of resources.

The affluent farmers in Sungai Bujur are by no means tongue-tied when it comes to explaining why so little *zakat peribadi* or *sedekah* is given to the poor. They make, in effect, three arguments, any one of which would be sufficient to justify their position. The first is nearly a point of law, inasmuch as the non-handicapped, working poor do not fall into any one of the eight categories of recipients who, according to Islamic regulations, are eligible to receive *zakat* gifts. Sa'idin, a literate landowner much given to quoting the rules, claims that if these rules were followed the rich might still be able to offer *zakat peribadi* to such poor, but that most poor would be wrong in accepting it.

A second argument is that there is virtually no one in the village who is truly in need of charity. Thus Haji Ibrahim, the richest man in the immediate vicinity, asks rhetorically, "Why give *zakat* to those who are hard up; they have land, they grow paddy like us". We are, he implies, all on basically the same footing here and hence there is no need for *zakat* or *sedekah*. It is true, of course, that most of the poor in Sungai Bujur do own or rent riceland, however tiny its size, and that fact allows Haji Ibrahim to make something of an abstraction of the difference between those who rent one *relong* and those who own twenty. Another rich villager, Lebai Awang, avails himself of the same argument, and adds that since those who thresh his paddy are paid and usually have some land of their own, any further gifts would be "too much". If one accepts this logic, then it becomes pertinent to wonder why the practice of giving *zakat peribadi* to wage laborers was so widespread until at least 1975. Why, if this logic is applicable today, was it not applied earlier? The anomaly, I believe, is resolved by considering *zakat peribadi* as, in part, a system of labor control which was necessary when harvest labor was scarce but is no longer required now that combine-harvesters are easily available. Ismail Bakar, a landless laborer, captures what has occurred in precisely these terms:

> The well-off gave out *zakat peribadi* so that they could call forth the work (*panggil kerja*). Poor people went everywhere. They called and we went. Now we go even without *zakat peribadi* because we need the work.

It is certainly possible that wealthy villagers always considered the *zakat* given to harvest workers as an illegitimate imposition – perhaps even as a form of labor blackmail. The difference may simply be that now, thanks to the combine-harvester, they are able to make their opposition to *zakat peribadi* stick.

The third and last line of defence against *zakat* to harvest workers is one which is familiar by now – the claim that many, if not most, of the village poor are not fitting objects for charity.

Prosperous villagers invariably mention the poor villagers whom they consider more or less disreputable to explain the decline in *zakat* and *sedekah*. The charges include lying, cheating and laziness. To the extent that this category begins to include most of the village poor the problem of charity is thus solved at one stroke. Giving help to such people, they imply, would only reward and therefore encourage such behavior. And here too we can see that the practice of *zakat peribadi* serves the purpose of social control as well as that of labor control. The rich put the poor on notice that only those who conform closely to their standard of correct conduct are eligible for their largesse. The only notable exception to this pattern is when death intervenes and even the poorest villager is accorded the minimal decencies.

As for *kenduri*, there are still a few well-off villagers who have a reputation for not scrimping. Hassan Osman and the headman, Haji Hassan, in particular, rarely let a season go by without a sizeable *kenduri* to which most of the village is invited. Other substantial villagers typically admit, sometimes with a trace of embarrassment, that they have become more clever (*bijak, cerdik*) about feasts to avoid wasting their money.

The potential beneficiaries of *zakat* gifts, alms, and feasts have, as one would imagine, a quite different view. There is, of course, the lament for the loss of income they and their families have suffered; each of them can recount exactly what they have lost in grain and from whom. But that is by no means the whole story. There is also anger and bitterness, made all the more galling by the fact that their losses have come at a time when prosperous villagers have been reaping the profits of double-cropping. The blame, as usual, is personalized; it is laid at the door of the rich, whose desire for further profit has led them to repudiate their obligations to their poorer neighbours. When the poor say, as they frequently do, that the rich are becoming stingier, it is above all the refusal of charity they have in mind.

There is also the *humiliation* of asking for *sedekah*, and occasionally for *zakat*, and being refused – an experience that is far more common today. Aziz, who is after all one of the more "reputable" poor, speaks with more feeling about this humiliation than about the grain he is denied. Before the harvest last season, when work was scarce and his family had nearly run out of rice and cash, he asked some of his usual employers for loans of rice as an advance on future wages. The results were meagre.

> I felt embarrassed asking friends [for help]. It's a pity; it reaches the point where I have to go every day to ask. I'm ashamed.

When his mother died, he had to ask for help with funeral expenses. Halimah, with few resources of her own, gave him $M 150 immediately, but Pak Haji Mat Isa, the richest man in Sungai Bujur, for whom he often worked, gave him nothing.

> Poor people can't complain. When I'm sick or need work, I may have to ask him again. I am angry in my heart.

Here then is the bitterness of a man who has decided to conduct himself according to the rules imposed by the rich – to be available, discreet, and deferential – unlike his brother Razak and unlike others of the poor who rarely ask for help. Aziz's deference clearly costs him much swallowed bile, which is only compounded by the rebuffs he receives when he asks for the small favors to which he believes his good conduct entitles him.

The village poor are caught in a situation where the old assumptions are no longer valid. Before, they could expect *zakat* from employers and ask for *sedekah* or advance wages with a reasonable expectation of sympathy. Now they may ask, but possibly at the price of a humiliating rebuff. A gift refused in this fashion is not simply grain foregone but it is, above all, a stark social signal that the relationship between rich and poor, which the requests for gifts assume to be in force, has been unilaterally declared null and void. The rich have given notice that they are no longer responsible for the pressing needs of the village poor. Small wonder then that the poor should read this behavior as stinginess, as selfishness, and as betrayal.

In the decline of the feast-giving cycle in Sungai Bujur, the poor see the same symptoms of social withdrawal and selfishness by the well-to-do. No longer, says Ismail Bakar, are there feasts which last the whole night and at which three or four cows are eaten. Instead, the rich "think about money; they just want to invest their money". The rich, he concludes, "think only of this world".

In this last comment by Ishak we can capture the religious tone of his accusation. To think *beyond* this world is to think of Allah's judgement (*hukum Allah*), and thus to be generous and sympathetic to those who are less fortunate. This perspective is reflected in the prestige enjoyed by those few comfortable villagers who continue to honor the *kenduri* tradition. Nor, according to village folk beliefs among the poor, is the punishment for a failure of generosity confined to Allah's judgement. Aziz, along with others, believes that generosity with feasts, *zakat*, and *sedekah*, serves to protect rich people against such misfortunes as accidents and illnesses. This is why, he says, those who make the pilgrimage to Mecca always give a *kenduri* before setting out. When I wonder out loud how this applies to Pak Haji Mat Isa, whose tight-fistedness is renowned but who appears to enjoy robust health, Aziz reminds me immediately of Mak Haji's long stay in the hospital, her fall down the steps, and Pak Haji's recurring back trouble. All of these misfortunes, he implies, are a sign of Allah's displeasure. It is hardly far-fetched to read into this interpretation an attempt, albeit feeble, by the poor to exert their own modest form of social control over the rich. Lacking the economic or coercive sanctions to influence the behavior of the wealthy, they must necessarily turn to less mundane forms of persuasion. Nor is it far-fetched to suggest that there is only a *very short step* between believing that the miserly rich will be punished in this world and the next, and actually *wishing on them* the misfortunes and judgements which, by their conduct, they have called down upon their own heads.

Ideological Commodity Production

Andrew Turton

. . . What might be the non-state ideological institutions of the dominant classes? No attempt will be made here to provide an inventory, but some indications may be given. A number of social forms combine a possible "dominant" aspect with a greater degree of potential autonomy, for example: some "non-governmental" development, educational, religious and welfare associations, professional groups, privately owned media and publishers, some kinship and domestic structures, the more so in the case of ethnic minorities. It can be argued that such institutions serve, or serve as, dominant ideology even more effectively because their domination effect is concealed as such; on the other hand, there may be greater room within these institutions for alternative and oppositional ideas to develop. However, the most important of all is apparently neither "ideological" nor "repressive", nor even institutional in the obvious sense: namely the capitalist system of production, exchange, and consumption itself, with all its organizational structures, agencies, media, etc. In an institutional sense they include the more substantially economic associations such as chambers of commerce, and the larger producers' and exporters' associations, and the less substantial but more ideological ones such as Rotary and Lions Clubs etc. (cf. Gramsci, 1971: 286). But I want to suggest the need to look beyond such formal structures to the processes of inculcation of new patterns and ideas, norms and values, of work and consumption, ideas which can be conceptualized as being simultaneously both forces of production and ideology (see Thompson, 1977:18; 1978:84).

Time (clock time, money time) and money have become the measure, if not of all things, then of much that they formerly had no power to control. In the small and rather remote upland valley of northern Thailand where I worked in the late 1960s and early 1970s, wage labor on any scale had only been recently introduced. Clocks had for some time been local prestige items (grandfather clocks had caught on among the aristocracy in the nineteenth century) and watches were only just beginning to be seen as other than jewelry, especially when the pawnbroker gave so little for them. Town squares were beginning to be graced with clock towers, sometimes presented by the local Rotary Club or equivalent. The old system of reckoning the dawn hours by the successive crowing of cocks was beginning to be faintly ridiculed, and giving way to phrases like "before the bus leaves" or "after the dawn market closes", though purely village meetings were still called for "after breakfast/supper", a leeway of an hour or two. By 1980, in the same area, experience of working in Bangkok metal factories, even in the Middle East on construction sites, was quite commonplace; the rhythm of buffalo ploughing was inadequate for double cropping; and festivals were sometimes not held "for lack of time". We could call this the "lengthening of the working year". Villagers are certainly conscious of the lengthening of the working day, including night shifts on factory farms, and of intensification of work within it.

Consider patterns of consumption. Advertising, especially by the transnational companies and their subsidiaries and agents, is very fierce, epitomized in rural areas by travelling sales promotion teams in fleets of vans. In earlier years, before the feeder roads were constructed, they had often provided villagers with their first experience of cinematography, images of foreign lands, and the ways of life of urban classes. Now they demonstrate, if they do not sell, not just toothpaste, pills and powders, but electrical food processors and vacuum cleaners in villages without electricity. Capitalist ideological elements may be present long before the local implantation of capitalist relations of production. There is occasional resistance too to the new consumerism. The cost of bottled sauces, now a "must", or jeans, or bottled drinks is frequently discussed in tones of exasperation. A few resist bottled drinks in favor of the many traditional beverages (including alcoholic ones), or object to monosodium glutamate on health grounds. Whole villages have been known to resist the advent of electricity, not as such, but because it is perceived as encouraging new and expensive "needs", not just lighting, but fans, television, refrigerators etc.; and with television comes more gambling (on boxing) and more money spent in the local drink shop. In local terms this consumerism can be criticized in the light of Buddhist values, as fostering "greed" and so leading to unhappiness. At another level we might refer to Marcuse's concept of the production of "repressive needs" (Marcuse, 1964: 246). Also Habermas's proposition about the ideological function of consumerism, albeit in the context of advanced capitalist society, is of some relevance here:

> The less the cultural system is capable of producing adequate motivations for politics, the educational system, and the occupational

system, the more must scarce meaning be replaced by consumable value (Habermas, 1976: 93).

The pharmaceutical field is one of several that require detailed study in this context. the unregulated over-importing, over-stocking, and marketing of drugs in Thailand is now well known; in many cases Thailand is used as a testing ground for dangerous drugs. Apart from the general effects of commoditization, high prices, down-grading traditional medicines etc., many drugs have a direct effect on production: from analgesic, anti-depressant, addictive compounds, which are the opiates of those not already on opiates, to expensive ways of consuming caffeine and glucose. There is a widespread use of amphetamines and other stimulants, whether taken voluntarily, sometimes as part of the pay packet, or surreptitiously put into the workers' food or drink in mine, factory, large farm etc. It is noteworthy that many of the efforts of poor farmers to set up their own associations, in conditions where political organization is most difficult, take the form of medical self-help projects, combining education about the risks of some modern drugs, wholesale purchasing of basic drugs, and selective revival of traditional medicines and practices. In this they are often helped by some of the alternative developmental organizations, recently formed consumer groups, and some concerned sectors of Thailand's highly advanced, but unequally distributed medical system.

Mental ill-health can also be seen to some extent as an effect of ideological domination. In an important recent work, Irvine [1982] has shown how villagers perceive the connections between health and the new economic irrationality, for example in their use of the terms "economics madman" (*ba setthakit*) and "money madness" (*ba ngoen ba kham*) used, in preference to available supernatural concepts, to refer to those, mainly young men, who succumb to anxieties brought about by economic hardships.

The supernatural itself has become commoditized. Of course non-capitalist commercialization and exploitation still exist, for example, the purchase of ecclesiastical office, and the "requisitioning of the labor of the poor" (*wat ken raengngan khon con*), as one villager put it, by the temple or rather its controlling committee of notables. A revealing example of the latter occurred in a northern village where the temple committee proposed an increase in cash contributions, and a change in the ratio between richer and poorer – already an index of locally perceived differentiation – from 5:3:1 to 6:4:2 (an increase of 20% for the wealthiest and 100% for the poorest). But the poorer villagers were alert to this kind of trick, and natural justice and plain arithmetic prevailed.

Let me give some indication of what I mean by commoditization of religion, its incorporation into the circuits of capital. Some temples have become small capitalist enterprises in their own right, and some monks are individual entrepreneurs. One monk, now deceased, whom I knew, ran a bus company while a district ecclesiastical officer. These and others may have all the personal consumer goods of high ranking officials and businessmen: cars, bank accounts etc. Whereas formerly everything required by monks and the temple could be locally manufactured – even books – now almost everything has to be bought from specialist urban suppliers. Temples are destroyed, and with them fine local craftwork and skills, not just because of "traditional" values of making merit by rebuilding, but because high pressure entrepreneurs tout design books and credit systems. The organization of festivals and fundraising may now be taken on by commercial contractors. In an example given me, the company guarantees a gross 80,000 baht to the temple; the villagers provide the labor (estimated cost 30,000); and the company nets 200,000. Monks may give their services directly for the ideological furtherance of capitalist causes, for fees. Sulak (1981:94) illustrates this, and the wider theme:

> The capitalist system regulates everything nowadays, not only the economic system, but also society, politics and religion; so that monks who go to chant [for example not only at funerals etc. but at openings and product launches organized by banks, oil companies etc.] earn more than merchants going about their ordinary business. They decline to chant if they are not offered 1000 baht; *Caokhun* and *Somdet* [senior ecclesiastical officials] get 5000 and 10,000 baht a time. The new economy intervenes. As I am always saying, those fans [strictly for preaching behind, and also used as badges of rank within the Thai *sangha*] which are presented to the monks, are advertising gimmicks persuading the people to accept the capitalist system and the power system. . . .

Part VI

Ethnic Histories and Minority Identities

Introduction

Vast areas of Southeast Asia, especially mountainous and forested regions, are home to more or less indigenous minority peoples. They are often referred to as "tribal" or "hill people" people, which can be a misleading term since many have not had the degree or kind of overall political organization or localization which the term usually connotes, while some have aspired to nationhood. The term also encourages unwarranted assumptions of "primitiveness". Most have long histories – centuries, even millennia – of varying degrees of incorporation and marginalization, dependence and independence, adaptation and resistance in relations with dominant outsiders, notably lowland states. Some have striven successfully to maintain their identity and distinctness; others have had new, sometimes unwelcome identities imposed upon them; yet others have constructed new or wider identities and forms of social organization in the face of changing situations. The following studies – unlike those earlier anthropological reports which negated history and depicted static, isolated views of individual cultures – reveal the historical dimensions of current predicaments of "development". They also allow insight into the depth and resilience of the historical "cultural experience" accumulated and deployed in the course of past and present struggles.

The issue of the "terms of incorporation" of such minorities into contemporary states and "national" societies, is particularly acute, and the costs of "development" often high. Insofar as they are now peasants within larger political and economic systems, they suffer some of the worst conditions of the poorest sections of the peasantry as a whole. Insofar as they are distinct linguistic, cultural and social groups, they suffer additional social and cultural disparagement and disadvantage, as well as economic marginalization. Many would readily accept social and economic integration on equal terms, but resist exploitation and policies of cultural assimilation. Given their ecological location, most practise forms of swidden agriculture, an extensive use of land which can be efficient and conservationist if

211

there is space and freedom to operate systematically. But this use of land – indeed their very occupation of large, sometimes geographically peripheral, tracts of land – is widely seen by state planners and developers as posing a threat to national resources, national development, and national security. Ironically, minorities receive misplaced blame, while the hills are increasingly occupied by lowland farmers, mining and timber companies, plantation owners, etc. responding to conflicting economic pressures and priorities. The latter are likely to have far fewer scruples in their management of natural resources. The economic dilemma – in some cases catastrophe – for the minorities, is compounded by political, legal and other forms of social discrimination at state and local official levels.

Alting von Geusau analyzes the long experience of being a vulnerable minority of the Akha on the margins of Chinese, Shan and now Thai states. They have reached the "end of the road" in their search for land and a desired "middle way" between extremes of isolation and incorporation. They are faced with critical depletion of natural resources, lost to industrialized processes of extraction, road building, forestry schemes and encroachment by lowland farmers. Tragic changes in their way of life are not new to the Akha. Their "cultural experience", rehearsed in songs, stories and rituals, reveals a realistic, "dialectical" understanding of the fluctuations in their social fortunes and economic well-being, in their varying dependence on stronger, majority groups, and in their ecological location. Their traditions link contemporary events with both cosmic processes and historical memories. They demonstrate a flexibility and adaptability of thought and practical solutions, which counter views held of them – as of many other minorities – as fundamentally conservative, bound by religion, historically isolated and technologically stagnant.

Like the Akha, the Hmong are relatives newcomers to Thailand, but have a long history of contention with Chinese states. Tapp deals here with a specific problem of economic development: the production of opium. The Hmong are only one of many ethnic groups who have long grown opium for mainly medicinal uses. They were encouraged for more than a century by colonial and other governments to increase production of opium, variously for export by government monopolies or for import substitution. Opium taxes and profits constituted large proportions of state revenues and early capital accumulation. Only for the past three decades have they borne the brunt of criticism for producing an illegal crop. But as the Hmong say: "Opium doesn't go looking for money; money comes looking for opium". The first stage of marketing involves local warlords and KMT (Kuomintang) remnants, some of whom have fulfilled counter-insurgency roles on behalf of Thai police and army. Little effort is made to restrict these middlemen and their local official allies; and half-hearted programs of crop destruction, crop substitution, and resettlement have almost entirely failed.

The Kalinga of Northern Luzon, Philippines, are one of many highland peoples whose economic and political development has been distorted by colonial irruptions. Magannon, himself a Kalinga, gives an account of the way in which highland cultures have been downgraded and separated from a generalized lowland Filipino culture. Contemporary Kalinga historical consciousness is grounded in their experience and values of centuries of existence in autonomous village communities, in the practice of a highly developed form of irrigated rice cultivation on terraced fields, and their continuous and fierce resistance to integration, assimilation, and the plunder of their environment. At the same time, they assert their claims to participate equally and responsibly in the construction of a more inclusive, equitable, and self-directed national society.

The Iban of Sarawak, East Malaysia, are a people who appear to have retained much of their traditional culture and ecological integrity, and have only recently become involved on any scale in a cash crop economy, alongside their subsistence swidden agriculture. However, Uchibori argues, their incorporation into the paternalistic and idiosyncratic state of the British "Rajah" Brookes fundamentally altered their social world and conditions of existence. The Brooke state had a deliberate policy of insulating the Iban way of life from the capitalist world economy, but integrated them nonetheless into a colonial state as part of the coercive apparatus of that state, providing military services and taxes. In the process the previously dispersed Iban acquired a sense of Iban identity, but were prevented from developing this into a stronger sense of ethnic community, let alone nationhood. Their continued practice of swidden agriculture is seen as a constrained response to their lack of capital and late arrival in the market economy: they are "trapped in the impasse of an involuted subsistence economy".

The Interiorizations of a Perennial Minority Group

Leo Alting von Geusau

It is a known fact that many of the "hill tribes" found on the Southeast Asian subcontinent have not always, during their history as ethno-linguistic groups, been living in the mountains. Thousands of years of migrations, predominantly southwards, punctuated by struggles in fertile valleys for power over resources, for labor and water, continually changed the ethno-linguistic situation. Former pre-state (that is, tribal) valley dwellers were often forced into less accessible and often less attractive higher areas. But also the inhabitants of valley chiefdoms, kingdoms, and even empires, which once seemed to have established their power firmly over soil, water, and people, and to have anchored their ancestries firmly in heaven, have made their way up into the mountainous jungles, and often back to a pre-state, non-class-stratified tribal existence. Not only cross-sections of these societies, but also segments, like defeated armies and dispossessed peasants, groups without a chance of economic and cultural integration into expanding and unifying valley kingdoms, either joined existing groups or just became highlanders, more independent of markets, armies, and tax collectors than those they left behind. Some of them were able to re-establish power in the form of chiefdoms or warlordships over, or at least in protection against, neighboring valley peoples or fellow highlanders; those who failed to re-establish power had to accept some kind of dependency on more differentiated and powerful economic, social and political forces in the valleys, or their allies in the mountains. This certainly means that most hill tribes cannot be called "primitives" in the current sense of the word, and that most of them have, if not remnants of former literacy, in any case, a cultural experience and memory of remarkable depth, only comparable to those Latin American Indians, who are the remote descendants of the Incas and Aztecs.

Because of their minority situation and relative isolation over a long period of time, many mountain cultures have a greater consistency and time depth than most Western, modern Thai, Burmese, or Laotian lowland cultures. Some bring us in touch with the pre-Han and pre-Tao strata of cultures from Chinese territory, or with the pre-Buddhist strata from Tibet. And in spite of osmosis with valley cultures and diffusion of culture traits, there are greater differences between the Tibeto-Burmese Lisu, Lahu, and Akha social organization, material culture, songs, ceremonial texts, and language, than, say, between the Dutch, the German, and the Swedish traditions, belonging equally to one linguistic family. One of the similarities of the hill tribes of northern Thailand is, however, the experience of being an ethnic minority for a very long time. When I say a very long time, that might vary from group to group from 300 to 3000 years. Also the concept "minority group" is very ambiguous. Without going into a lengthy discussion here, it can be said that all hill tribes of northern Thailand in one way or another have for a long period of time not only been smaller groups, continually confronted with larger ones, but, more fundamentally, they have been vulnerable, generally non-stratified groups, which for production and for reproduction of their societies risked being dependent at any time on ethnically different, more powerful, larger, highly and pyramidically class-stratified valley societies. A stratified society has classes of soldiers, artisans, peasants, and traders. In a non-stratified society this specialization does not exist, at least not in the same way. Every family has to participate in cultivation, hunting, defence, construction technology, and so on. The only division of labor is between men and women, elders and younger. This makes the pre-state people more universal, and specialization less exclusive, but it makes tribal people weaker.

Being a minority is not a constant in the history of many hill tribes, that is, being a minority was not felt the same way all the time. We can, for instance, say about the Loloish hill tribes of northern Thailand (that is, the Lisu, the Akha, and the Lahu) that at least they were in one way or another part of the so-called Lolo kingdoms scattered between Tibet and Szechwan and the southern Yunnanese borders of China, and that their situation as a minority has gradually deteriorated. Their history since then seems to be that of vulnerable pre-state societies, faced originally with small, but stronger, valley kingdoms, but increasingly with even stronger and bigger national political, economic, and ethnic systems or migrating groups. The gradual Hanification of China and the migrations, for instance, of the Thai groups southwards were a consequence of what was already a centuries-old process, long before mercantilist and colonial powers made their impact after the sixteenth century. Colonial unification of Burma and Indo-China, radical nationaliz-ation of China in the last few centuries, and the recent birth of modern states and modernizing economies of different ideologies, created a situation of increasing inequality between hill dwellers and valley majorities in the search for resources and political power, decreasing the chances of integration into national cultures, economies, and political systems. Because of the quickly proceeding exhaustion of natural resources (particularly the forests), and the impossibility of moving either southwards downhill to the water or higher up into forested mountains, as they had in former times, hill tribes are now at the end of their long journey, confronted with an increasing disparity between their collapsing economies and national economies, between their own and valley political systems, between national discriminatory mythologies about them and the realities of their lives and symbolico-mythological systems, and between their own realistic ideas about the solution of their problems and the often unrealistic national or international planning for "development" of the hill areas. This last phase of the minority problem has a parallel in many other modernizing countries all over the world. It also makes the dichotomy, valley majority – highland minority, obsolete insofar as the powers precipitating the process of marginalization of the hill tribes, involve international as well as national economic interests operating from commercial and political centres far away, whereas the immediate valley population is often itself impoverished, and because of that has developed a more predatory attitude towards highland resources (natural and human) than in earlier times.

The Tibeto-Burman hill tribes currently living in northern Thailand have this in common: that in a known past they have not been able to build up political or territorial power, at least not for a substantial period of time. It seems, therefore, that being a perennial minority has become, in different ways, part of their cultural experience. By "cultural experience" I do not only mean people's memory as it has been crystalized in stories of origin, mythology, songs, and ceremonial recitations, and in the whole of what I call the symbolico-mythological complex. Cultural experience has also contributed to giving shape and form to modes of production and reproduction, the preferred ecological niche, kinship, and technology, as well as to the manner in which outside relations are handled.

The almost 19,000 Akha people now living in northern Thailand are only a small part of the estimated half million Akha speakers, spread over Yunnan in China, the eastern Shan state in Burma, upper Laos, and northern Thailand. Although there is a great variety of dialects, mythology, and material culture in linguistic subgroups, Akha culture as a whole shows a remarkable unity, consistency, and complexity, built up over two and probably more millennia. This is even more remarkable since the Akha, after they were forced out of their city-state in Yunnan, in their own counting about thirty generations ago, seem to have been consistently egalitarian in their social organization, and attach much value to individual, family, and village autonomy.

Limiting ourselves to Thailand, Akha immigrations are much more recent than commonly believed. The first Akha settlements near the northern Burmese-Thai border date from 1903. Until well into the 1950s the number of Akha remained in the few thousands; the numbers who came were never large, and some preferred to go back to Burma where the soil was believed to be better. Political development in Burma, particularly after 1960, rapidly increased the number of Akha refugees, from 6270 in 1964 to 18,863 in 1979. There are at this moment a reported 136 Akha villages in Thailand.

With most parts of the upper north almost completely deforested, the people are left largely without a new cash crop to serve as a substitute for the traditional cotton and peppers. Moreover, the yearly yields of nutritious hill rice have steadily declined, and the protein intake has also dropped below the level of needs, which threatens an imminent increase in both mortality and vulnerability to infection, for which neither their elaborate traditional medical system nor modern medicine have a real solution. In response to the diminishing fertility of the soil and continuing deforestation, the people in larger Akha villages, unable to move away to less populated areas because they lack the status of citizenship, are forced to segment into smaller and smaller communities. This, and the construction of new roads, has made them very vulnerable to bandits from stronger lowland and highland groups. Although the control of the Border Patrol Police has improved lately, quite large quantities of cash, silver, cattle, and terraced land have been taken from them in the last ten to fifteen years.

A lack of hope for a better future, and the considerable difficulties of either assimilating or integrating into the national Thai culture, have contributed to both the high rates of opium addiction and a breakdown in the traditional value system of *Àkhàzán* in several communities. Obvious poverty in some of the more accessible communities has certainly not helped improve a negative public image and mythology, which has deteriorated over the last ten years. The Akha are also much more frequently subject to adverse comment than other groups. In general this is due to a lack of information about Akha culture, which in turn is partly a function of the remoteness of their villages, and the fact that they arrived in Thailand more recently than other hill peoples.

The poverty of a growing number of Akha villages and their

increasingly marginal situation, particularly in the upper north, is not unique to the Akha but is a phenomenon to which several Lisu, Lahu, Hmong, Yao, and an increasing number of Thai villagers, in similar ecological, economic, and demographic circumstances, are also subject. Just as the forebears of these groups were likely to have been prosperous in times when economic, political, and demographic conditions were better, so also many Akha fathers and grandfathers who are now poor were once wealthy. Villages that are now somewhat apathetic and poor were often well-off and hardworking as recently as ten or fifteen years ago. On the other hand, there are still a certain number of relatively prosperous Akha communities, due either to the availability of forest, the presence of alternative sources of cash income (near the border, this means, in a few cases only, the growing of opium, or alliance with politically stronger groups like the Kuomintang), or help from outsiders, such as missionaries.

With respect to this economic situation, the Akha do not differ very much from other groups. A selected summary of a report on developments in Thailand's economy, made by the World Bank's survey mission in 1978, shows clearly the process of gradual impoverishment of whole areas, among them the upper north. We can expect that highlanders who often do not have citizenship and its attendant privileges, and who have vulnerable social structures, would be the first to experience the effects of that process. Input of funds (along with the work of increasingly skilled and dedicated personnel) by the Social Welfare Department, particularly through the Hill Tribe Development and Welfare Center in the Mae Chan area, has not been able to reverse a trend that has resulted from the character of national political and economic structures, the growth of demographic pressure, and the exhaustion of resources.

Within this general process of the deterioration in the position of the greater part of the highlander population, some ethnic minority groups react differently from others to crisis situations. Such reactions are based upon what I call their cultural experience, as perennial minority groups. I will concentrate on this aspect of the problem.

It is the intention of the following study to investigate the dense and highly formalized traditional system prescribing the Akha way of life, called *Àkhàzáŋ*, depository of their cultural experience. I will particularly try to explore those aspects of *Àkhàzáŋ* that are the result of their long-standing minority situation. . . . A characteristic of *Àkhàzáŋ* is that it includes the whole of Akha life at all levels, in other words, the whole of what American anthropology calls "culture". It describes when, where, and how forest has to be cleared and burned; rice and vegetables have to be planted and harvested; hunting by traps or driving have to be performed; villages and houses have to be founded or built; husbandry tasks have to be taken care of; game and animals have to be slaughtered and divided; food has to be cooked; children have to be conceived and brought up; and transactions have to be managed. *Àkhàzáη* also contains prescriptions indicating how to relate to many different categories of groups and persons within the Akha milieu, including family, lineage, and clan, in matters concerning marriage, penal and judiciary rules, as well as outsiders. . . .

In *Àkhàzáη* most behaviour seems so much described that a dividing line between ritual and non-ritual behavior is sometimes hard to draw. Nor is there in the very realistic Akha cosmology a clear line between sacred and profane. The sacred is not really sacred in the widely accepted sense of a *mysterium tremendum et fascinosum*, nor is there anything profane in the sense of only having to do with secular affairs. There is a dividing line between the living and the dead, between humans and spirits, but once they all lived together, and then separated only because they were stealing from each other. Otherwise, humans and spirits (villages and the ancestor villages) are perfect mirror images of each other. . . .

The main concern in *Àkhàzáη* is not with the past as past, but with linking human events to cosmic processes and cycles. The songs literally speak of "openings", where men enter cosmic cycles through ceremonies and recitations, a linkage through which mundane human events, such as the performance of tasks like planting rice, hunting, and gathering at crucial moments, are synchronized with favorable ecological and cosmic conditions, and by which these are manipulated. Everything in cosmic space and time is interrelated, from the crowing of the rooster to the rising of the sun, from the concerts of cicadas to the emerging rice. So also the human word is related to its significatum, the symbol to its meaning. A great deal of *Àkhàzáη* is actually devoted to a meticulous articulation of the harmony of the human microcosmos and its harmonious links with ecological and macroscosmic processes, as much as with their interpretation. A great deal of time is spent determining the right time (in terms of good days and bad days, good months and bad months, etc.) and place (wrong or right spot) for all human activities. Errors can bring hazards, and a series of taboos and an intricate etiquette prevent major catastrophes. . . .

One could almost expect that flexibility and adaptability to continuous change would be characteristic of such a small, intimate society, where relations to house, land, utensils, animals, and neighbors are not of long duration. Perhaps it is largely because of the "semi-nomadic" nature of swiddening itself, and the obvious transience of the human condition. Houses are mostly built out of bamboo, which quickly decays. Mortality rates for people and animals alike are high. Then there are the natural and human hazards endemic to life in the highlands: climate and pests; bandits; infringements from both majority groups and stronger minority groups; armies and administrators from the valley. As far back as anybody can remember, troubles caused by these elements have always been a part of life. Here a Heraclitean attitude is evident: "Everything flows, nothing remains the same". Perhaps their Lolo ancestors knew the *yin* and *yang* of Tao, if not as a philosophy, at least as an attitude. The stable and static aspects of Akha cosmology, then, appear as a countervailing construction to offset the high incidence of change and of the tragic and unexpected.

The texts of their songs, myths and rituals confirm this interpretation. . . . A detailed study of their content counters a widely held myth, especially favored by urban-based "developers" from Bangkok, New York, and Chiang Mai, who have somehow taken it into their heads to propagate a mythology of their own which assumes that the Akha are more conservative than other ethnic groups, and less willing to accept agricultural improvements because of their "religion". This is far from true. They are interested and willing to accept beneficial changes, but only if they believe that drudgery will be reduced, that some profit will accrue, that they will be treated like equals by those who advise a change, and that they can trust their benefactors not to exploit them.

There are several *Àkhàzáŋ* stories which, because of the considerable climatic differences among southern China, northern Burma, and Thailand, record quite radical changes in the past relating to the whole timing of planting and harvesting. Because of the need for cash to supplement their incomes, *Àkhàzáŋ* was changed to allow the Akha to work as wage laborers on the lowlands of Burma between August and November. Old Akha texts very accurately report why and from whom they learned, much earlier in history, to build the type of house they have now (the Mountain Khmer), to create the patterns on their jackets (the Mountain Shan), to cultivate tobacco (the Chinese), etc. *Záŋ* thus seems quite open to change and innovation.

Oppositions and Contradictions Built into Zán

The basic humanistic realism of *Àkhàzán* seems, however, to have taken one more step in the adaptation to continuous change and to extreme vulnerability to human and natural ecological hazards, that is, in the adaptation to a life in which the contingency of human existence is continuously manifest. *Zán* does not accommodate the contradictions of human existence by constructing an idealized after-life free from pain, suffering, disease, and poverty. Neither is there a Utopian eschatology, that is, a future stage in history in which "all tears will disappear from all faces", nor an idealized invisible reality behind the visible one. There are hardly any traces of messianic or vitalistic movements so far, and even the past (that is, the time of ancestors) is looked up to with great realism, as we will see.

Àkhàzán, on the contrary, developed a system in which reality is seen in the form of present oppositions and contradictions. This also means that in *Àkhàzán*, after all, the static and cyclical does not prevail when interpreting the macrocosmos and the microcosmos, that is, nature and society; rather, the dialectical movement prevails. In other words, *Àkhàzán* is used to interpret reality, not as a collection of binaries but as movement between extremes, in which man has to try, all the time, to reach middle ground. In the Akha view of reality not everything of course is shaped in binary form. Akha are neither structuralists, who like binary games, nor philosophers. There obviously has not been a *class* of philosophers or priests reflecting in a more systematic way on the philosophy implicit in *Àkhàzán*. They use the simile of a girl or boy thinking too much about the ideal wife or husband, and not marrying at all in the end, to express their doubts about thinking as an occupation. . . .

I want now to concentrate on some contradictions and oppositions in *Àkhàzán* which seem to relate to the Akha experience of fluctuations as a swiddening minority group. We are not dealing here with word games, but with basic and often tragic events affecting the Akha economy, their ecological niche, and their social organization. Among those oppositions which seem to be present in *Àkhàzán*, the first is that between *wealth* and *poverty*; the second that between the Akha as a *minority* group, faced in various ways with strong *majority* groups. The third opposition is that between *uphill* and *downhill* with its economic implications.

The Poverty–Wealth Contradiction

The opposition between *poor* and *rich* is an often-repeated theme in *Àkhàzáŋ*, so much so that even a relatively well-to-do young man or woman, while courting or going to the fields, will sing about his or her poverty as compared with the wealth of the beloved or of others. . . .

When the wealth of others is spoken of, the difference is then between the rich, who have a broom of horse-tail as compared with the elephant-grass brooms of the poor; an iron cooking pot instead of a clay pot; and an aluminum cup instead of a bamboo cup. The poetic concern with the opposition poverty/wealth reminds one somewhat of Black-American "blues" and the Portuguese "fado", but the comparison cannot be pursued very far. There is a clear sense of *overcoming the contradiction*, not so much in a nativistic, mystic direction but in a realistic down-to-earth manner. The poor courting boy remarks that his "rich" girl's family will lose its "wealth". . . .

Opposition between wealth and poverty, mediated by work for survival, whether by gathering food or accepting wage labor, occurs in many places and in texts which have been preserved over quite a long period of time. From most texts we get the impression that the Akha view personal wealth as a situation of temporary good fortune. (And it should be noted that wealth is not only possessing plentiful supplies of food, but also silver and gold, the surplus reserves for times of hardship.)

Given the nature of swiddening and the frequency of both natural and man-made disasters, this is hardly surprising, but for further explanation of the wealth–poverty dichotomy we have to look to another opposition.

The Minority–Majority Contradiction

It is an essential part of Akha experience that throughout their history they have been dependent on other ethnic groups, particularly on economically, militarily, and politically stronger valley kingdoms or empires. They ascribe their original existence in mountainous jungle, if not the origin of the tribe as a whole, to conflicts with stronger ethnic groups. References to different types of Chinese (valley people, war-lords, middlemen, magicians, wise men, and smiths), to the Shan, Thai, Burmese, and Mountain Khmer, occur often. Their habits, costumes, products, and handicrafts are described in ceremonial texts and songs, often in comparison with their own. Chinese middlemen and war-lords, and the Burmese and the valley Shan obviously do not have their sympathy, whereas the Chinese wise men, the Mountain Shan, and the Mountain Khmer seem to have a better image. . . .

The Akha mention two periods in their history in which they had war-lords (generals), and later chiefs or kings (*sànpà*) associated with walled cities. . . . This experience of statehood, during which clans were formed out of phratries, and many rules were laid down, ended badly. The first ruler-king was killed by three of his nine village headmen, all of them clan founders. The fate of the second ruler is even more interesting. Through his mother's clumsiness, one of the wings of the heavenly horse was broken, but it was mended with wax. On the next flight the heat of the sun melted the wax; he plunged to earth and was killed. During the time of the third ruler, the power to rule, although thought of as reified for all time, was either lost or burned, the art of writing disappeared, books were eaten, and because of pressure from the Chinese and Shan, the clans, one after another, had to seek refuge in the mountains.

This period of city life is said to be the only period during which the Akha actively conducted warfare. They commanded Chinese masons to build the walls for them, but the city did not become a "Jerusalem of the heart". Just as this aggressive behavior is reported as being unusual, so the attempt to build a city stands out as a departure from the norm. The Akha trace their ancestry back sixty generations, thirty generations beyond the advent of their city-state, to reach the true land of their genesis – an egalitarian village. It is to this home that the dead return.

Most stories report the Akha as "born losers". The city fell because of internal disputes and external threats, including Tai movements. In other situations of confrontation the Akha always lose. They have to withdraw to avoid fighting, and occasional victories are credited more to cunning and trickery than force of arms.

This self-image has been interiorized, and reinforces the minority situation of the group. The minority–majority opposition is a constant theme in all oral literature. But here, once again, the manner is dialectical; Akha common sense provides a counterbalance. Although myths record past defeats, and daily talk recounts charges of stealing, killing, and discrimination by majority peoples, ritual texts ignore these problems. Mention of any type of disaster, be it either ecological or human, is avoided, because it is feared that such talk will provoke the very situation described, as a self-fulfilling myth. Texts are designed to restore confidence in the face of hostile experience, and many emphasize the *superiority* of the Akha in several fields. . . .

There is a tendency to confirm identity in opposition to valley people, or in comparison with them. Sometimes in the texts a feeling of superiority is conveyed: from the mountain, the Akha overlooks the whole world of the Chinese, the Shan, and the Burmese.

The Upslope–Downslope Contradiction

Contrary to what one would expect from members of a minority group who portray themselves as losers, the Akha feel themselves very much at the center of the universe-disc. The Chinese, Burmese, and Shan are cast as inhabitants of the periphery, and from that point of view they remind us of that famous minority group which centers itself on Jerusalem. The centre of the Akha universe is, however, not a city, either past or future. Nor is it, as one would expect, a village *on top* of a high mountain, far away from rivers and valleys. It is a village half-way up, half-way down, that is, *mid-slope*. The choice of site mediates between, and attempts to overcome the contradiction between *upslope* and *downslope*. . . .

The upslope-downslope dichotomy, with the Akha firmly placed in an intermediate position half-way up, is not a dialectical game. This is clearly explained in Akha mythology and literature. The hill fields located on slopes cleared from the forest, are not entirely unlike the terraces and irrigated fields in valleys, located next to secondary rivers and constructed after the forest has first been cleared and burned. Because of the availability of water, irrigated and terraced fields represent a more stable mode of production and thus are a basis for a more or less permanent settlement, which as we know, facilitates the development of land ownership and class stratification. Akha mythology suggests that after their rulers died they went into the jungle, where they started to build terraces and irrigated fields next to secondary rivers. After a Shan married into the community, he started to send messages on wood-chips downstream, inviting other Shan to join him. The result was a physical contest as well as a test of intelligence, in both of which the Akha lost. After this defeat the Akha had to move uphill, and south into the territory of the Mountain Khmer. *Zán* records that swiddening then became the dominant mode of land use, and the hill field became the symbol of security.

Ambiguous references to hill and terrace fields remain in songs and recitations, and, from what is known from Burma, it is clear that several Akha communities there retain both types of fields.

Many Akha communities still prefer to give the name of a *river*, rather than of a *mountain* to their village.

All this seems to suggest that the ecological niche preferred by the Akha, a mountain ridge half-way uphill, and preferably near to a secondary river, is the product of their experience as a minority people, who, on their journey south, tried to settle near water and lowland markets, but were continually displaced by valley people (and at some point also by malaria).

The upslope–downslope contradiction has up till today retained its validity. Akha, like others, have been pushed, often by violence, over the high mountain ridge which marks the Burmese–Thai border area into the north of Thailand and moved down to secondary rivers near the market places on ridges between the 450- and 700-metre altitudes. In several places they started to build irrigated paddy fields next to rivers, still clearing and burning hilly slopes for swiddens. Almost invariably they lost the irrigated land because of simple occupation by lowlanders, who profited from their lack of legal status. Construction of roads often added to their insecurity by making them accessible to bandits, and many villages since the mid-1960s have preferred to establish villages at medium altitudes away from thoroughfares. Nevertheless, within this decade, the borderline between highlanders and lowlanders, with roads as infiltration points, have often, in the competition for scarce resources, taken on many of the characteristics of a war front. In conflicts, highlanders invariably end up as the losers.

The Market–Subsistence Contradiction

There is an *economic correlate* to the ecological upslope-downslope contradiction, namely, the *market-subsistence* contradiction. Although it is mistakenly thought by foreign and Thai developers that the Akha, like other hill minorities, once lived a life of self-sufficient plenty, in complete isolation from markets, this is simply not so. One only needs to begin translating rituals and songs to find how many different vivid and realistically detailed stories exist about going to markets to buy salt, iron, buffalo, buttons, and the like. These old texts seem to antedate the kerosene and industrial–mechanical epoch. Exact names of market cities in Burma and China, and rivers to be crossed, are also mentioned. From the early industrial era there is mention of cash crops, like massive plantings of short-fibre cotton, sesame, and peppers – typical swidden and higher-altitude products – sold to Chinese middlemen in exchange for "silver frogs", but also, in Burma, to Indian middlemen in exchange for Indian rupees. Silver plays a role in almost any ceremony and in all fines imposed after judicial processes. Before silver, cowrie shells were obviously used as a "currency", and they are still highly valued.

Besides the cultivation of tobacco, sesame, and peppers, particularly the cultivation of cotton, weaving, and coloring with an ingenious pre-industrial bamboo-technology has traditionally been at times an important source of cash income.

All of this builds up the strong impression, reinforced by the previous contradictions of fluctuating ecological location and economic situation, that the Akha have been involved in market systems and have practised a type of mixed economy for hundreds of years. They seem to have been involved not only in local markets, but equally in mercantilist and colonial market systems, both in China and in Burma. This is particularly clear in the case of massive cotton growing for Indian middle-men in Burma in the nineteenth and twentieth centuries. Opium, which has become since the 1840s one of the more classical examples of a colonial and neo-colonial cash crop in Yunnan, China, and later in the "golden triangle" in Burma and Thailand, is not mentioned in ritual texts or songs. There is no *zán* for it, they say, which means that the ancestors did not know it, and thus were not able to define rules either for its growing or for its consumption. And although in the last twenty years opium addiction among the Akha has been escalating dramatically in the face of the disaster of an inescapable collapse of their economy, opium is not commonly grown by them as much as it is by the Hmong, Yao, and Lisu groups. One reason why only a low percentage of Akha communities has been involved in opium cultivation is that opium grows only at altitudes above 1000 to 1200 metres, locations not preferred by them. At this particular moment, hardly 10%, or 13 out of 140 Akha communities in Thailand, grow opium.

While the Akha have traditionally been involved in the market economy, they have been so only peripherally. They lacked a class of middlemen and traders, a role that is well filled in lowland societies. They also lacked easy access to markets and had to rely on typical mountain cash crops, which to compete profitably on the lowlands had to bring in returns which exceed the high cost of transport. They have been, more than lowlanders, vulnerable to fluctuations in the market, more dependent on the prices middlemen offered. In the case of opium they are often subject to intimidation, bandits, or to corruption on the part of administrators or police. This means that the contradictions, poverty–wealth, upslope–

downslope, subsistence–market, minority–majority, not only stand parallel, but also add up to a historical course in which poverty, some remoteness from valleys, and the subsistence economy were, so to speak, forced upon the Akha *in spite of* the attraction that irrigated cultivation, markets, and the cash economy, and also integration into lowland cultures, promised.

As a consequence, the hill field and the pink-to-purple hill rice, ennobled over the centuries, rich in minerals and vitamins (there were about thirty different species known to the Akha in the two villages in which I lived), have become in *Àkhàzáη* the symbol of survival, of independence from the market economy, and of ethnic identity. Most ceremonies in *Àkhàzáη*, during the year, have to do with rice cultivation, and most traditional Akha daily life centers around it. Irreversible declines in yields because of "stabilization" in areas of Thailand where hardly any forest is left, and where the Akha have the impression that their minimum-subsistence economy is more or less consciously destroyed by the authorities, provoke demoralization and disintegration. . . .

The Akha have never had any ideological objections to integration into lowland cultures as long as such incorporation is based upon equality of rights and equal access to resources. But lowland political organization, acceptance of economic and political inequality, military abuse, and differences of culture have always impeded integration and even systematic assimilation. If anything, this resistance seems to be growing, and has been reinforced and rationalized into discriminating valley mythologies (monkey-mythology) by lowlanders who make up the ethnic majorities. It is largely in reaction to this that Akha thinking has developed a mythology of the "born loser". This has further complicated the chances of either integration or assimilation into the more differentiated and powerful Chinese, Shan, Burmese, Laotian, and Thai economic and political valley cultures. This mythology, along with the Akha sense of cultural and ethno-linguistic identity, has reinforced the density and importance of *Àkhàzáη*. *Àkhàzáη* can for these reasons be considered to be a depository of the Akha adaptation to a harsh natural and human environment, that is, of a *swiddening minority group*.

Akha have incorporated migratory movements and fluctuations in their economic, political, and ecological fortunes into *záη*, in the form of contradictions. In Akha cosmology these contradictions often take the shape of dialectics, which advise: take the middle road in order to move forward in history; compromise to make something acceptable in order to survive; remain flexible so that you can adapt to majorities and other outside pressures.

The Akha have become a part of Thailand. Akha faces appear on brochures designed to attract tourists, and to show the cultural multiformity of this culturally rich and diverse country. Akha handicrafts are for sale in most tourist shops. The Akha have come to stay. May the Akha, who came into Thailand as refugees, be given the chance to play a full part in national life, granted an equal voice in the political process, accorded fair accesss to educational opportunities, and bestowed the benefits of economic growth and legal protection, based upon their unique cultural identity.

The Hmong – Political Economy of an Illegal Crop

Nicholas Tapp

Introduction

Numbering nearly six million, the Hmong people who inhabit the rugged highlands of southwestern China and the northern parts of Laos, Vietnam and Thailand, descend from a people who once vied with the Chinese for supremacy over the lower banks of the Yangtze River. Known to some as aboriginal Chinese because they retain in their customs and social organization so many traces of an archaic Chinese civilization, their culture has developed over the ages slowly and organically to the point where now it stands at the crossroads between violent change and total destruction. . . .

The Hmong are criticized for being illegal producers of opium. Over the past decade and a half it is they who have borne the brunt of government programs receiving international assistance aimed at eradicating poppy cultivation. Yet originally it was pressure from these same government agencies which encouraged the Hmong to concentrate on the growth of this crop. Opium has now become the mainstay of the Hmong economy and without it they would not be able to survive.

Opium Production

The opium poppy (*papaver somniferum*) is an extremely difficult crop to grow. It has been calculated that it takes an individual cultivator five minutes to incise a hundred poppy heads, and more than eight minutes to scrape them. Assuming eight hours of continuous work per day, it would still take a laborer over a month to harvest a single *rai*, with an average of 2.3 *rai* cultivated per head (1 *rai* = 0.4 *acre*). While the hired labor of other ethnic groups partly reduces the time required, such labor is not preferred at harvest time, since it is feared outsiders may steal the poppy sap. Poppy cultivation is an immensely time-consuming task. The combined efforts of women and children are required at harvest time, for the hoeing and clearing of stones which must precede planting, and for the two weedings and thinnings which must take place. The risks are also great. Too-heavy rains occurring near the time of harvest can wash the poppy sap away, or cause uneven germination and necessitate transplantation at early stages of the growing process. Incision must be neither too deep nor too shallow and take place at exactly the right time.

The Background

Although opium was probably first introduced into China by Arab traders in the eighth century AD, it was cultivated only on a small scale and for medicinal purposes. It was the British East India Company which, confronted with the reluctance of the Chinese to exchange goods such as tea and silk for the currency which was all British India had to offer, began to export opium to China in the late eighteenth century. By 1767 for example 1000 tons of opium were being exported annually.

After a series of unsuccessful edicts against the trade by the Chinese government the first Anglo-Chinese opium war broke out. The Nanking Treaty of 1842 which brought an end to the fighting forced the Chinese to accept the trade. In an attempt to stem the flow, China legalized imported opium in 1858 and began to tax it. By 1883 Chinese home production of opium had increased to twice the amount imported, and British opium imports began to decline. It was at this time that the Hmong first began to cultivate poppies as a cash crop.

In 1899, less than a decade after establishing control over the Laotian principalities, the French set up a centralized opium monopoly in Indochina, importing opium from China and India, taxing it at 10% of its value, and selling it by licence to addicts. Opium revenues increased by 50% in four years and accounted for more than one-third of the total colonial revenues. After a temporary halt to the opium trade during the Japanese occupation of the Second World War, tribal opium production was again encouraged in the post-war years. In Laos officials were authorized to collect taxes from the Hmong in the form of opium, and as taxes doubled, so did the production of opium.

During the period in which the US secret forces built up a guerrilla Montagnard army in Laos to resist the Communist Pathet Lao, American and other advisers condoned the trade in opium. The revenues which General Phoumi Nosavan, former Premier of Laos, derived from the opium trade were a major cause of the success of his leadership of the right-wing faction in Laos in the early 1960s.

Indeed Air America, a CIA-chartered airline, was known to be transporting Hmong opium as late as 1970. Opium, as many commentators have written, became the financial bastion of anti-communism in Indochina. In Thailand, the situation has essentially been no different.

Bangkok's Stance

The Thai government, following the ending of legal foreign importation of opium, for the first time authorized local poppy cultivation in its northern provinces in 1947. Despite strong international pressure, the government did not ban the sale and consumption of opium within Thailand until 1958. Production was declared illegal the following year. During those dozen years, the Hmong and other poppy cultivators were attracted into the region from neighboring Laos, and local opium production and trade increased dramatically. The 1958 Act ended the Royal Thai Opium Monopoly established, owing to British pressure, by King Mongkut in 1852.

During the Second World War, Thailand's occupation of the Shan states of Burma, the major opium-producing area of the region, forged links between the Shan and Chinese leaders of those areas and high-ranking officials in the Thai administration who became involved in the opium trade. The Thai government thus derived considerable profit from the trade before Marshal Sarit Thanarat's coup of 1957 removed both the Premier, Phibul Songkram, and Police General Phao Sriyanond, who had been a major beneficiary of the opium trade. The Hmong were therefore first encouraged to grow the crop to such an extent that it became an integral part of their economy, yet over the past two decades they have been penalized for their successful response to the challenge.

In the Village

Why then do the Hmong continue to grow opium? Opium as a cash crop has various advantages. Although it requires more care and weeding than any other crop, once the sap has been gathered it keeps for a long time, is easy to store, and fetches a good price on a guaranteed market – a higher price per weight than anything else available. Traders are prepared to travel up to the mountain villages every year to purchase it. They sell rice on credit during the off-season and collect the repayment in opium. This means that opium does not have to be transported the long distance to the lowlands where more perishable foodstuffs and livestock are often sold at half their real value. Opium functions as a general currency in the hills between villages and the members of different ethnic groups, and most things can be exchanged for it. The opium poppy grows well on soils of low fertility, and opium swiddens can be used two or three times longer than those growing upland rice. Many villages, especially in the Chiang Mai area where the largest concentration of Hmong live, cannot now produce enough rice for their yearly needs. Opium must often be sold to purchase sufficient rice to last seven months of the year. In addition, there are important cultural and medical reasons for the cultivation of the opium poppy. . . .

Estimates of the amount of opium internally consumed by Hmong villages vary widely, but it is quite common for a village to have only 40% of its opium produce left for sale after internal consumption and wage needs have been met. Even if opium were to be abandoned as a cash crop, therefore, there would still be medical, social and cultural reasons for its continued production on a small scale.

The real cause of large-scale opium production is the demand of the world market, the national agencies which pursue a policy of suppressing poppy cultivation with one hand while encouraging it with the other, and the local networks of extortionate traders and officials who market the drug, supply credit for its production and protect its transportation. These are all forces beyond the control of the Hmong, who may reasonably be seen as unwitting victims of an alien and hostile market.

Many Hmong in Thailand are now aware, thanks to ceaseless government propaganda, and improved radio communications, of the severe social problems arising from the marketing of their cash crop, and earnestly wish to turn to other forms of cultivation. But there are none available. Nor have there been since the inception of crop substitution programs designed to replace opium with alternative crops more than a decade ago. The demand continues. The traders still visit Hmong villages yearly to set up shops there, and the government, which in the past seemed at best half-hearted in its attempts to do anything about the problem, now increasingly resorts to the type of armed force which proved so counterproductive in the 1960s. Addicts still need to grow opium for themselves, and illness remains prevalent.

The Traders

As the Hmong themselves say, "Opium doesn't go looking for money. Money comes looking for opium." And those who bring it are the traders, who have never effectively been suppressed.

The major traders of opium are the Muslim Chinese originating from Yunnan and known locally as "Haw" or "Ho". Many have mountain connections with the remnants of Chiang Kai-Shek's National Chinese Army, the Kuomintang (KMT), which fled China for Burma after the success of the Chinese 1949 Revolution. They are presently settled in northern Thailand. . . .

The Market

The Thai government has long known of the crucial role played by Haw, Yunnanese and KMT trading networks.

As early as 1962, a government survey report identified the Haw as the major opium dealers in the area, and urged the need for "decartelizing the Haw combine" to halt their smuggling of opium from the Shan states of Burma into Thailand. The report barely mentioned the KMT, whose presence on Thai soil the government did not officially recognize, but it did admit that there had been a fair degree of understanding and cooperation between the Haw traders and "military refugees from Yunnan". The 1967 UN Survey Report also made surprisingly few references to the KMT remnants, despite suggesting that a considerable proportion of the opium production in the Shan states, possibly some hundreds of tons per annum, was being smuggled through Thailand. In fact this was, and is, the case and, of the total amount produced in the "Golden Triangle" (comprising part of Thailand, Laos and Burma), it was estimated by the United Nations that between 300 and 600 tons was produced in Burma annually, as compared with 200 tons in Thailand. About a thousand tons of opium was harvested overall in the region. In an EEC report in 1982 it was estimated that 500 to 600 tons came from Burma and 50 to 110 tons from Thailand. In 1982, 80% of the Triangle's production was estimated to have come from Burma.

Quite clearly, the amount harvested by the Hmong of north Thailand is an insignificant percentage of the total crop of the Golden Triangle. Most opium is harvested in Burma and transported by KMT irregulars and other paramilitary forces through Thailand. Much of the opium produced by the Hmong themselves is sold through these organizations. Yet, while occasional seizures are made which are given enormous publicity, little or no attempt is made to prevent or curtail the activities of such organized traders.

The reasons for this are political. The KMT remnants and other rebel military groups such as the Shan United Army (SUA) have all received sanctuary on Thai soil during their struggle against the

Burmese government. These right-wing organizations have in the past fulfilled important counter-insurgency functions in the areas which they control, on behalf of the Thai police forces and army. For political reasons no measures are taken to curtail the activities of these middlemen and producers. Instead all efforts are directed against the unfortunate, and poverty-stricken people of the hills, who are stigmatized and castigated as enemies of the nation, and unhealthy producers of a dangerous drug. . . .

So long as Thailand continues its policy of sheltering the enemies of neighboring states such as Burma, China and Laos, these large and powerful armies of brigands will continue to manipulate local opium producers, and Burmese opium from the rebel Shan states of Burma will continue to pass through Thailand.

The price of opium spirals as it leaves these traffickers in the hills. At the end of 1966, on the basis of Thai police and Federal Bureau of Narcotics information, the United Nations Survey Team calculated that the price of one kilogram of raw opium in a remote village would be US$20 to $30 and $40 nearer the towns. In Singapore this would become $125 to $175, a minimum increase of over 300%. Small quantities of heroin selling for $1400 in Bangkok would fetch $28,000 wholesale on the streets of New York and $50,000 in other US cities. The Halpern Report of 1972 calculated that $120 worth of opium purchased from the farmers brought in returns of $430,000 when it was sold as heroin on the New York streets. These sorts of figures, and estimates, could be multiplied. What these figures show is that beyond the network of producers and middlemen lies a ready and avaricious market of consumers. The prime mover of the process, of which the Hmong economy is the unfortunate result, are the social problems of the industrialized capitalist nations.

As had happened earlier in Shanghai and Hong Kong, the Thai government's ban on opium in 1959 had the effect of encouraging the manufacture, sale and consumption of heroin, which is less easily detectable than opium. The market grew when American soldiers, serving in South Vietnam and resting in Thailand became addicted and took the habit back home with them. Today, the heroin trade from Thailand, which accounts for some 60 tons of opium per annum, is run through a series of undercover organizations based on the connections of the old Chinese Triad societies, Corsican syndicates and Mafia families.

The amount of opium needed to supply the US heroin market can be grown in an area as small as about 20 square miles, but the American response to addiction has been to try to end the cultivation of poppies altogether. As former President Nixon stated: "The only effective way to end heroin addiction is to end opium production and the growing of poppies. I will propose that as an international goal." However, the eradication of opium cultivation in one area simply results in its transfer elsewhere. Left to themselves the Hmong suffered few, if any, ill effects from growing opium. It is the demand from the West, particularly from the United States, that has caused them. It is this which needs to be destroyed. . . .

Bangkok and the Tribespeople

In 1958 the sale and smoking of opium were outlawed, and with the ceremonial burning of 40,000 opium pipes in the following year production became illegal. In fact, the ban on production was never fully enforced. The government had no effective control over large areas of the highlands where opium is produced and attempts to enforce the ban are impractical and provoke the resistance of the local people. The government claimed that the non-implementation of the law was prompted by humanitarian feelings, rather than such practical difficulties. For the Hmong, however, the ambiguities of their legal position cause considerable hardship and suffering.

Graft

This policy of false leniency has led to the absurd situation where the hill people are engaged in an illegal mode of production for which they can be penalized (harvests confiscated, poppy fields burned or bombed, cultivators arrested). At the same time the Thai authorities in the hill areas often turn a blind eye to the traders and peddlers who come to purchase the illicit substance. The opportunities for graft are great. Tolls are levied on frightened traders and taxes exacted from individual farmers by local Thai bureaucrats who derive comfortable revenues from the business they supervize and deplore. The whole policy of attempting to suppress opium production at source is fundamentally an error. Neither preemptive buying nor strategic controls such as crop substitution can be effective unless combined efforts are also made to deal with addiction and the networks of middlemen which link demand to supply at the local level.

The policy as it stands places the producers in the most ambiguous, unenviable and invidious of positions. Some individual growers do manage to take advantage of the situation and exploit the local structures of authority successfully. But these are few, and as more and more pressure is brought to bear on the Hmong to increase poppy cultivation, a heavy strain is placed on the reserve of labor. Extra labor is provided by women and children and especially by other ethnic groups such as the Karen. More often than not the Karen are bound to the Hmong producers by debt.

Most commentators in the north Thai hill areas have blamed expanding population pressure in the hills (brought about by natural increase, refugees migrating from the conflicts in Burma and Laos, and the upward movement of landless Thai peasants) for a general resource scarcity. As available land diminishes, so the argument goes, fertile soil is cultivated for ever longer periods with ever shorter and less adequate fallow periods, so that rice yields drop dramatically while cultivation of the poppy, a sturdy crop which can be grown on the same plot of land for longer periods of time, expands. Such arguments provide a justification for attempts to reduce the tribal populations by family planning and resettlement.

However, given the ever-expanding market for opium in Thailand and abroad, it would be surprising if the producers had not been encouraged, threatened, cajoled, blackmailed and bullied into expanding their own cultivation of the poppy by those who buy it from them. It is these pressures, dictated by financial considerations, that help to explain the growing dependence of the Hmong on the cash economy of the poppy plant. . . .

With such a double-edged policy, which way is the Hmong opium farmer to turn? In 1982, rumors that the government was to destroy all poppy fields in the hills received some backing from local development workers and the national press. Many Hmong wanted to give up poppy cultivation since they were aware of the problems it caused elsewhere. But, as they and their families would starve if their fields were destroyed, they saw it as their duty to protect their crop as best they could. In the event, after a high-level policy disagreement, the fields in question were not destroyed (although they had been in previous years). Instead, some villagers were paid to destroy their own crops, and photographs were distributed to the press attesting to the success of the government's eradication policies.

Development Projects

In general, the government welfare and development programs for the hill people, and the United Nations sponsored crop substitution scheme initiated in 1971, have been unsuccessful. Left largely to the tender mercies of local officials and the propaganda exercises of the border patrol police, a paramilitary organization funded and part-trained and equipped through United States Operations Mission (USOM) during the 1950s, opium producers found themselves the victims of a government operation – the *nikhom*, or Land Settlement Program.

The aim was primarily to persuade the scattered hill tribes to move into the project areas and settle down permanently. Centers with stores, dispensaries and schools were set up in various provinces. They had supervisors to administer them, and it was expected that the hill people would move into them. Very soon it became apparent that this radical attempt to transform the fundamental features of shifting cultivation was not going to work, as the anticipated mass migration of uplanders into these lowland sites failed to occur.

Instead government policy changed. In 1963 the Hill Tribe Welfare and Development Division in the Department of Public Welfare was established to co-ordinate projects in the uplands. The government transformed resettlement sites into bases from which development could be brought to the people. Mobile development teams consisting of an agricultural, a health, and a social welfare worker, visited individual villages for periods of up to a month. Propaganda work was undertaken, surveys were conducted, and a notion of self-help put forward to generate support for local projects such as mobilizing villagers to build roads. The teams of mobile development workers worked very much as the old border patrol police teams had done.

The increased contacts between highlands and lowlands brought about by such projects, however, has exacerbated rather than reduced frictions. In 1967 a major rebellion broke out among the Hmong, convulsing large areas of the highlands in Chiang Rai and Nan, and continuing sporadically until 1971.

A new substitute crop approach was ushered in with the signing of the Thai–United Nations Agreement on December 17, 1971. It met with little more success in eradicating opium production or changing the livelihood of its farmers than the earlier programs. Centering on five key project sites in Chiang Mai province of north Thailand, the United Nations Program for Drug Abuse Control (UNPDAC) project has sought to introduce a variety of alternative crops to the opium poppy. However, the program has allegedly been plagued by the lack of marketing facilities, inefficient administration, insensitivity to the needs of the producers, and lack of foresight.

In essence, this extremely expensive program has been conducted on a trial-and-error basis in which research has been carried out concurrently with development projects. Suwannabubpa calculated that by June 30, 1974, 25.85% of the total five year budget – about two million dollars – had been spent; of this 75.78% had been expended on salaries, furniture, transport and office equipment.

In the early stages of the program, UNPDAC was forced to buy up the total crop of red kidney beans they had persuaded villagers to grow, because there was so little demand for them. Despite promises of compensation in case their experimental crops failed, the Hmong were never compensated for failed sesame and kidney bean crops. According to the Hmong villagers in the Khun Wang area, potatoes planted in 1972 to be sold to the project at a guaranteed price, were never bought. The same was true for castor beans which were also grown extensively. Peaches which took seven years to grow sold well in 1976 but dropped to a third of their price in 1977, so that the cash value of the fruit did not even cover the cost of transporting it to market. Coffee, planted on a wide scale in the late 1970s, has met with disease and failure. There was no program of training for the Hmong producers wishing to plant this new cash crop. Nestlé of Switzerland's agreement to buy up all UNPDAC coffee beans could not be taken up since so little coffee was successfully produced. When there was a market, production could not meet it, and when farmers did produce a crop successfully there was virtually no demand for it.

Tobacco, cotton and peanuts were originally ruled out as substitute crops in order to avoid competition with existing United States monopolies in Thailand. The experimental nature of the whole attempt was well demonstrated in 1978 when the New Zealand premier presented the Thai King with thousands of lily seeds for distribution to the hill people.

Criticisms have been made about the inability to find a viable economic alternative to the cultivation of the opium poppy. The failures of such projects, which are not unique to the Thai United Nations Project but are characteristic of attempts to introduce alternative crops, result from poor marketing and insufficient demand. Opium, however, suffers from no such disadvantage. The Hmong producers are ensnared by these economic realities. . . .

Perhaps the unkindest cut of all is that the Hmong are no longer, if indeed they ever were, the major opium producers. Over the past 20 years there has been an increased incidence of landless northern Thai peasants moving up into the hills and cultivating the opium poppy. Thai farmers often cultivate without any regard for ecology. Also many Karen communities have begun cultivating small poppy swiddens. Furthermore, Burma-based groups such as the Lahu and Lisu, and the Nationalist Chinese are responsible for the vast majority of the opium in transit through Thailand, and also for an increasing proportion of the opium produced within Thailand. Since the majority of upland farmers are now Thai rather than tribal, the continuing identification of opium production with the Hmong appears increasingly unjustified. . . .

Kalinga History and Historical Consciousness

Esteban T. Magannon

Community and Identity

The Kalinga are one among seven ethnolinguistic groups which inhabit the Central Cordillera region of Northern Luzon, Philippines. The other six are: the Ibaloi, Kankanai, Bontoc, Ifugao, Tinguian, and Isneg. . . .

All ethnic appellations presently applied to the populations of the Central Cordillera region of Northern Luzon, Philippines, are inventions by their lowland Filipino neighbours, by invading colonialists, anthropologists, and linguists. The name Kalinga itself is a very good illustration. It is the designation given by the Ibanag of the Cagayan Valley to the people living on the mountains in the higher reaches of the Chico River. These highlanders used to come down to the valley and raid Ibanag settlements for human heads and cattle. For that reason, they were called *kalinga*, which in Ibanag language means *enemy*. If these ethnic names have any meaningful sense at all, it is that they reflect the outsiders' and foreigners' perceptions of the Cordillera inhabitants and the kind of relation they have had with them.

How then do the Kalinga call or identify themselves? While the exigencies of modern life have made them accept the ethnic label which they now carry, traditionally they referred to themselves collectively as *tagu* (humans). And when a Kalinga is further pressed about his individual identity and to distinguish himself from other men and groups, he answers by giving his personal name and follows it, not by a family name for the Kalinga do not have family names, but by the name of his *ili* (village) of origin. In short, the Kalinga identify themselves as men living in villages, which indeed continues to be the actuality of their social existence. . . .

It is no accident that the Kalinga, when identifying themselves, add to their personal name that of their *ili* of origin as if it were their family name. It is a specification of identity which touches on the very cornerstones of human social organization and social theory. When the Kalinga name their *ili* as the second element of their identity, they mean to say that the *ili* is their second self, their social self, a second definition of their human existence. What are the characteristics of this second self? What is its mode of being?

The word *ili*, as used by the Kalinga, first of all refers to the settlement, the clustered complex of houses, the human community. Space in the community is classified into three categories. 1) The surrounding space constituting the edge of the settlement called *pidong*. This area, generally planted with coconut trees and other fruit trees in addition to natural vegetation, serves not only as dustbin for all kinds of refuse materials and as a "communal toilet" for the inhabitants of the *ili* but also as a buffer zone between the settlement and the rice terraces. 2) The empty, unoccupied residential lots called *sa'ad*. These lots, very much like the *pidong*, are often used as depositories for refuse and dirt. As such, they are likewise considered as convenient habitats for agents of disease and lurking places for invading *aran* (spirits of the locality) from foreign lands, especially at night. However, during community festivities, such as the inauguration of a peace-pact or celebration of a marriage, one of these lots is cleaned and becomes the setting for dancing and general merrymaking. 3) The settled lots, *da naboboroyan*, the agglomeration of houses called *boboroy*.

Secondly, *ili* refers to a wider geographical area which establishes the ultimate boundaries, called *ka'is*, of the village community. This wider area comprises the *pappayaw* (rice terraces) and the *taron* (forest). The *taron* encompasses the communal forests where all members of the community can go and gather firewood, root-crops, fruit, berries, and other edible plants; the hunting grounds; the fishing grounds; and the areas where people of the locality can build their *uma* (swiddens). This wider expanse constitutes the territory of the *ili* both as an economic and political entity. Moreover, it is recognized by neighboring groups as the proper domain of the group occupying it.

Thirdly, this wider territory also constitutes the religious world of the Kalinga. It is a religious world in the sense that, in this particular territory, *tagu* (humans) and *aran* (spirits) are destined not only jointly to elaborate a common mode of social existence but also to cooperate in protecting the *ili* from outside attacks.

The ethic of this social mode of existence stems from the *ngilin* and *paniyaw* (taboos and prohibitions) surrounding the personality and status attributed to spirits, people, animals, places, times, social relations and activities.

The Kalinga recognize *kigad* (boundaries) in space as they do in time. In the *ili* territory, the forests and lakes, except those put to cultivation by man, belong to the nature deities, who build their dwellings on big trees, mountain tops, the curve of pathways, the banks of rivers, brooks, lakes etc. Graves, corners of rice fields, entrances to the village settlement and nearby groves are the habitats of the spirits of the dead. The territorial domains of man are the village settlement and all the areas which he has subjected to culture. Wild life, acquatic life, and wild plants associated with their settlements are likewise considered to belong to the spirits as their property. Man's animals are of course those he has domesticated for food and work. His plants are those he has cultivated for food, ornament, and medicinal use.

The spatial boundaries specify where both *aran* and *tagu* should construct their settlements and situate their activities. The temporal measures determine not only when *aran* and *tagu* should take leave of their settlements and be on the common pathways, but also when they should undertake their work and various activities. Adhering to these spatial and temporal *measures* – in other words, observing the prescriptions of the different *ngilin* and *paniyaw* – enables both spirits and men to avoid not only conflictual relations among and between themselves but also the waste of precious time and productive labor: situations which bring in their wake illness, misfortune, and death on the side of man, especially so when such conflictual relations and waste of time and labor are deliberate.

Breaches of peace and harmony in the *ili* world are resolved, on the side of *tagu*, by the performance of prescribed rituals, like the *sap'uy* (blowing), the *sis'si'wa* (dissipation), or the *dawak* (seance of mediation) depending on whatever is required. These rituals are carried out not only to appease victimized neighbors or offended spirits but also to restore the integrity of the spatial boundaries or temporal measures which have been transgressed, rendering them once again safe for their spirit and human inhabitants to live in and to undertake their productive work and other vital activities.

In conclusion, then, the *ili* is the second self of the Kalinga not only because it is the permanent home of his people and spirits, thereby embodying both his familial and religious affections and loyalty, but also because the *ili* literally bears on its surfaces the imprints of the Kalinga people's economic, political, social, and religious work. . . .

Ecology and History

In the past, the region of Southeast Asia has tended to be treated as merely a meeting point of cultural influences derived from neighboring parts of the world: as a southward extension of East Asia or an eastward extension of India. Kroeber's (1943) presentation of the growth of Philippine civilization as a succession of layers of external cultural influences from China, India, and from the West, each time burying deeper the original Malay culture, exemplifies best this classical view with regard to the Philippines. While the importance of Indian cultural influence in the region as a whole, and that of Chinese influence in certain areas (and of course that of the West in the whole region in the modern period), are not to be denied, the foregoing view has obfuscated the construction of a history or histories of the region in its own terms and in accordance with an indigenous historical consciousness, and therefore of histories of the countries which compose it. Philippine historiography is a good illustration. Based mainly on Spanish and American documentary materials and elaborated in the perspective of the development of the Philippine colonial state, existing historical writings give a myopic view which limits the purview of Philippine history from 1521, the year of the discovery of the Islands for the Crown of Spain and for the West, to the present. Fortunately, archaeological, linguistic, and ethnological researches, especially during the last two decades, have uncovered evidence showing that indeed Southeast Asia has historical and cultural characteristics specific to it, and that therefore its history and civilization can be reconstructed on terms and concepts proper to it. . . .

Up to modern times, the life situation in the Luzon Highlands seems mainly to have consisted of a search for the resources and means for survival. In accordance with such prevailing conditions, the pattern of technological development presents an evolutionary line. Ethnographic accounts first present the peoples of the region gathering fruits, root-crops, and other food items readily given by the forest environment. From this stage, they are reported a little later, about the fourth decade of Spanish colonization, to be cultivating taro, yam, and *camote* (sweet potato) in hill swiddens. Together with taro, yam, and *camote*, they were also domesticating vegetables in garden plots. With these cultivated legumes, hunting and fishing catches formed the supplementary diet to the taro, yam, and sweet potato to make subsistence living more comfortable.

A later and much improved technology, which transformed not only the physical face of the region but also its social and political configurations, was the cultivation of rice. The first stage in this innovation is what anthropologists commonly refer to as dry-rice shifting cultivation. As practised today in the Central Cordillera, it involves first of all cutting forest undergrowth and such smaller trees as can be done with the use of a bolo or the bigger head-axe. These then are left to dry. When the cleared area is dried, it is fired; the remnants of the burning are then cleared away to the perimeter, serving as a fence for the entire swidden plot. Once cleared of the cinders and other debris, the swidden is then weeded and planted to rice, beans, corn, etc. After the swidden has been harvested, it is allowed to lie fallow for a period of two years, if the plot is new, and four years on the average, if it is an old one. In the meantime, another plot is constructed somewhere else to take care of the rice needs of the cultivator while the previous plot lies fallow.

The second technique of rice cultivation which has been found to be the most effective means of providing a continuous and permanent supply of rice for the population of the region, is the wet-rice terracing technique. It consists of constructing terraces on slope-gradients, on the sides of mountains or hills, and on flat alluvials along the banks of rivers and streams. The terraces are then planted twice in a year, in most areas of the Central Cordillera, the soil of the field lying fallow only between these two harvests. The construction of wet-rice terraces and the use of the new technique not only made the population of the region more secure and comfortable subsistence agriculturalists but also turned the region into the site of what has been called the "eighth wonder of the world". . . .

With the development of wet-rice terracing agriculture came spatial or residential permanence and stability of the source of subsistence, including the domestication of animals for food and work. This gave rise to the aggregation of the formerly semi-sedentary bands into areas of settlement. This concentration of different kin groups into one place forming a clustered community is what is called *ili* (village) in the languages of the Central Cordillera peoples. Political authority and leadership in the *ili* are provided by some form of council of elders constituted by the various heads of the kin groups comprising the population of the *ili*. This council, whether loosely constituted, as for example in Kalinga, or formally organized, as in the Kankanai and Bontoc *ato* (ward), made decisions on the internal affairs of the *ili*. The *ili* was self-sufficient in its subsistence, and autonomous, independent, and sovereign in its decisions, not only *vis-à-vis* its constituents but also with respect to other villages.

These self-sufficient, autonomous, sovereign, and independent *ilis* are found near river banks, slope-gradients, hill and mountain sides where water is readily available all over the Central Cordillera. With their respective *ili* identitities established by the definite and mutual recognition of territorial boundaries, these different groups started to establish trade and commerce, and diplomatic relations, among themselves and with some of the lowland communities down in the surrounding foothills. They were well advanced in a process of uniting themselves with one another by means of inter-*ili bodong* (peace-pact), and by the increasing physical linkages between *ili* in terms of the construction of trails and common irrigation systems. In fact, it has been postulated that if these *ili* communities had joined their respective territories when forming the *bodong* system, there would have been tribal federations in the Central Cordillera similar to the sultanates among the Muslims in the southern Philippines. . . .

This well-adapted and integrated development, if it had not been disturbed by the coming of the colonialists and then continuously disrupted up to the present attempts at so-called integration by a neo-colonial state, would surely have given rise to a very different socio-economic and political history of the region. One thing which has remained through to the present is the highlanders' pride, independence, and defiance of all forms of domination, all rooted in this cultural base. The *ili* community, embodying the cultural achievements gained by these populations throughout the preceding centuries, lies at the back of their consciousness as the cornerstone and reference point of their sense of history. . . .

Integrating Cultural Minorities

The Philippines were "discovered" for Spain in 1521 by Ferdinand Magellan. Contacts with Northern Luzon began in 1572, but the Spanish met with considerable resistance, from Kalinga and others, to attempts at "pacification" and Christianization. Spanish coloniz-ation had the effect of separating highlanders from the increasingly hispanized lowlanders. Spanish rule came to an end in 1898 with the establishment of a short-lived Philippine Republic. The subsequent Philippine-American war ended with the setting-up in 1902 by the Americans of a colonial civil government.

During the entire American colonial administration in the Philip-pines, the aim of "assimilation" was described as clear-cut, and so it is when regarded from the viewpoint of Filipino nationalism: the Highlanders of the Central Cordillera, the Muslims of Mindanao, and the other non-Christian populations must be made fully partici-pating citizens in the social, economic, and political life of the newly acquired American Pacific colony. The same policy, but now pursued under the name of "integration" by all the succeeding administrations of the Independent Republic of the Philippines since 1946, has also been continually regarded as clear and simple. More closely analyzed, however, the term integration is obscure, as was the previous word assimilation. . . . Filipinos of today are deeply rooted in *local* backgrounds and loyalties: more than anything else, they are Tagalogs, Ilocanos, Cebuanos, Pampangos, Bicolanos, etc. And this does not make them any less Filipino. Indeed, there is as yet little *Filipino* culture as distinct from such localisms, and the latter are regarded by most Filipinos as in the main harmless, enriching, and interesting variations, not at all subversive of the ideal of national solidarity. Those, in government or otherwise, who have steadily defined the future of the so-called Cultural Minorities as "integration" have failed to specify with any clarity what kind of *local* Filipinos they want to make of them.

In the meantime, despite the various laws passed ostensibly to protect the Cultural Minorities – especially their ancestral lands, distinctive customs, arts, and other traditions – the everyday circumstances of modern life have caught up with them. In the case of the Central Cordillera and its population, the establishment of Baguio as a hill station and summer capital of the country in Ibaloi territory in 1903, and the subsequent construction of trails, ferries, telephone and telegraph lines, and finally of roads for automobile traffic, opened the formerly impenetrable mountain fortress; and it opened it not only to lowland Filipino migrants but also to foreign business and to the world in general. This opening up, while it broadened both physical and cultural contacts and brought along with it some of the benefits of modern social services, such as education, transport, medicine, etc., simultaneously introduced negative effects which tend to impoverish the region and to further disadvantage the already weak position of the native population, developments which are increasingly drawing discontent and resentment from the highlanders.

Attempts by the Spaniards to bring the region into the purview of the Spanish colonial administration never succeeded. The population of the region effectively resisted Spanish attempts at subjugation and colonization. Spanish administration therefore never had a chance to tamper with the indigenous political system and government.

At the initial entry of the American administration into the area, they met with the same opposition and resistance. However, gradually they were able to establish a foothold. They were able to do this because, learning from the errors of the Spanish policy of outright subjugation, and perhaps from their own experience of having once been a colony, they modified their initial policy of direct assimilation to one of more slow and gradual absorption. They soon realized that there could be no single and uniform pattern of asimilation. Thus, in dealing with the Muslims of Mindanao and with the highlanders of Northern Luzon, they tried to show sympathy to and understanding of the traditional cultures. In so doing, the form and structure of government which the Americans established, and which was adopted by the Republic of the Philippines, have taken root in both the Muslim areas and in the Central Cordillera.

From the beginning of the American administration to the early 1950s, officials in the Central Cordillera region were appointed by the national government. Since there were not too many educated people in the area, the officials appointed were outsiders, Americans and lowland Filipinos, with some of the articulate traditional leadership playing secondary roles in the local administration. This situation has largely persisted to the present as the general pattern of government leadership in the Mountain Provinces. While a number of these outsiders appointed to administer government in the region did their best to bring beneficial development, and for which they have earned the permanent gratitude of the region's population, most entrenched themselves in their positions to constitute a migrant elite. In the process, the real development of the region was greatly neglected. In the meantime, natives who had acquired sufficient education to qualify them for higher positions in the local administration, seeing the neglect around, aspired to those positions in the hope that they could bring about the necessary development of the region. But two things militated against them. Access to those positions was no longer by appointment but by election. But these elections were controlled by the monied migrant elites who always bought their positions from the easily manipulated populations. The only other way, therefore, in which these illustrious sons of the region could enter the higher positions of local government was to appeal to the regional sentiments of the traditional leadership who still controlled the grass-roots population of the villages. This appeal has been heeded. But the lowland governors are still there. How and why they are still in power, the population of the region attribute to manipulations by the national government. At present this cleavage and contradiction has taken the form of a liberation movement on the part of some of the Central Cordillera groups. . . .

For the contemporary Kalinga, historical consciousness is grounded in now "invisible events" going back to their Austronesian background and origins, and leading to their now settled life in *ili* (village) communities in the Central Cordillera of Northern Luzon,

Philippines. From the perspective of the internal development of the *ili*, colonization was viewed by the Kalinga and the other Igorots as the very antithesis of their social and historical existence. Therefore their resistance took the form of pure and simple rejection (overt during the Spanish period, mainly covert during most of the American period). They fought both Spaniards and Americans with head-axes. Current historical tensions focus on open and dramatic resistance to increasing and accelerated pressures and processes of incorporation into the Philippine nation-state. This course of events is viewed by them as inevitably leading to the destruction of their entire existence, both physical and cultural.

Present Kalinga attitudes towards so-called modernization and development are of one and the same kind as lowland Philippine peasant reactions to social injustice and exploitation which have been variously depicted as "agrarian unrest", "millenarian movements", "revitalization movements", and "peasant revolts". The only difference between them is that the latter, unprotected by forbidding mountain walls, have been muted for a while, but now they rejoin the former. The movements of both are genuine clarion calls of the native pride which heaved in the stout hearts of ancient Maly *tao* (men) to defend their *barangay* settlements against the predations of foreign intruders. In the context of contemporary nation-states, such as the Philippines, which are still riding high on the waves of continuing decolonization, such resistance should not be interpreted as treasonable separatism. For it is one of the normal manifestations of the inherent contradiction still permeating the national social structures of such states. Properly understood, it is at the same time both a legitimate demand for the recognition and respect for native cultures, which are the genuine and real foundations of an authentic, independent and democratic nation, and a clamor for meaningful and responsible participation in, and a claim for an egalitarian share in the tasks and the benefits of self-conceived and self-directed national construction.

Transformations of Iban Social Consciousness

Motomitsu Uchibori

... The ethnic group currently called the Iban is one of several proto-Malay peoples living in western Borneo. Their population at present numbers approximately 320,000 in Sarawak, and possibly exceeds 400,000 if we include those residing in West Kalimantan of Indonesia. This makes the Iban one of the largest indigenous ethnic groups on the island of Borneo. More significantly they form the most numerous single ethnic group in Sarawak, constituting almost one-third of the total population of the state. In fact, unlike any other indigenous people the Iban now reside in all seven administrative divisions, a consequence of their relatively recent migration from the southern parts of Sarawak. They are thus geographically distributed throughout the state. Furthermore, the number of Iban who dwell in the state capital, Kuching, and other provincial towns is gradually increasing. This situation should be taken into account even when we focus our attention on the social circumstances under which rural inhabitants in up-river areas lead their regionally confined lives. Although their daily communications and transactions are conducted within a narrow local circle, extended networks of kinship and friendship make those remoter areas and towns somewhat familiar to them. This combines with the existing custom of *bejalai* ("travelling") to widen the experiential world of the Iban.

The Iban were traditionally shifting (swidden) agriculturalists, cultivating dry-rice on the slopes of low, though often steep, hills along river valleys. The majority of Iban still maintain this subsistence economy, though it has been modified by the introduction of cash crops, such as rubber and pepper. Up-river inhabitants rely heavily for their daily diet on hunting, fishing, and gathering, which are carried out individually or in groups within, or in the vicinity of, their communal territory (*menoa*). Their meagre income from cash crop production is spent on clothes, kerosene, salt, sugar, tobacco, and various utensils, unless it is consumed totally in the purchase of rice in case of bad harvests or in the "hungry season" (*maia lapar*) before harvesting. Earnings from seasonal labor migration to Sabah and Brunei – also termed *bejalai*, using a cultural

250

idiom for "travelling" of all kinds – may be a source of occasional income, though a high proportion of labor migrants return home almost empty-handed. Trading of jungle products has only marginal significance, except for the selling of wild boar meat by some communities.

Iban agriculture has been fully studied both for the "pioneering area" of the Baleh region (now in the Seventh Division), and for the "long-settled area" of the upper Batang Ai in the Second Division. Despite the overall uniformity in technology and land tenure, there is one crucial difference in land usage between these two historically and ecologically divergent areas. In the "pioneering area" Iban cultivators show a marked proclivity towards opening new tracts of field in primary forests, whereas cultivators in the "long-settled area" rotate field sites on a fallow basis.

The Iban are known in anthropological literature as one of the most migration-oriented shifting cultivators, practising the most wasteful use of land resources. For example, Geertz . . . goes so far as to say that the Iban regard "natural resources as plunder to be taken", showing "superior indifference toward agricultural proficiency", and thus deserve the name "less of shifting cultivators than *mangeurs de bois*" (Geertz, 1963: 27). This popular image of Iban agriculture is derived from the practice predominant in the "pioneering area". In this view, the preference for opening virgin forest found among pioneer cultivators is regarded as the cause of Iban expansion. As I see it, this view makes curious equation of *migration* with *expansion*, while in fact those two phenomena are not logically identical. In order to give a full picture of the phenomenon of expansion, we have to pay due attention not only to migration and "pioneering area", but also to the continued occupation of established territories and the utilization of already cultivated lands. Without the latter there would be no expansion, at least, as it is observed among the Iban. . . .

Contemporary Iban ethnography cannot be properly presented without understanding the nature of the people's historical experience since their first encounter with a colonial power. Sarawak was established as a "private raj" by James Brooke in 1841, and continued to be ruled by him and his inheritors for the next hundred years. Although the Brooke state was a colonial state in the sense of a foreign administration imposed upon native inhabitants, it does not fit squarely into the normal typology of colonial regimes. Most important in this respect is the fact that Sarawak was not a part of any greater imperial whole. . . . It was an autonomous state, with the Brooke Rajahs being almost absolute rulers who ran the state on a largely personal basis. It is perhaps a corollary of this personal rule that the Brooke state had a general suspicion, if not explicit antipathy, towards foreign capitalist enterprise. Sarawak remained practically closed to capitalistic development throughout the period of the Brooke regime, to such a degree that it gained a rather sarcastic reputation of being an "anthropological zoo". In fact the stated ideal of Charles Brooke, the second Rajah (1868–1917), was to protect native "virtue" from possible degeneration as an outcome of contamination with external civilization. . . . The innocent *bons sauvages* image of indigenous "tribal" inhabitants was thus consolidated during the Brooke period. Needless to say, this image was not so much a result of close observation of the natives' conditions as an outdated romantic stereotype. Nevertheless, what is significant is that it played a definite role in determing the trajectory which the Iban would follow in their entry into the modern world.

Sarawak, especially the indigenous sector of its inhabitants, remained largely at the level of subsistence economy well into the second half of the twentieth century. To be sure, some Iban succeeded in smallholding rubber plantation in the 1920s, but this was restricted to the Saribas and Krian regions. For the rest of the Second Division, cash crop production by Iban is a remarkably new activity, traceable only to the 1950s in most up-river communities. There are a number of reasons for this retardation. One major reason is that the up-river areas of the Second Division had suffered perennial unrest, caused by violent conflict between the Brooke government and "rebellious" Iban, from the end of the eighteenth century until as late as 1920. The upper Batang Ai was the home of the "rebels", and was attacked a number of times by government forces, and especially by pro-Brooke Iban, whereas the upper Skrang became a vulnerable target of counter-attack by revengeful "rebels". In both areas emigration ensued on the scale of an exodus. Still worse, the upper Skrang once became almost deserted in 1930s when a "rebellion" broke out in the Entabai just across the watershed between the Skrang and the Kanowit-Entabai. This incident was traumatic for the upper Skrang Iban because resettlement was enforced by government, who feared they might take the side of the "rebels", many of whom were their relatives.

The affliction suffered by the upper Skrang Iban was a typically tragic result of the peculiar way the Brooke government handled Iban affairs. It was one of the primary concerns of the Brooke state from its inception to suppress Iban headhunting and "piracy", and thus to bring about peace to troubled peoples. It was even a professed *raison d'être* of the state. Ironically, in order to carry out this policy, the Brookes had to rely on the use of troops composed of subdued or allied Iban, since they did not possess their own suppressive apparatus. In this way, some Iban became instruments of Brooke policy. So the Iban as a whole stood in an ambivalent position *vis-à-vis* the government. In concrete situations there emerged an often violent antagonism between pro-government Iban and anti-government "rebel" Iban. The paradox is often noted that Iban warfare and headhunting were all the more exacerbated by the Brooke policy of suppressing this bellicose complex (Wagner, 1972). Thus the Europeans continued to hold a warrior image of the Iban, which somewhat contradicted the *bons sauvages* image, but was equally romantic.

Generally speaking, Brooke policy towards the Iban was intentionally conservative. However, this does not mean that there was no change in the conditions of life of the Iban during the Brooke period or thereafter. On the contrary, their life was thrown into an entirely different and alien context by the advent of state power. Their subsistence economy seems to have changed little, but the wider context within which it persists is fundamentally different from that of the past. Their legendary "warrior" orientation appears to be an inheritance from the distant past, but it is in fact just as much a product of their historical experience of the Brooke period. The "anthropological zoo" was always a myth. The most significant transformation in Iban life, namely their incorporation into the Brooke state, was denied in that state's view of its mission to conserve a traditional Iban way of life; and yet the terms and strictly limited nature of this incorporation did allow a degree of continuity in the Iban mode of existence, particularly their subsistence economy, which veiled the significance of the transformation even from them. . . .

Iban society in the pre-Brooke period was in a condition of perpetual, if often latent, warfare. The notion of "enemy" (*munsoh*) is thus of special importance in Iban social consciousness. It is an element of cognitive style particularly relevant to the self-contained world of the Iban in those earlier times. For it constitutes, however negatively, the definition of the outermost limit of the range of "we-ness", and as such plays a role similar to that of an ethnic label. More significantly, the contents of this notion have changed through historical experience, reorganized in accordance with actual socio-political relations. Here the policy taken by the Brooke state was decisive.

It says much for the ingenuity of the Brookes that they took advantage of the highly evocative notion of *munsoh* when they mobilized Iban warriors. It not only heightened the morale of the warriors, but also had the more important effect of uniting troops of different regional origin, some of whom had previously been enemies. Thus a kind of ethnic consciousness was generated among them. The single ethnic label Dayak, under the banner of the unitary Brooke state, created for the Iban a new sense of identity so that they thought of themselves as a group transcending their traditional parochial loyalties. Yet, paradoxically, while the Brookes enhanced the growth of ethnic unity of various Iban subgroups, at the same time they relied on the traditional allegiances of more circumscribed regions. For in most cases the *munsoh* of the Brookes were ethnic Iban "rebels" in up-river areas. The most serious consequence of this use of Iban against Iban was the amplified antagonism between pro-government Iban and "rebel" Iban. As mentioned earlier, their repeated mutual raids had devastated large up-river areas of the Second Division around the turn of the century. This situation contrasted sharply with the undisturbed area of the Saribas and Krian, where considerable economic development took place later in the 1920s and 1930s. The use of Iban warriors within the state apparatus thus eventually led to intra-ethnic collision, and gave rise to mutual suspicion which still lingers today, and to differentiation of life environments between regions. In this respect, Brooke policy towards the Iban prevented as much as it enhanced the formation of Iban ethnic consciousness.

Nonetheless it is still true to say that the present ethnicity of the Iban is essentially a product of Brooke policy or, more precisely, of the Iban-Brooke interaction. The Brooke state treated the Iban as a definable entity, gave them a single ethnic label and, more importantly, it allocated to them a privileged status within the state system. Except for the Malays in the Second Division, they were the only Sarawak subjects who were, when necessity arose, obligated to serve on government military expeditions. For this reason, all the Iban in the state received special treatment in taxation.

The formation of Iban ethnicity during the Brooke period, as reviewed above, took place without radical socio-cultural disjunction of the Iban. The Brookes relied more on traditional Iban values in their use of Iban as the major state force than on any new forms of organization more pertinent to a modern state. This fact alone may explain the striking absence among the Iban in the Brooke period of anything like the nativistic or millenarian movements which occurred elsewhere in Southeast Asia. The numerous "rebellions" in up-river areas lacked any ideological content other than a vague notion of a form of freedom which could only be found in a stateless society. In fact most "rebellions" were retaliations in response to prior government military action, and seem to have had no intention to establish any new order. Of course, the lack of disjunction does not mean the absence of transformation. It simply means that the actors were able to rely on pre-existing socio-cultural practices and idioms in order to cope with changing socio-political environments. Transformation took place not in the form of the overthrow of the old socio-cultural systems, but as the distorted persistence of those systems under entirely new circumstances.

Let us now return to present-day Iban consciousness of social identity, especially of ethnic identity. It is not certain to what extent we can speak of specifically *ethnic* consciousness of rural Iban, particularly in everyday life situations. Despite the now ubiquitous acceptance of the ethnic label Iban, its relevance to Iban social identity is still very ambiguous. Probably we have to speak of a "pre-reflective" consciousness of ethnicity, rather than of an elaborated conscious form. An "ethnic category" may be a mode of existence and of consciousness distinct from an "ethnic community"; the former referring to the absence of any sense of "community", which in turn is characterized by memories of a common fate in past history, by a shared sense of liberation from former afflictions, and by some form of unifying agency or organization. Applying these indicators to the present case, we can say that the Iban have not yet formed an "ethnic community"; at least this is true for those in the Second Division. Of particular importance is the near absence of agencies which could thematize or articulate the potentialities of ethnicity in continuous social and political processes. . . .

The genesis of Iban ethnic identity was largely due to policies imposed by the Brooke state, but the Iban did not substantially develop their identity as an "ethnic category", given by their incorporation into the state system, to the level of "ethnic community". I have mentioned a number of possible reasons for the "failure" of the growth of ethnic consciousness, all derived from the specific historical experiences of Iban with the Brooke state. Ethnic consciousness, if it is to be able to serve as a driving force for social reformation of any sort, must be formed or transformed through struggles with opposing power, usually of other ethnic origin. A curious paradox is that the Iban did not nurture this kind of ethnic consciousness despite their repeated "rebellions" against the Brooke state. The defeated "rebels" were easily drawn into the state order, and thereafter often took an active part in government military operations. The "paternalism" of the Brookes, as is often pointed out, was certainly a significant factor. The Iban could safely, and maybe also falsely, feel that they were allied with, rather than subjugated by, the Brooke state.

Subsistence Economy and Consciousness

One way in which the Iban define themselves is by stressing their traditional hill rice cultivation. It is the core of the Iban "way of life" (*adat*) as against hunter-gatherers in the past, and as against modern town dwellers. The majority of up-river Iban are still emotionally involved in this subsistence activity, and are even ready to sacrifice time and labor, which could possibly be used for the more profitable work of rubber tapping and pepper growing, for the intensive work necessary in the rice fields. As for basic cultivation techniques, one can see scarcely any traces of change or improvement from what could have been observed in the last century. It is as if subsistence rice cultivation had been trapped in this backward corner of the world, unable to find a way out.

Iban consciousness, or rather pre-consciousness, of their own mode of subsistence is deeply embedded in religious notions and activities. It can even be said that rice cultivation forms the core of the entire religious system of the Iban. It thus defies the narrowly developmental study approach, though this is not totally irrelevant. We need to remind ourselves of the fact that for those who adhere to the traditional religion, the rice plant is something like a reincarnation of their ancestral spirits who return from the Land of the Dead. The Iban have an attitude almost of veneration towards the souls or spirits of rice (*semengat padi* or *antu padi*) on the various ritual occasions which mark the stages of growth of rice plants. Such an attitude has an important bearing on activities usually regarded as strictly economic. . . .

Nevertheless, the persistence of a largely subsistence economy in up-river areas has to be explained in historical terms, particularly in view of the contrast with the degree of economic development (remarkable by Sarawak standards) and perceptible transformation among the lower Saribas and Krian Iban. The single most important historical factor is to be found in the violent turmoil endemic in up-river areas from the end of the nineteenth century well into the 1930s. This was in retrospect a period of crucial importance for the economic transformation of many rural areas in the Malay-Indonesian world. The introduction of the rubber tree (*Hevea brasiliensis*) into the region, and the subsequent rubber boom after 1900, led peasants in various parts of Malaya and Indonesia to engage in rubber production on smallholdings. The boom was naturally carried over to Sarawak. First introduced by the government, rubber planting quickly spread to the Saribas Iban. The Sarawak government, or more personally Rajah Charles Brooke, endeavored to foster smallholder rubber cultivation in the state. It did not encourage the introduction of large-scale plantations, particularly by foreign (European) investors.

The Iban of the upper Skrang were not ignorant of the merits of rubber plantation. In early 1930s, when the majority of them were temporarily – if for as long as ten years – resident in the upper Layar (Saribas), many of them were employed as wage laborers, or worked on a share-cropping basis (the tapper and owner each taking half the product) or rubber plantations in the lower Saribas. However it is only after the new rubber boom in 1950 that the upper Skrang Iban finally managed to transplant saplings brought from the Paku, where they had once again been working. This turned out to be a fatal delay, if we regard the introduction of a cash crop as a necessary initial step towards wider social development. For in the 1970s the price of rubber continued to remain at a very low level and the proceeds from rubber production were little more than a supplement to daily consumption. This re-emphasized the reliance of local Iban on a subsistence economy based on rice cultivation.

We may therefore speak of a phenomenon almost of involution in this outdated and heavy reliance on the subsistence economy. There is a real difficulty for the Iban to get out of this impasse. One possibility is to take the opportunity to switch drastically from hill rice cultivation, to the exclusively commodity production of a cash crop, especially pepper, which maintains a high price level. There are a few exceptionally adventurous young people in the upper Skrang who express their intention exclusively to produce pepper, provided that conditions permit. The generation gap between those young people, often married couples, and the old who are sentimentally attached to the subsistence economy, is not acute for the present. A number of reasons can be given for this apparent lack of gap between generations. The major reason is that transition to exclusively commodity production cannot be carried out all at once, if only because of lack of initial capital. Unlike rubber, pepper plants are extremely delicate, requiring intensive care especially during the three years before the first harvest. Chemical fertilizer, for example, is a necessity. Therefore, most up-river inhabitants begin by planting no more than one or two hundred plants. What is worse, even this modest attempt is often in contradiction with the labor cycle of rice cultivation; for quite often the busiest seasons of the two cultivation cycles coincide. Households which have enough hands may cope with such a situation, but many small households are unable to manage. Thus the vicious circle closes. The majority of people, even if they want to engage in pepper cultivation instead of rubber tapping, are compelled to return to rubber. Another reason for the lack of a generation gap is more a question of social ethics. Not even those Iban youths who have an adventurous spirit can freely dismiss their older parents' aspiration for success in rice cultivation as being simply old-fashioned. The social ethics involved in the unity of the *bilek*-family as the unit of production are still solid.

It is evident, therefore, that the Iban in up-river areas who seem to be clinging to a traditional subsistence economy are in a sense being compelled to do so. Surrounded by a predominantly cash economy, and themselves willy-nilly encroached upon by it, they are trapped in the impasse of an involuted subsistence economy. At the same time it is true that they are also consciously attached to traditional Iban subsistence ethics.

One might even say that the up-river inhabitants in question are, in their consciousness, subsistence cultivators *par excellence*. And yet this form of consciousness is a reaction, a kind of anxiety reaction, to their own transformed and threatened existence. The meaning of subsistence economy, both subjectively and objectively, for these "traditionalized" cultivators is totally different from that of the genuinely traditional cultivators of former days. Once again, a most profoundly significant transformation in Iban life has taken place, and yet has been occluded from consciousness by the apparent persistence of earlier forms.

Bibliography of Texts Cited

Abdul Aziz Mahmud 1977. "Malay Entrepreneurship: Problems in Development – A Comparative Empirical Analysis". Ph.D. Dissertation, University of Southern California.

Adas, Michael 1974. *The Burma Delta*. Madison: University of Wisconsin Press.

Anan Ganjanapan 1984. "The Partial Commercialization of Rice Production in Northern Thailand (1900–1981)". Ph.D. Dissertation, Cornell University.

Anderson, B. 1983. *Imagined Communities*. London: Verso.

Arief, S. and Sasono, A. 1980. *Indonesia: Dependency and Underdevelopment*. Jakarta: Institute for Development Studies.

Asad, T. 1972. "Market Model, Class Structure and Consent", *Man*, 7, pp. 74–94.

Badgley, John 1969. "The Communist Parties of Burma", in Robert A. Scalapino (ed.), *The Communist Revolution in Asia*. Englewood Cliffs: Prentice-Hall, 2nd ed.

—— 1974. "Burmese Communist Schisms", in John Wilson Lewis (ed.), *Peasant Rebellion and Communist Revolution in Asia*. Stanford: Stanford University Press.

Barth, Frederik 1959. *Political Leadership among Swat Pathans*. London: Athlone.

Boserup, E. 1970. *Women's Role in Economic Development*. London: George Allen and Unwin.

Bruner, Edward M. 1974. "The Expression of Ethnicity in Indonesia", in *Urban Ethnicity*, A. Cohen (ed.). London: Tavistock.

Butwell, Richard 1969. *U Nu of Burma*. Stanford: Standford University Press, 2nd printing.

Cady, John F. 1958. *A History of Modern Burma*. Ithaca: Cornell University Press; supplement, 1960.

Chakravarti, N. R. 1971. *The Indian Minority in Burma*. London: Oxford University Press.

Charlesworth, Harold K. 1974. *Increasing the Number of Bumiputra Entrepreneurs*. Shah Alam: Institut Teknoloji MARA.

Chee, Peng Lim, *et al.* 1979. *A Study of Samll Entrepreneurs and Entrepreneurial Development programmes in Malaysia*. Kuala Lumpur: University of Malaya Press.

Chen Siok-hwa 1968. *The Rice Industry of Burma, 1852–1940*. Kuala Lumpur: University of Malaya Press.

Cocks, S. W. 192?. *Burma Under British Rule*. 2nd edn. Bombay.

Donnison, F. S. V. 1953. *Public Administration in Burma*. London: Royal Institute of International Affairs.

——— 1970. *Burma*. London: Benn, 1970; New York: Praeger, 1970.

Feder, Ernest 1976. "The New World Bank Programme for the Self-Liquidation of the Third World Peasantry", *The Journal of Peasant Studies*, vol. 3, pp. 343–54.

Friedman, Jonathan 1974. "Marxism, Structuralism and Vulgar Materialism", *Man*, 9, pp. 444–68.

Friedmann, H. 1980. "Household Production and the national economy; concepts for the analysis of agrarian formations", *The Journal of Peasant Studies*, vol. 7, no. 2, pp. 158–81.

Furnivall, J. S. 1948. *Colonial Policy and Practice, A Comparative Study of Burma and Netherlands India*. Cambridge: Cambridge University Press; reprinted New York: New York University Press, 1965.

——— 1950. "South Asia in the World Today" in Philips Talbot, (ed.), *South Asia in the World Today*, University of Chicago Press.

Geertz, Clifford 1960. *The Religion of Java*. Glencoe, Ill.: Free Press.

——— 1963. *Agricultural Involution, the Process of Ecological Change in Indonesia*. Los Angeles: University of California Press.

——— 1963. *Peddlars and Princes*. Chicago: University of Chicago Press.

——— 1965. *The Social History of an Indonesian Town*. Cambridge, Mass.: MIT Press.

Gilsenan, Michael 1977. "Against Patron-Client Relations", in *Patrons and Clients*, Ernest Gellner and John Waterbury (eds). London: Duckworth, pp. 167–83.

Godelier, M. 1984. *The Mental and the Material*. London: Verso.

Gramsci, Antonio 1971. *Selections from the Prison Notebooks*, ed. G. Nowell-Smith and Q. Hoare. London: Lawrence and Wishart.

Habermas, Jurgen 1976. *Legitimation Crisis*. London: Heinemann.

Hall, D. G. E. 1932. *Dalhousie-Phayre Correspondence*. London: Oxford University Press.

——— 1945. *Europe and Burma*. London: Oxford University Press.

——— 1950. *Burma*. London: Hutchinson's University Library; 2nd edn., 1960.

——— 1955. *A History of South East Asia*. London: Macmillan; 4th edn, 1981.

Hart, G., Turton, A. and White B. (eds). 1988 (forthcoming). *Agrarian Transformations: Local Processes and the State in Southeast Asia*. Berkeley: University of California Press.

Harvey, G. E. 1974. *History of Burma*. London: Faber and Faber, 1946; reprinted New York: AMS Press.

Heyzer, N. 1986. *Working Women of South-East Asia: Development, Subordination and Emancipation*. Milton Keynes: Open University Press.

Higgott, R. and Robinson, R. (eds). 1985. *South-East Asia: Essays in the Political Economy of Structural Change*. Melbourne: Routledge and Kegan Paul.

Houtart, François and Lemercier, Geneviève 1981. *Sociologie d'une commune vietnamienne*, CRSR, Université Catholique de Louvain.

International Bank for Reconstruction and Development (IBRD) 1959. *A*

Public Development Program for Thailand. Baltimore: The Johns Hopkins Press.

Irvine, W. 1982. "The Thai-Yuan 'Madman' and the Modernising, Developing Thai Nation, as Bounded Entities Under Threat: A Study in the Replication of a Single Image". Ph.D. Thesis, University of London.

Jay, Robert R. 1963. *Religion and Politics in Rural Central Java*, Cultural Report Series no. 12. New Haven: Yale University Southeast Asia Studies.

—— 1969. *Javanese Villagers: Social Relations in Rural Modjokuto* Cambridge Mass.: MIT Press.

Jomo, Sundaram 1977. "Class Formation in Malaya: Capital, State and Uneven Development". Ph.D. Dissertation, Harvard University.

Kaplinsky, R. 1984. "The International Context for Industrialization in the Coming Decade", *Journal of Development Studies.* 21/1, 1984.

Kwan Kuen-Chor and Lee Soo Ann 1983. "Japanese Direct Investment in Singapore Manufacturing Industry" in Sueo Sekiguchi (ed.), 1983, *ASEAN-Japan Relations: Investment.* Singapore: Institute of Southeast Asian Studies.

Leach, E. R. 1960. "The Frontiers of 'Burma'", *Comparative Studies in Society and History*, pp. 49–68.

—— 1965. *Political Systems of Highland Burma.* Boston: Beacon Press.

Lehman, F. K. 1967. "Ethnic Categories in Burma and the Theory of Social Systems", in Peter Kunstadter (ed.), *Southeast Asian Tribes, Minorities and Nations.* Princeton: Princeton University Press, vol. I, pp. 93–125.

—— Maram La Raw 1967. "Towards a Basis for Understanding the Minorities in Burma: The Kachin Example", in Peter Kunstadter (ed.), *Southeast Asian Tribes, Minorities and Nations.* Princeton: Princeton University Press, vol. I, pp. 125–46.

Lévi-Strauss, Claude 1966. *The Savage Mind.* London: Wiedenfeld & Nicolson.

Li Causi, L. 1975. "Anthropology and Ideology: The Case of 'Patronage' in Mediterranean Societies", *Critique of Anthropology*, 4 and 5, 1975, pp. 90–109.

Liddle, R. William 1972. "Ethnicity and Political Organization: Three East Sumatran Cases", in *Culture and Politics in Indonesia*, Claire Holt *et al.* (eds). Ithaca: Cornell University Press.

Lyon, Margo 1970. *Bases of Conflict in Rural Java*, Research Monograph Series. Berkeley: Center for South and Southeast Asian Studies, University of California.

Marcuse, H. 1964. *One-Dimensional Man, Studies in the Ideology of Advanced Industrial Society.* London: Routledge and Kegan Paul.

Marx, K. 1973. *Grundrisse.* Harmondsworth: Penguin.

Maung Maung [Dr] 1961. *Burma's Constitution.* The Hague: Martinus Nijhoff, 2nd ed.

—— 1969, *Burma and General Ne Win.* New York: Asia.

Maung Maung [Brigadier Retired] 1980. *From Sangha to Laity, Nationalist Movements of Burma, 1920–1940.* New Delhi: Manohar.

Mendelson, E. Michael   1975. *Sangha and State in Burma*, John P. Ferguson (ed.). Ithaca: Cornell University Press.

Milne, R. S. and Mauzy, Diane K. 1978. *Politics and Government in Malaysia*. Vancouver: University of British Columbia Press.

Molyneux, M. 1981. "Women in Socialist Societies: Problems of Theory and Practice", in K. Young *et al.* (eds.), *Of Marriage and the Market*. London: CSE Books.

Mortimer, R. (ed.) 1973. *Showcase State: The Illusion of Indonesia's 'Accelerated Modernization'*. Sydney: Angus and Robertson.

Moscotti, Albert D. 1974. *British Policy and the Nationalist Movement in Burma, 1917–1937*. Honolulu: University of Hawaii Press.

Moshe, Yegar   1972. *The Muslims of Burma*. Wiesbaden: Otto Harrassowitz.

Nartsupha, C. *et al.* 1978. *The Political Economy of Siam, 1851–1932*, (2 vols.). Bangkok: Social Science Association of Thailand.

Nash, Manning   1965. *The Golden Road to Modernity*. New York: Wiley.

Ngo Vinh Long   1973. *Before the Revolution: The Vietnamese Peasants under the French*. Cambridge, Mass.: MIT Press.

Nu, U. 1954. *Burma under the Japanese*. London: Macmillan.

Pang Eng Fong and Lim, Linda   1977. *The Electronics Industry in Singapore: Structure, Technology and Linkages*. Singapore: Chopmen Enterprises.

Pham Cuong and Nguyen Ba   1976. *Revolution in the Village, Nam Hong, 1945–75*. Hanoi: FLPH.

Popenoe, Oliver   1970. "Malay Entrepreneurs: An Analysis of the Social Backgrounds, Careers and Attitudes of the Leading Malay Businessmen in West Malaysia". Ph.D. Thesis, London School of Economics.

Puthucheary, James   1960. *Ownership and Control in the Malayan Economy*. Singapore: Eastern Universities Press.

Pye, Lucian W. 1962. *Politics, Personality and Nation-Building: Burma's Search for Identity*. New Haven: Yale University Press.

Raffles, Sir T. S. 1817. *The History of Java*, vol. I. London: John Murray.

Robison, Richard   1978. "Capitalism and the Bureaucratic State in Indonesia: 1965–1975". Ph.D. Thesis, Sydney University.

Sarkisyanz, E. 1965. *Buddhist Backgrounds to the Burmese Revolution*. The Hague: Martinus Nijhoff.

—— 1978. "Buddhist Backgrounds of Burmese Socialism", in Bardwell L. Smith (ed.), *Religion and Legitimation of Power in Thailand, Laos and Burma*. Chambersburg: Anima.

Silverstein, J. 1977. *Burma: Military Rule and the Politics of Stagnation*. Ithaca: Cornell University Press.

—— 1980. *Burmese Politics, the Dilemma of National Unity*. New Brunswick: Rutgers University Press.

Smith, D. E. 1965. *Religion and Politics in Burma*. Princeton: Princeton University Press.

Snodgrass, Donald   1980. *Inequality and Economic Development in Malaysia*. Kuala Lumpur: Oxford University Press.

Spiro, Melford   1970. *Buddhism and Society*. New York: Harper and Row.

Srivaraksa, Sulak   1981. *Yu yang thai na samai satawat this sam haeng krung rattanakosin* (Living in the Thai Way in Bangkok's Third Century). Bangkok: Kledthai Press.

Stanis, Vladimir 1976. *The Socialist Transformation of Agriculture*. Moscow: Progress Publishers.

Steinberg, D. I. 1981. *Burma's Road Toward Development: Growth and Ideology Under Military Rule*. Boulder: Westview Press.

Swift, Michael G. 1971. "Minangkabau and Modernization", *Anthropology in Oceania*, Lester R. Hiatt and Chandra Jayawardena (eds). Sydney: Angus & Robertson, 1971.

Taylor, John, G. 1979. *From Modernisation to Modes of Production: a Critique of the Sociologies of Development and Underdevelopment*. London: Macmillan.

Thompson, E. P. "The Peculiarities of the English", *The Poverty of Theory and Other Essays*. London: Merlin Press.

—— "Folklore, Anthropology and Social History", *Indian Historical Review* 3, 2: 247–66.

Thomson, J. S. 1959. "Marxism in Burma" in Frank N. Trager (ed.), *Marxism in Southeast Asia*. Stanford: Stanford University Press, 1959.

Tinker, Hugh, 1967. *The Union of Burma*. London: Oxford University Press, 4th ed.

Trager, Frank N. 1966. *Burma: From Kingdom to Independence*. London: Pall Mall.

Turton, Andrew 1978. "The Current Situation in the Thai Countryside" in Andrew Turton *et al.*, *Thailand: Roots of Conflict*. Nottingham: Spokesman Books, pp. 104–42.

—— 1982. "Poverty, Reform and Class Struggle in Thailand" in Steve Jones, P. C. Joshi and Miguel Murmis (eds), *Rural Poverty and Agrarian Reform*. New Delhi: Allied Publishers, and ENDA, Dakar, pp. 20–45.

—— and Tanabe, S. (eds) 1984. *History and Peasant Consciousness in South-East Asia*, Senri Ethnological Studies No. 13. Osaka: National Museum of Ethnology.

United Nations, Center on Transnational Corporations 1981. *Transnational Banks: Operations, Strategies and their Effects in Developing Countries*. New York, ST/CTC.16.

UNIDO 1984. *World Industrial Restructuring and Redeployment*. Vienna: ID/Conf. 5/3.

Utrecht, Ernst 1972. "Some Remarks on Class Struggle and Political Parties in Indonesia", in *Indonesia's New Order* (Association for Radical East Asian Studies and the British Indonesian Committee, 1972).

Wagner, Ulla 1972. *Colonialism and Iban Warfare*. Stockholm: OBE-Tryck.

Wain, Barry (ed.) 1979. *The ASEAN Report*. Hong Kong: Don Jones Publishing Company.

Walinsky, Louis J. 1962. *Economic Development in Burma, 1951–1960*. New York: Twentieth Century Fund.

Wertheim, W. F. 1969. "From Aliran towards Class Struggle in the Javanese Countryside", *Pacific Viewpoint*, 10, 2: 1–17.

—— 1984. *East-West Paralles: Sociological Approaches to Modern Asia*. The Hague: W. van. Hoeve.

Wheelwright, E. L. 1966. *Industrialisation in Malaysia*. Melbourne: Melbourne University Press.

Wong, J. 1979. *ASEAN Economies in Perspective: a Comparative Study of Malaysia, the Philippines, Singapore and Thailand*. London: Macmillan.

World Bank 1980. *Thailand: Toward a Development Strategy of Full Participation*. Washington DC East Asia and Pacific Region Office.

Worsley, P. 1984. *The Three Worlds: Culture and World Development*. London: Weidenfeld and Nicolson.

Zuidberg, C. L. and Hasyir, Anidal 1978. "Family, marriage and fertility in Serpong", in A. C. L. Zuidberg (ed.), *Family Planning in Rural West Java: the Serpong Project*. Amsterdam: Ge. Nabrink and Son.

General Bibliography

Basic Texts for Southeast Asia and its Constituent Countries

History

Bastin J. S. 1968. *A History of Modern South East Asia*. Englewood Cliffs: Prentice-Hall.

Coedès, G. 1968. *The Indianised States of Southeast Asia*. Honolulu: East West Center Press.

—— 1966. *The Making of South East Asia*. London: Routledge and Kegan Paul.

Hall, D. G. E. (4th edn) 1981. *A History of South East Asia*. London: Macmillan.

Heine-Geldern, R. 1956. "Conceptions of State and Kingship in Southeast Asia" (first published in 1942). Data Paper no. 18, Southeast Asia Program. Ithaca: Cornell University.

Keyes, C. F. 1977. *The Golden Peninsula: Culture and Adaptation in Mainland Southeast Asia*. New York: Macmillan.

Purcell, V. 1966. *The Chinese in South East Asia*. London: Oxford University Press.

Steinberg, D. J. (ed.) 1985. *In Search of Southeast Asia: A Modern History*. London: Pall Mall.

Politics: 1945 to the Present (with general background)

Kahin, G. McT. (ed.) 1969. *Governments and Politics of Southeast Asia*. Ithaca: Cornell University Press.

Kunstadter, P. (ed.) 1967. *Southeast Asian Tribes, Minorities and Nations*. Princeton: Princeton University Press.

McAlister, J. T. (ed.) 1973. *Southeast Asia: the Politics of National Integration*. New York: Random House.

McVey, R. (ed.) 1978. *Southeast Asian Transitions: Approaches through Social History*. New Haven: Yale University Press.

Osborne, M. 1970. *Region of Revolt: Focus on S.E. Asia*. New South Wales: Pergamon.

Pandey, B. N. 1980. *South and South-East Asia, 1945–79, Problems and Policies*. London: Macmillan.

Pluvier, J. 1974. *South-East Asia from Colonialism to Independence*. Kuala Lumpur: Oxford University Press.

Selden, M. (ed.) 1974. *Remaking Asia: Essays on the American Uses of Power*. New York: Pantheon.

Taufik, Abdullah and Siddique Sharon (eds) 1986. *Islam and Society in Southeast Asia*. Singapore: Institute of Southeast Asian Studies.

Time-Life Books (Consultant M. Williams) 1987. *South-East Asia* (Library of Nations Series). Amsterdam.

Economies and Geography

Buchanan, K. 1967. *The Southeast Asian World: an Introductory Essay*. London: Bell.

Dobby, E. H. G. 1969. *Southeast Asia*. London: University of London Press.

Fryer, D. W. 1970. *Emerging Southeast Asia: a Study in Growth and Stagnation*. London: Philip.

Furnivall, J. S. 1956. *Colonial Policy and Practice: a Comparative Study of Burma and Netherlands India*. New York: New York University Press.

Golay, F. H. *et al.* (eds)   1969. *Underdevelopment and Economic Nationalism in South-East Asia*. Ithaca: Cornell University Press.

Hansen, G. E. (ed.)   1965. *Southeast Asia*. Englewood Cliffs: Prentice-Hall.

Heyzer, N. 1986. *Working Women of South-East Asia: Development, Subordination and Emancipation*. Milton Keynes: Open University Press.

Higgott, R. and Robison, R. (eds)   1985. *South-East Asia: Essays in the Political Economy of Structural Change*. Melbourne: Routledge and Kegan Paul.

Krausse, G. (ed.)   1986. *Urban Society in Southeast Asia, Vol. 2: Political and Cultural Issues*. Hong Kong: Asia Profile Publishers.

Myint, H. 1972. *Southeast Asia's Economy: Development Policies in the 1970s*. Harmondsworth: Penguin.

Wong, J. 1979. *ASEAN Economies in Perspective: a Comparative of Malaysia, the Philippines, Singapore and Thailand*. London: Macmillan.

Rural Economy and Peasantry

Burling, R. 1965. *Hill Farms and Padi Fields: Life in Mainland Southeast Asia*. Englewood Cliffs: Prentice-Hall.

Hart, G., Turton, A. and White, B. 1988 (forthcoming). *Agrarian Transformations: Local Processes and the State*. Berkeley: University of California Press.

Hayami, Y. and Kikuchi, M. 1982. *Asian Village Economy at the Crossroads*. Baltimore: Johns Hopkins Press.

Jacoby, E. H. 1961. *Agrarian Unrest in Southeast Asia*. London and New York: Asia Publishing House.

Popkins, S. 1979. *The Rational Peasant: the Political Economy of Rural Society in Vietnam*. Berkeley: University of California Press.

Scott, J. C. 1976. *The Moral Economy of the Peasant: Rebellion and Resistance in Southeast Asia*. New Haven: Yale University Press.

—— and Kerkvliet, B. J. de Tria (eds)   1986. *Everyday Forms of Peasant Resistance in South-East Asia*. London: Frank Cass.

Turton, A. and Tanabe, S. (eds)   1984. *History and Peasants Consciousness in South East Asia*. Osaka: National Museum of Ethnology, Senri Ethnological Studies no. 13.

Brunei

State of Brunei Annual Report. Brunei Press Kuala Belait (Published Annually).

Burma

Adas, M. 1974. *The Burma Delta: Economic Development and Social Change on an Asian Rice Frontier, 1852–1941.* Wisconsin University Press.

Andrus. J. R. 1956. *Burmese Economic Life.* Stanford: Stanford University Press and London: Oxford University Press.

Badgeley, J. 1970. *Politics Among Burmans: A Study of Intermediary Leaders.* Athens: Center for International Studies, Ohio University Press.

Cady, J. F. 1965. *A History of Modern Burma.* Ithaca: Cornell University Press.

Htin Aung, M. 1967. *A History of Burma.* New York: Columbia University Press.

Leach, E. 1970. *Political Systems of Highland Burma.* London: Athlone Press.

Liberman, V. 1985. *Burmese Administrative Cycles: Anarchy and Conquest, c 1580–1760.* Princeton: Princeton University Press.

Mendelson, E. M. 1975. *Sangha and State in Burma: a Study of Monastic Sectarianism.* Ithaca: Cornell University Press.

Sarkisyanz, E. 1965. *Buddhist Backgrounds of the Burmese Revolution.* The Hague: Martinus Nijhoff.

Silverstein, J. 1980. *Burmese Politics and the Dilemma of National Unity.* New Brunswick: Rutgers University Press.

Smith, D. E. 1965. *Religion and Politics in Burma.* Princeton: Princeton University Press.

Spiro, M. 1971. *Buddhism and Society: a Great Tradition and its Burmese Viscissitudes.* London: Allen and Unwin.

Steinberg, D. I. 1981. *Burma's Road Toward Development: Growth and Ideology under Military Rule.* Boulder: Westview Press.

Taylor, R. H. 1987. *The State in Burma.* London: C. Hurst.

Tinker, H. R. 1957. *The Union of Burma.* London: Oxford University Press.

Walinsky, L. J. 1962. *Economic Development in Burma, 1951–60.* New York: Twentieth Century Fund.

Cambodia (Kampuchea)

Caldwell, M., and Tan, Lek Hor 1973. *Cambodia in the Southeast Asian War.* New York: Monthly Review Press.

Chandler, D. P. 1972. *The Land and People of Cambodia.* Philadelphia: Lippincott.

Coedès, G. 1963. *Angkor: an Introduction.* London: Oxford University Press.

Kiernan, B. 1985. *How Pol Pot Fell.* London: Verso.

—— and Boua, C. (eds) 1982. *Peasants and Politics in Kampuchea, 1942–1981.* London: Zed Press.

Osborne, M. E. 1973. *Politics and Power in Cambodia: the Sithanouk Years.* Melbourne: Longmans.

Ponchaud, F. 1978. *Cambodia: Year Zero.* Harmondsworth: Penguin.

Shawcross, W. 1979. *Sideshow: Kissinger, Nixon and the Destruction of Cambodia.* London: Andre Deutsch.

Steinberg, D. J. *et al.* 1959. *Cambodia: its People, its Society, its Culture.* New Haven: HRAF Press.

Vickery, M. 1984. *Cambodia: 1975–1982*. Hemel Hempstead: Allen and Unwin.
—— 1986. *Kampuchea: Politics, Economics and Society*. London: Frances Pinter.
Willmott, W. E. 1967. *The Chinese in Cambodia*. Vancouver: University of British Columbia.

East Timor
Budiardjo, C. and Liong, Lim Soei   1984. *The War against East Timor*, London: Zed Press.
Dunn, J. S. 1983. *Timor: A People Betrayed*. Milton, Queensland: Jacaranda Press.
Hicks, D. 1976. *Tetum Ghosts and Kin*. Palo Alto, California: Mayfield Publishing Co.
Hiorth, F. 1985. *Timor: Past and Present*. S.E. Asian Monograph, no. 17, James Cook University of North Queensland.
Jolliffe, J. 1978. *East Timor: Nationalism and Colonialism*. St. Lucia: University of Queensland Press.
Metzner, J. 1977. *Man and Environment in Eastern Timor*. Canberra: Development Studies Center, Australian National University.
Ormeling, F. J. 1956. *The Timor Problem*. Groningen.
Ramos-Horta, J. 1985. *Funu: the Unfinished Saga of East Timor*. New Jersey: Red Sea Press.
Schulte-Nordholt, H. G. 1971. *The Political System of the Atoni of Timor*. The Hague: Verhandelingen van het Koninkijk Instituut Voor Taal, Land-en Volkenkunde.

Indonesia
Anderson, B. and Kahin, A. 1976. *Interpreting Indonesian Politics: Thirteen Contributions to the Debate*. Ithaca: Cornell University Press.
Arief, S. and Sasono, A. 1980. *Indonesia: Dependency and Underdevelopment*. Jakarta: Institude for Development Studies.
Caldwell, M. 1968. *Indonesia*. Oxford University Press.
Crouch, H. 1978. *The Army and Politics in Indonesia*. Ithaca: Cornell University Press.
Feith, H. 1962. *The Decline of Constitutional Democracy in Indonesia*. Ithaca: Cornell University Press.
—— and Castles, L. 1970. *Indonesia Political Thinking, 1945–1965*. Ithaca: Cornell University Press.
Fox, J. J. (ed.)   1980. *The Flow of Life: Essays on Eastern Indonesia*. Harvard, Mass.: Harvard University Press.
Furnivall, J. S. 1944. *Netherlands India: A Study of Plural Economy*. Cambridge, Mass.: Cambridge University Press.
Geertz, C. 1963. *Agricultural Involution: The Process of Ecological Change in Indonesia*. Berkeley: University of California Press.
—— 1960. The Religion of Java. Illinois: Free Press of Glencoe.

Hansen, G. E. (ed.) 1981. *Agricultural and Rural Development in Indonesia.* Boulder: Westview Press.

Hart, G. 1986. *Power, Labor, and Livelihood: Processes of Change in Rural Java.* Berkeley: University of California Press.

Holt, C. and Anderson, B. 1972. *Culture and Politics in Indonesia.* Ithaca: Cornell University Press.

Kartodirdjo, S. 1973. *Protest Movements in Rural Java: a Study of Agrarian Unrest in the Nineteenth and Twentieth Centuries.* Singapore: Oxford University Press.

—— S. 1984. *Modern Indonesia: Tradition and Transformation, a Socio-historical Perspective.* Yogyakarta: Gadjah Mada University Press.

Liddle, R. W. 1970. *Ethnicity, Party and National Integration: an Indonesian Case Study.* New Haven: Yale University Press.

Mortimer, R. 1974. *Indonesian Communism under Sukarno: Ideology and Politics, 1959–65.* Ithaca: Cornell University Press.

—— (ed.) 1973. *Showcase State: the Illusion of Indonesia's 'Accelerated Modernisation'.* Sydney: Angus and Robertson.

Polomka, P. 1971. *Indonesia since Sukarno.* Harmondsworth: Penguin.

Ricklefs, M. C. 1981. *A History of Modern Indonesia.* London: Macmillan.

Robinson, R. 1986. *Indonesia: the Rise of Capital.* Sydney, Australia: Allen and Unwin.

Stoler, A. L. 1985. *Capitalism and Confrontation in Sumatra's Plantation Belt, 1870–1979.* New Haven: Yale University Press.

Tornquist, O. 1985. *Dilemmas of Third World Communism: the Destruction of the PKI in Indonesia.* London: Zed Press.

Weinstein, F. B. 1976. *Indonesia's Foreign Policy and the Dilemma of Independence.* Ithaca: Cornell University Press.

Laos

Adams, N. and McCoy, A. W. 1970. *Laos: War and Revolution.* New York: Harper and Row.

de Berval, R. (ed.) 1959. *Kingdom of Laos: the Land of the Million Elephants and the White Parasol.* Saigon: France-Asie.

Dommen, A. J. 1985. *Laos: Keystone of Indochina.* Boulder: Westview Press.

Evans, G. and Rowley, K. 1984. *Red Brotherhood at War.* London: Verso.

Halpern, J. M. 1964. *Government, Politics and Social Structure in Laos: a Study of Tradition and Innovation.* New Haven: Yale University Press.

Kahn, A. R. and Lees, E. 1980. *Employment and Development in Laos: Some Problems and Policies.* Bangkok: International Labour Organisation.

Lao Peoples' Democratic Republic, "Report on the Economic and Social Situation, Development Strategy and Assistance Requirements", Geneva, 1983. (Report prepared for the Asian Pacific Round Table Meeting on the implementation of the 'New Program of Action' for Less Developed Countries.)

Stuart-Fox, M. 1986. *Laos: Politics, Economy and Society.* London: Frances Pinter.

Vongvichit, P. 1969. *Laos and the Victorious Struggle of the Lao People Against Us Neo-Colonialism*. Vientiane: Neo Lao Haksat Editions.

Zasloff, J. J. 1973. *The Pathet Lao*. Lexington, Mass.: D. C. Heath and Co.

—— and Brown, M. 1986. *Apprentice Revolutionaries: the Communist Movement in Laos, 1930–85*. Stanford: Hoover Institute Press.

Malaysia

Alatas, S. 1977. *The Myth of the Lazy Native*. London: Frank Cass.

Andaya, B. W. and Andaya, L. Y. 1982. *A History of Malaysia*. London: Macmillan.

Bastin, J. S. and Winks, R. W. (eds) 1979. *Malaysia: Selected Historical Readings*. Nendeln: KTO Press.

Caldwell, M. and Amin M. (eds) 1977. *Malaya: the Making of a Neo-colony*. Nottingham: Spokesman Books.

Enloe, C. H. 1970. *Multi-Ethnic Politics: the Case of Malaysia*. Berkeley: University of California Press.

Fisk, E. K. and Osman-Rani, H. (eds) 1982. *The Political Economy of Malaysia*. Kuala Lumpur: Oxford University Press.

Gullick, J. M. 1969. *Malaysia*. London: Benn.

Husin Ali, S. 1975. *Malay Peasant Society and Leadership*. Kuala Lumpur: Oxford University Press.

—— 1984 (ed.). *Ethnicity, Class and Development. Malaysia*. Kuala Lumpur: Malaysian Social Science Association.

Jackson, J. C. 1968. *Planters and Speculators: Chinese and European Agricultural Enterprise in Malaya, 1786–1921*. Kuala Lumpur: University of Malaya Press.

Kessler, C. 1978. *Islam and Politics in a Malay State, Kelantan, 1838–1969*. Ithaca: Cornell University Press.

Lim, D. 1973. *Economic Growth and Development in West Malaysia, 1947–70*. Kuala Lumpur: Oxford University Press.

Lim, Mah Hui 1981. *Ownership and Control of the One Hundred Largest Corporations in Malaysia*. Kuala Lumpur: Oxford University Press.

Lim, Teck Ghee 1977. *Peasants and Their Agricultural Economy in Colonial Malaya, 1874–1941*. Kuala Lumpur: Oxford University Press.

Miln, R. S. 1967. *Politics and Government in Malaysia*. Boston: Houghton Mifflin.

Ong, Aihwa 1987. *Spirits of Resistance and Capitalist Discipline: Factory Women in Malaysia*. Ithaca: State University of New York Press.

Purcell, V. 1967. *The Chinese in Modern Malaya*. Singapore: Eastern University Press.

Roff, W. R. 1967. *The Origins of Malay Nationalism*. New Haven: Yale University Press.

Scott, J. S. 1985. *Weapons of the Weak: Everyday Forms of Peasant Resistance*. New Haven: Yale University Press.

Strauch, J. 1981. *Chinese Village Politics in the Malaysian State*. Cambridge, Mass.: Harvard University Press.

Sundaram, J. K. 1986. *A Question of Class: Capital, the State and Uneven Development in Malaysia.* Kuala Lumpur: Oxford University Press.

Wheelwright, E. L. 1965. *Industrialisation in Malaya.* Melbourne: University Press.

Wong Lin-Ken 1965. *The Malayan Tin Industry to 1914.* Tucson: University of Arizona Press.

Philippines

Agpalo, R. 1972. *The Political Elite and the People: a Study of Politics in Occidental Mindoro.* Manila: University of the Philippines.

Agoncillo, T. A. 1969. *A Short History of the Philippines.* New York: New America Library.

Baldwin, R. E. 1965. *Foreign Trade Regimes and Economic Development: the Philippines.* New York: National Bureau of Economic Research.

Burley, T. M. 1973. *The Philippines: an Economic and Social Geography.* London: Bell.

Constantino, R. 1976. *A History of the Philippines.* New York: Monthly Review Press.

De La Costa, H. 1975. *Readings in Philippine History.* Manila: Bookmark.

Fast, J. and Richardson, J. 1979. *Roots of Dependency: Political and Economic Revolution in Nineteenth Century Philippines.* Quezon City: Foundation for Nationalist Studies.

Golay, F. H. 1961. *Philippines: Public Policy and Economic Development.* Ithaca: Cornell University Press.

Guerrero, A. 1971. *Philippine Society and Revolution.* Hong Kong: Ta Kung Pao.

Kerkvliet, B. de Tria 1979. *The Huk Rebellion: a Study of Peasant Revolt in the Philippines.* Berkeley: University of California Press.

—— 1974. *Political Change in the Philippines: Studies of Local Politics preceeding Martial Law.* Honolulu: University of Hawaii.

Lachica, E. 1971. *The Huks: Philippine Agrarian Society in Revolt.* New York: Praeger.

Lande, C. H. 1965. *Leaders, Factions and Parties: the Structure of Philippine Politics.* New Haven: Yale University Press.

McCoy, A. W. and de Jesus, C. (eds) 1982. *Philippine Social History: Global Trade and Local Transformations.* Sydney: Allen and Unwin.

Singapore

Buchanan, I. 1972. *Singapore in S.E. Asia: an Economic and Political Appraisal.* London: G. Bell and Sons.

Chen, P. S. J. (ed.) 1983. *Singapore: Development Policies and Trends.* Singapore: Oxford University Press.

Deyo, F. C. 1981. *Dependent Development and Industrial Order: An Asian Case Study.* Singapore and New York: Praeger.

Krause, L. B., Koh Ai Tee and Lee (Tsao) Yuan 1987. *The Singapore Economy Reconsidered.* Singapore: Institute of Southeast Asian Studies.

Lee Soo Am 1973. *Industrialisation in Singapore.* Australia: Longman.

——— 1977. *Singapore Goes Transnational.* Singapore: Eastern University Press.

Mirza, H. 1986. *Multinationals and the Growth of the Singapore Economy.* London: Croom Helm.

Hassan, R. 1976. *Singapore: Society in Transition.* Kuala Lumpur: Oxford University Press.

Thailand

Chaloemtiarana, T. 1979. *Thailand: the Politics of Despotic Paternalism.* Bangkok: Social Science Association of Thailand.

Charoenloet, C. 1971. *The Evolution of Thailand's Economy.* Bangkok: Thai Watana Panich Press.

Darling, F. C. 1965. *Thailand and the United States.* Washington: Public Affairs Press.

Girling, J. L. S. 1981. *Thailand, Society and Politics.* Ithaca: Cornell University Press.

Ho, R. and Chapman, H. C. (eds)   1973. *Studies of Contemporary Thailand.* Camberra: Australian National University Press.

Ingram, J. C. 1971. *Economic Change in Thailand 1850–1970.* Stanford: Stanford University Press.

Morell, D. and Samudavanija, C. 1981. *Political Conflict in Thailand.* Cambridge, Mass.: Gunn and Hain.

Nartsupha, C. *et al.* 1978. *The Political Economy of Siam, 1851–1932,* 2 vols. Bangkok: Social Science Association of Thailand.

Neher, C. (ed.)   1979. *Modern Thai Politics.* Schenkman, Mass.

Rabibhadana, A. 1980. *The Organisation of Thai Society in the Early Bangkok Period.* Data Paper no. 74, Southeast Asia Program. Ithaca: Cornell University.

Riggs, F. W. 1966. *Thailand, the Modernisation of a Bureacratic Polity.* Honolulu: East-West Center.

Sifflin, W. J. 1966. *The Thai Bureaucracy: Institutional Change and Development.* Honolulu: East-West Center.

Silcok, T. H. (ed.)   1967. *Thailand: Social and Economic Studies in Development.* Canberra: Australian National University Press.

——— 1970. *The Economic Development of Thai Agriculture.* Itchaca: Cornell University Press.

Skinner, G. V. 1957. *Chinese Society in Thailand: an Analytical History.* Ithaca: Cornell University Press.

Suehiro, A. 1985. *Capital Accumulation and Industrial Development in Thailand.* Bangkok: Chulalongkorn University Social Research Institute.

Suksamran, S. 1976. *Political Buddhism in Southeast Asia: the Role of the Sangha in the Administration of Thailand.* New York: St Martin's.

Turton, A. 1987. *Production, Power and Participation in Thailand: Experiences of Poor Farmer's Groups.* Geneva: United Nations Research Institute for Social Development.

Turton, A., Fast, J. and Caldwell, M. (eds)   1978. *Thailand: Roots of Conflict.* Nottingham: Spokesman Books.

Vella, W. F. 1955. *The Impact of the West on the Government of Thailand*. Berkeley: University of California Press.

Wilson, D. A. 1962. *Politics in Thailand*. Ithaca: Cornell University Press.

Wyatt, D. K. 1984. *Thailand: a Short History*. New Haven: Yale University Press.

Vietnam

Buttinger, J. 1967. *Vietnam: a Dragon Embattled* (2 vols), New York and London: Pall Mall.

Chaliand, G. 1969. *The Peasants of North Vietnam*. Harmondsworth: Penguin.

Chomsky, N. and Herman, E. 1979. *The Political Economy of Human Rights* (2 vols, and particularly volume two on Indochina – After the Cataclysm). Nottingham: Spokesman Books.

Elliott, D. W. P. 1981. *The Third Indochina Conflict*. Boulder: Westview Press.

Fforde, A. and Paine, S. H. 1987. *The Limits of National Liberation: Problems of Economic Management in the Democratic Republic of Vietnam*. London: Croom Helm.

Gettleman, M. E. 1966. *Vietnam: History, Documents and Opinions in a Major World Crisis*. Harmondsworth: Penguin.

Hammer, E. J. 1955. *The Struggle for French Indochina, 1940–55*. Stanford University Press.

Kahin, G. McT. and Lewis, J. 1969. *The United States in Vietnam*. New York: Dial Press.

Lacouture, J. 1969. *Ho Chi Minh*. Harmondsworth: Penguin.

Le Duan 1965–7. *On the Socialist Revolution in Vietnam* (3 vols). Hanoi: Foreign Languages Publishing House.

Ngo Vinh Long 1973. *Before the Revolution: the Vietnamese Peasants under the French*. Cambridge, Mass.: M.I.T. Press.

Smith, R. B. 1968. *Vietnam and the West*. London: Heinemann.

—— (2 vols, continuing) 1983–5. *An International History of the Vietnam War*. London: Macmillan.

Turley, W. S. (ed.) 1980. *Vietnamese Communism in Comparative Perspective*. Boulder: Westview Press.

Zasloff, J. and Brown, M. (eds) 1975. *Communism in Indochina: New Perspectives*. Lexington, Mass.: D. C. Heath.

Southeast Asia: General Texts of Reference

Economic Survey of Asia and the Far East. United Nations ECAFE, New York. Annually 1948–1970.

Economic and Social Survey of Asia and the Pacific. United Nations ESCAP, Bangnon. Annually 1974– .

Far Eastern Economic Review Yearbook. Published annually by the Far Eastern Economic Review, Hong Kong, since 1960.

Southeast Asian Affairs. Published annually by the Institute of Southeast Asian Studies, Singapore.

Southeast Asia: Useful Periodicals

ASEAN Economic Bulletin, Institute of Southeast Asian Studies, Singapore.

Asia Quarterly, Centre d'étude de Sud-Est Asiatique et de l'Extrême-Orient, Brussels.

Asian Affairs, Royal Central Asian Society, London.

Asian Studies, Asia Center, University of the Philippines, Manila.

Asian Survey, Institute of International Studies, University of California at Berkeley. (The first two parts of the volume for each year provide a survey of individual countries for the previous year.)

Borneo Research Bulletin, Borneo Research Council, Williamsburg, Virginia.

Bulletin of Indonesian Studies, Australian National University, Canberra.

Bulletin of Concerned Asian Scholars, Claremont, Massachusetts.

Far Eastern Economic Review (weekly), Hong Kong.

Indonesia, Cornell University Modern Indonesia Project, Ithaca.

Journal of Contemporary Asia, Manila.

Journal of South East Asian Studies (formerly *Journal of S.E. Asian History, 1966–70*), History Department, University of Singapore.

Journal of Asian Studies, Association for Asian Studies, University of Michigan.

Malayan Economic Review, University of Malaya Economics Society, Singapore.

Modern Asian Studies, Cambridge University Press.

Pacific Affairs, Institute of Pacific Relations, Honolulu.

Sojourn: Social Issues in Southeast Asia, Institute of Southeast Asian Studies, Singapore.

Southern Asian Journal of Social Science, Singapore.

Index

Note: this index deals with the main subject areas covered in the text. It only lists authors when their work is discussed in the text.